Witness in Our Time

D1516147

WITNESS IN OUR TIME

WORKING LIVES OF DOCUMENTARY PHOTOGRAPHERS

Ken Light

INTRODUCTION BY KERRY TREMAIN | Second Edition

Smithsonian Books | Washington

The text in this book is based on interviews conducted by Ken Light with support
from an Erna and Victor Hasselblad Foundation grant.

The interviews were edited by Ken Light, Melanie Light, and Kerry Termain.

COPY EDITOR: Lise Sajewski

Library of Congress Cataloging-in-Publication Data
Witness in our time: working lives of documentary photographers, 2nd Edition/
[edited by] Ken Light ; introduction by Kerry Termain.
    p.   cm.
Includes bibliographical references and index.
ISBN 978-1-58834-298-0 (paper)
    1. Photographers—Interviews.   2. Documentary photography.   3. Photojournalism.
I. Light, Ken.
TR139 W58 2010
070.4'9'0922—dc21   00-020889

British Library Cataloguing-in-Publication Data is available

Manufactured in the United States of America

15 14 13 12 11 10 1 2 3 4 5

For Stanley Light, my father,

who gave me my first camera and taught me about the human condition,

and Melanie Light, my wife,

who has been patient, reassuring, and wise.

Contents

Photographers

Editors and Curators

In the Field

Acknowledgments

The second edition of *Witness in Our Time* would not have been possible without the support, comments, discussion, and editing by Melanie Light, my wife and partner. She generously allowed me to bounce ideas off of her, argue with her, and always gave wise, thoughtful feedback despite my stubbornness. Without her support this book would not have been possible. My daughter, Allison, was always present with a smile and a "How was your day, Daddy?" and then attentively listened to my reply, which is a wonderful gift from a teenager busy with her own active world.

A generous grant from the Erna and Victor Hasselblad Foundation originally supported my travel and my time to conduct interviews with the photographers, and a grant from the National Press Photographers Research Foundation (NPPA) gave a much-needed boost. Without this support I might have never originally undertaken this project.

The first edition could not have happen without my colleague and co-conspirator Kerry Tremain, nor would it be in its present narrative form, or graced with such an insightful introduction. As we began this updated edition, Kerry's original introduction still rang true. The research he did for the first edition, and his collaboration on the biographies that introduce those interviews made the 2000 edition more readable. Our conversations and his editing skills, passion, and faith in the ideals of documentary photography were a welcome breath of fresh air and made a critical contribution to the book's final form.

Many have given to this work. Amy Pastan, my former acquisitions editor at the Smithsonian Institution Press, first agreed to the publication of this manuscript and nurtured it into draft form. My thanks to Mark Hirsch, former senior editor at the Smithsonian Institution Press, on whose desk this project landed as a book without a home. His unwavering support restored it back to health and finally to its present form. The first edition editor, Robert Poarch, and designer, Janice Wheeler, both helped create a more dynamic publication.

Over the years, as *Witness in Our Time* has been adopted by colleges and read by thousands of photo students and documentary photographers, I wondered what would become of this book as huge changes impacted the photo world. To my surprise, Carolyn Gleason, director of Smithsonian Books, asked me if I might revise the book. Christina Wiginton stepped in as editor, and it has been a great pleasure to have such an enthusiastic supporter of this work.

Many thanks to the photographers who took their precious time to answer my questions and who were so very patient, offering photos, reviewing text, and correcting mistakes that can so often happen in a recorded interview.

My students and assistants at University of California, Berkeley Graduate School of Journalism—Doreen Bowens, Jill David, Matt Golec, Christina Koenig, Kimberly Lisagor, Matt McClesky, and Sophia Ray—helped with the tedious transcriptions of the recorded interviews and indexing in the first edition. Fortunately Ananda Shorey stepped forward to do the transcriptions in the new edition, and proved to be accurate and quick, making my job that much easier.

My colleagues at the graduate school have continued to inspire me, and Neil Henry, dean of the school, has been a great supporter of the photography program and my work. My intern and assistant Max Cohen has helped me at every turn and given me insights about the next generation. My friend Jay Berg offered his apartment on my visits to New York to use as a home base for some of the interviews.

This book originally started with my colleague and friend Kim Komenich as we bemoaned the lack of a text for our students from which they might gain insight into the lives and work of documentary photographers. Long after we took separate paths toward this goal, he remained a steadfast supporter and cheerleader for this project's completion.

Finally to the readers who have shared this book with others, and to all of those working to keep the documentary tradition alive, thank you.

Ken Light

Thanks to Valerie McGuire for researching the biographies. For reading and commenting on the edits and introduction, thanks to Mike Feeback, Carl Fleischhauer, Melanie Light, Joe Loya, Brad Matsen, Susan Meiselas, Joshua Phillips, Jon Polansky, Barbara Ramsey, Fred Ritchin, Bill Smock, Marilyn Snell, Patti Wolter, and especially to Jane Melnick, who first ignited my interest in documentary photography, and Peter Solomon, master wordsmith.

Kerry Tremain

Introduction

Seeing and Believing

KERRY TREMAIN

I

When mujahedin soldiers captured Antonin Kratochvil in Afghanistan, where he traveled in 1978 to photograph their war with the Russians, one of them pressed the barrel of an AK-47 rifle into Kratochvil's temple, read his passport, and shouted to the others that their prisoner was born in Czechoslovakia. The mujahedin knew Czechoslovakia. Czechs manufactured Russian guns. The soldier told the photographer he was going to blow his brains out.

Ironically, Kratochvil had risked his life to escape communist Czechoslovakia eleven years earlier. While still a teenager, he had walked to the Czech-Austrian border, a coil of barbed wire in a swath of fine gravel raked to allow the police patrol to track trespassers' footsteps. A friend of his had been killed nearby. In the dark he crawled under the barbed wire on his belly. Upright, euphoric, he spit on the Czech side of a stone that marked the border.

In Afghanistan Kratochvil sat silently while a guide he had hired just a few hours before pleaded furiously with them to spare the photographer. "He is not a spy; he hates the Soviets. He will tell the world about your revolution. You know my cousin who fixed your truck."

For two hours, the guide begged. Finally, the mujahedin fighter lowered his rifle and freed Kratochvil.

Polluted Garden, Romania, 1995
(© Antonin Kratochvil)

I met him in 1989, the year the Velvet Revolution liberated Czechoslovakia, the year he returned to Prague, where his parents had died after decades of persecution by communist authorities. While the TV broadcast only happy celebrants, he photographed a hysterical boy covered in Vaclav Havel placards screaming to a large, empty plaza.

Like the best documentary photographs, Kratochvil's images conveyed an invaluable, if imperfect, truth. His natural elation about the liberation was chastened by an angry knowledge that the century's tragedies—the ethnic hatreds, the political recriminations, and environmental disasters—had not yet fully played out in Eastern Europe.

I published these photographs, and later we became friends. On trips to New York City I would visit the one-room apartment near the Lincoln Tunnel he shared with his wife and young son and piles of prints. There, he once showed me his pictures from Afghanistan and more recent photographs from a prison in Venezuela, one of which was a group of starving prisoners huddled in the dark behind a door nearly rusted shut.

In the movies the photographer is often a romantic action figure— James Bond with a Nikon. But there was no gold or glory to be gained from those prison photographs. Instead, they made me ask: Why would you spend your savings to go to a hellhole near Caracas where the guards and the prison gangs, both armed, would just as soon kill you and trade your camera for food? I found part of an answer to this and similar questions in the stories recorded in this book.

As a child, Jill Freedman would sneak into her parents' attic each day and cry over pictures of Auschwitz and Dachau that she found in magazines stored there. When she grew older, she saw parallels to those pictures in magazine photographs of civil rights activists set upon by dogs in the American South. Outraged when Martin Luther King Jr. was shot and killed in 1968, she quit her job to camp in a plywood lean-to on the Washington Mall and photograph the Poor Peoples' March, which King had conceived before his death.

Donna Ferrato was shooting a feature on "love" for Japanese *Playboy* when a man began beating his wife in front of her. Stunned, unable to respond, Ferrato threw the film in a drawer the next day. But she found the courage to develop and print those pictures, then devoted her work in the years that followed to photographing victims of domestic violence and establishing an organization to help them.

Joe Rodriguez, who kicked a heroin habit as a young man, spent months gaining the trust of East Los Angeles gang members before asking to photograph them. Then LAPD officers, for unknown reasons, lied to the gang. They said that Rodriguez was helping them on drug busts. Although his life was now in grave danger, he went back to the neighborhood and slowly started to rebuild trust.

Like Kratochvil, Rodriguez risks his life to plea furiously, through photographs, for others to escape a future he once faced.

Documentary photographers often see things that do not officially exist. Indignities. Cruelties. People pinned to a wall with fire hoses because they want to vote.

During the Civil Rights movement, Klansmen ran Eugene Richards out of Arkansas for taking their pictures. Earl Dotter made portraits of miners dying from black-lung disease, while both the coal companies and corrupt union officials denied the problem. Susan Meiselas photographed the corpses of villagers in El Mozote after they were shot and burned by the Salvadoran army. It took ten years before a congressional inquiry and an exhumation forced authorities to admit the massacre had happened.

A transformation occurs when you see something important that is denied by those who have not or will not see it.

"Look. I've got a picture," you say. "I was there." Excuses are made: pictures can lie.

"But I don't."

The first time it happens, you become enraged. You dig in. You get better at shooting in low light and at developing a relationship with your subjects.

The camera gives you entry, but you don't shoot at first. You put it away. You stick around. You come back again and again. You explain yourself. Eventually you think: I've earned it.

No way.

"You just grit your teeth and bitch and moan and call home all the time and complain and try to keep away from the alcohol and don't get too depressed and go back the next day," said Richards.

In Red Hook, in Brooklyn, the crack addicts he had gone to photograph in the early nineties figured that he and the writer working with him were cops. "Then about the fourth week we had a breakthrough moment. We witnessed a violent chase and people recognized we were journalists instead of cops. The doors opened."

If intense engagement with your subjects is the first requirement, keeping your head is the second. You can be too involved, or not involved enough.

The only thing to do is to get it right. The only way to get it right is to keep asking yourself if it is.

"You attempt to tell the truth," is how Richards described it. "You try to find the tools, the metaphors, the shapes, the shadows to translate the event or personality as truthfully as possible."

When it is done, you hope the work is faithful to the people you have spent weeks or months or years with. You notice things you missed, nuances. The truth is not completely here; it is slightly out of the frame. In the darkroom, other truths are unexpectedly revealed.

Work on the story is done but the work to get it published, intact, is just beginning. Richards spent months in cocaine-ravaged neighborhoods, but black activists like Al Sharpton denounced him as a white interloper, and intimidated editors avoided the photographs.

Dayanita Singh documented the growing Indian upper middle class into which she was born, but her photographs did not show what the editors wanted: poor India, exotic India. "This is not India," Singh recalled one editor saying. "This is Indians in London or Indians in New York."

"Look. I've got the pictures. I was there."

II

Social documentary photographers have rarely had a secure home.

The American tradition was first encouraged by late nineteenth-century Progressives. To remedy a problem, they reasoned, we must first see it. And people of goodwill, once they see it, will work to correct it.

Jacob Riis, proud of the artlessness of his photographs, campaigned to improve immigrant ghettos with Teddy Roosevelt's support. Lewis Hine, on the other hand, proved that beautifully crafted images of ugly conditions could move the nation. His tireless work eventually helped create child labor laws.

Franklin Roosevelt's New Dealers, successor to the Progressives, offered documentary photographers a new and more spacious home. The Farm Security Administration established the country's first national documentary project and hired photographers like Dorothea Lange, whose images of California field hands helped influence Congress to legislate rural reform.

Life, founded in 1936, together with magazines like *Vu* in France and the *Picture Post* in Britain, provided the richest home yet. During World War II, these new magazines turned documentary photographers into photojournalists and photojournalists like Robert Capa, Margaret Bourke-White, and W. Eugene Smith into heroes. The photographers' politics were antifascist, the magazines their bread and butter.

After the war, even as political consensus frayed, photo-essays by photographers like Smith and Gordon Parks in *Life* helped stoke the "can-do" energy of the times. In the decades that followed, photographers alerted the country to the viciousness of racial bigotry and, in Vietnam, to the contradictions of the cold war.

Documentary photographs from the dust bowl to Da Nang changed our perceptions and remain lodged in our memories. By the seventies, however, television was king; the big-picture magazines were dying. The liberal Left entered a grim period of division and decay when the reform political coalition FDR had built forty years earlier shattered, preparing the way for Ronald Reagan and Margaret Thatcher.

The eventual decline of photo magazines and the sixties' social movements dealt documentary photographers a triple blow—a loss of revenue, influence, and a secure political home.

Ironically, at the same time the art world's interest was growing, along with the prices of vintage Depression-era photographs. Galleries and small publishers expanded, offering photographers the display space and editorial control they had lost in magazines.

To offer documentary photography a warm home, however, art's driving forces—formal innovation tied to celebrity genius tied to big money—would have had to undergo a fundamental renovation toward community engagement around controversial social issues. Except for a handful of sympathetic curators, documentary photography struck most as a dowdy interloper in the house of high culture—a house that underwent a renovation, but toward conceptual purity, not the nitty-gritty necessities brought in the back door by documentarians.

Contemporary art proved no more hospitable a home than did contemporary media, its middlebrow cultural rival. Documentary photographers have moved between them like resilient foster children, grabbing what they could from each. Astonishingly, they managed to produce a body of work that in its depth, breadth, intelligence, and pictorial inventiveness equals that of any previous era.

The documentarians' move into the art world also brought their work under the stern gaze of high-culture critics who did not always like what they saw. Documentary photographers, severe critics said, are voyeurs who profit from the misery of the poor by stealing and prettifying their visages, then parading them in exhibitions for the privileged. And photographic realism, they argued, perpetuates the myth that photographs are objective, rather than projections of the cultural values of those who make and distribute them.

This criticism, as we have seen, misconstrues why and how documentary photographers work. These photographers reject the quick, sensational pulse of news pictures in favor of long-term engagement with the people they photograph. Some have recently made more explicit this moral contract with their subjects, like Fazal Sheikh, who makes collaborative portraits of refugees. And just as there is a difference between a lecherous and a friendly look, the gaze of the voyeur and that of the witness are not the same.

Still, without a secure home—without a connection to an influential progressive movement or the financial support and power of popular media—documentary photographers were vulnerable to the sting of the art critics. They are aware that the truths they frame are fragile and tentative. Some, like Eugene Richards, devise pictorial strategies to make their own subjectivity transparent. Most, like Dayanita Singh, know firsthand how the media can distort meaning.

They have experienced, even in mundane ways, the difficulties of trespassing borders of language and culture with people they photograph. And they hold only a slender hope that they can prevent the sort of tragedies they witness.

A friend, who spent years documenting the lives of Andean people, told me, "My photographs changed nothing for them. In the end, the images had more to do with me." This widely shared sentiment draws on two truths—that photographs are always the product of personal concerns and that photographs alone are rarely capable of radical social change—to imply a false conclusion, that acts of witness are unimportant. We all see others by seeing our different selves in others. That is why Joe Rodriguez returned to the barrio, Donna Ferrato to those living rooms, and Antonin Kratochvil to places where people are trapped. Their own suffering, their memories of their suffering, made them seek the suffering of others.

Their pictures did not end drive-by shootings nor domestic or ideological violence. Photographs will not end centuries of oppression. Human tragedy requires many acts of empathy. Each of us is only capable of our own.

"A photograph that brings news of some unsuspected zone of misery cannot make a dent in public opinion unless there is an appropriate context of feeling and attitude," wrote Susan Sontag in *On Photography*. But what creates "an appropriate context of feeling and attitude"? Some remain convinced that historical forces like class conflict or nationalism will set us free, but the last century bears a tortured testimony to the results of those convictions.

Many documentary photographers, as do I, maintain a faith in the force of our collective acts of empathy and witness.

III

Airplanes, televisions, satellites, and computers have so intensified cross-cultural contact that we share our foods and our viruses, our music and our hatreds.

Engineers from Bangalore, India, educated at Stanford University now discuss software design at French bistros in Dublin. Serbian nationalists wear T-shirts adorned with multicultural cartoon creatures from *The Lion King*.

Culture clash and assimilation are ancient. What is new is the speed at which we perceive it, transmit it, turn it over, devour it. And this development, in large part, depends on images—on photographs.

The Kayapo people of the Amazon rain forest make videos with rock star Sting to extend their "traditional" culture, a way of life now as dependent on European environmentalists as on the forest itself. Mexican photographer Graciela Iturbide shoots images of muscular Zapotec matriarchs in an ancient pueblo, which suddenly becomes a pilgrimage site for feminists who have seen the photographs in North American magazines.

Inevitably, intensified intercultural contact has made us question the old truths and spawned new ones that are more fluid and temporal. We are exhilarated to experience a world of cultural options to choose from, but terrified because the comforting certainties of any single tradition are ripped apart.

An explosion of global words and images has made us question how truths are made—and why. In photographs there is more to see, but our trust in what we see has been shaken. "We began the twentieth century by believing what we saw in a photograph was true and ended the twentieth century by distrusting every document," says curator Anne Wilkes Tucker of Houston's Museum of Fine Arts.

Faced with this confusion, many turn to imagined pasts. Perhaps the most notorious are the religious fundamentalists, such as the Talibans, but there are also those who long for a return to pre-Stalinist communism or to a world of hunters and gatherers attuned to nature. Some photographers also long for a more heroic era, like the one in which Robert Capa and W. Eugene Smith confronted fascism and traveled around the world for *Life*.

Although theoretically committed to the new, even so-called "postmodern" photographers and artists have, in practice, recoiled from the future. Instead, they have sought security in derivative theories of representation that they are as certain of as Rome's bishops once were of the Ptolemaic universe, and that are argued in a cultural equivalent of Latin. Given the complexities of representing the "other," many urge photographers to stick to their own kind, often a racial or gender category that they defend with the vigor of nineteenth-century Spencerians. Confronted with the myriad difficulties of accurately reporting, for example, the carnage of the Rwandan holocaust, they prefer to condemn Western media hegemony from their studios.

Believing that reality is hidden from us by the powerful, these artists implicate documentary photographers for promulgating a lie that photographs are true. But paranoia is just another way to give the truth a unity it does not really possess. Suspicious, ironic art seeks disengagement from an impure world, not immersion in the cross-cultural tumult so richly available to the more daring.

The world is both a promising place to make photographs and a broad stage for self-discovery. The alternative to narrowing our vision to the studio is widening it to include more varied international participants. As cultural encounter intensifies, the globe becomes the important and visually inexhaustible arena for understanding our times. And with new modes of communication, there are opportunities to be seized.

Sebastião Salgado, who believes that "there is no person in the world that must be protected from pictures," sees the documentary photographer as a vector connecting the different realities of people around the world. This could double as a vision for the Internet, perhaps the most powerful media tool ever invented. At the very least, the Internet gives international photographers a way to share their interests and debate their concerns.

The World Wide Web also offers documentary photographers a place among media and reform organizations. They can work as part of creative teams of writers and video and audio documentarians to create compelling issue-based experiences.

While sensible about the difficulties of adapting to the Internet, thoughtful producers like Susan Meiselas understand that "We have to find ways of taking people someplace they don't expect to go." Her web site, www.akaKurdistan.com, posts images of Kurdish culture from diverse contributors, contemporary and historical, for visitors to view and discuss. In effect, the site hosts public debates about ways of representing truths.

In public forums communities of photographers, like those of writers and scientists, can examine the evidence and censure those who deliberately lie, digitally or otherwise. In this way, as curator Anne Wilkes Tucker described, "Photographers are liberated from trust being inherent in their medium. Our acceptance or rejection of the information they present will have to do with the reputation of the photographer, the declared intentions of the maker, and what else we know about that subject. In some ways it's probably the best thing that's happened in documentary."

Meiselas's www.akaKurdistan.com also suggests that accelerated cultural interaction need not imply the wholesale abandonment of cultural and political traditions—it may instead be an occasion for their renewal.

Certainly, we can appreciate traditions like democracy and humanism that promote commonality amid difference, mutual respect, and lawful resolution of conflict. Each shares a cultural genealogy that is traceable through Ashoka, Gandhi, and King as well as Erasmus, Jefferson, and Mandela. They are neither natural nor inherent in human societies, as Hitler and Pol Pot have surely taught us. Democratic values urge us to resist the false comfort of utopias but encourage our better selves. For over a hundred years they have guided documentary photographers.

As they evolve and mature, democratic and humanistic traditions recognize that our commonality lies not just in our similarities, but in our multiplicity, and that this multiplicity cannot be contained within any one country, culture, or ideology. We can value each other although we are not the same. We can experience one another through one or another aspect of our own multifaceted selves.

Good photographs are complex records of this exchange between photographer and subject. They give us access to the experience of both and evoke and widen feelings within the viewer.

A widened consciousness of other human beings and cultures invites compassion and yields some working truths: there is no final conflict, no shelter from tragedy, no release from suffering, and no end of history. It is the perfect theories and the dreams of a perfect state that deceive us.

During the communist occupation in Czechoslovakia, writers won our admiration by courageously passing around copies of samizdat books of literature and social criticism. Others, like Antonin Kratochvil's father, a filmmaker and "class enemy" of the regime, made photographs on paper smuggled into the country. By witnessing a lie, these writers and photographers gave us glimpses of truth. They kept alive their human feeling, their sense of humor, and their sense of purpose.

"We've got pictures," they told us. "We were there."

Photographers

Hansel Mieth
1909–1998

The Depression and the Early Days of *Life*

In 1937 Hansel Mieth began work as a photojournalist for *Life*, only the second woman, after Margaret Bourke-White, to be hired full-time by the magazine.

Born in Germany in 1909, Mieth began photography as an amateur while traveling through Yugoslavia, Austria, Bosnia, Bulgaria, Romania, and Hungary with her boyfriend, Otto Hagel. After migrating to the United States in 1929, the couple worked among migrant farm laborers and photographed the extreme poverty of the Depression. These photographs were the basis of their book, *The Great Hunger*. In 1934 Mieth and Hagel made a film about the California Central Valley cotton strike, ironically titled *A Century of Progress*.

At *Life* Mieth photographed hundreds of stories, including Texas cowboys, the Meninger clinic, young railroad hoboes, the census, and unwed mothers. In 1941 Mieth left *Life* magazine and, with Hagel, returned to the West Coast to resume work on social documentary projects. During the 1950s, they were unable to work as photographers after being blacklisted, and many of their friends were afraid to be seen with them.

Mieth's last major project was on post–World War II Germany. Mieth and Hagel returned to their hometown to photograph the devastation and broken people. Their collaborative effort, *We Return to Fellbach*, was published in 1950. After her husband's death in 1973, Mieth remained on their ranch in Northern California where she painted, photographed, and wrote until she died in 1998.

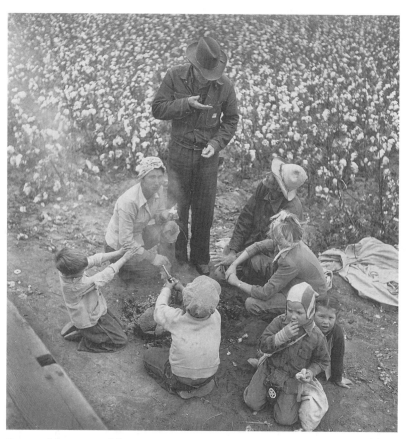

Cotton pickers around fire, 1934
(Hansel Mieth/Otto Hagel)

Otto and I had started photography in Germany in the late 1920s. Otto had a little camera. The first photographs he took were of his grandfather's funeral when he was twelve years old. He took a whole series of him dying and then being buried and the people bringing him to the cemetery. To see from these that eventually we would become photographers, you would have had to have a good imagination.

In Yugoslavia we took some pictures here and there and sent them in with little articles to newspapers. We hardly made anything. I don't even know if and how they were used, because we were traveling. We made ourselves a little booklet where we wrote our credo and the things we were looking for in the world. When we went to these various countries and towns and villages, we found out whether there were any writers or known people living there. If we could befriend them they would write in their life's urges and credo in our little book.

But we couldn't stay in Germany anymore because of the growing conditions under the Nazis.

I was about eighteen or nineteen years old when I came to the United States in 1929. I worked in San Francisco factories, sewing or hat making, and they paid me by the piece. The girls next to me were also on piece labor. I made piece by piece the same amount of material as them, and the boss gave me six dollars a week. They made twelve dollars a week. Now I was not against them getting twelve dollars, but I was against me getting six dollars. So I told the boss that he made a mistake. He said he didn't make a mistake. I tried to tell him, "Yes you did, you counted only half." He told me that people like me don't get anywhere in life because they want to know too many things. So I said, "I guess I have to leave you. Good-bye." And that happened a few times. They were telling me I was a "green" woman. When you had just come from another country to a new country, you didn't get the same wages that somebody who was here a long time was getting.

The camera I brought with me from Germany was stolen right in the beginning. So, when Otto was cleaning up somebody's attic he found a very small camera that didn't work. He went to the lady he worked for and asked if she would sell it to him. She said he could have it because it wasn't working. So he fixed it up. He had started as a watchmaker at home, so he took it apart and fixed it up, and he used that little camera. All the North Sacramento Hooverville pictures were taken with it.

It was during the Depression that we came to America, and we knew that the Depression couldn't last forever. Otto was really the person who took the lead. He said we must record the situation now—all the people who have no homes, who have no roof over themselves, who have dishes and who have nothing to cook, and who are on the road. We were in the same position as these people then. We couldn't buy the individual magazines of 35mm film, so we bought a hundred feet, or whatever length, they come in and rolled the film in the changing bag. We had our own cartridges then.

The thing that was a little hard was the developing and printing. You needed a stationary place and usually we had to come back for a week or two to San Francisco or Berkeley with some friends and borrow their darkroom. Or we rented a place in San Francisco, usually in the North Beach section, for $8.25 a month. There was a kitchen and a bedroom, and the bedroom we used as the darkroom. At the time they had flat roofs, and we could put a tent up there and sleep. Most of what we earned went to gasoline and film.

We got a job for a few weeks in North Sacramento from a Frenchman who had bought a place, and he wanted to get it cleaned up. We had to go by these Hoovervilles everyday. We started [photographing] Hoovervilles in 1931, 1932.

Otto and I, we went in and we talked to the men. We were all of one kind of language, I mean we could understand each other. We saw an Indian family there. We had cheap film and cheap paper, and everything came out pink, so we always call them the "pink Indians." We helped people if they had any construction problems. If a woman was not feeling well, I took care of the kids for her a bit. We just got acquainted, so the relationship was not just one way, it was many ways. It was quite a large Hooverville, I would think about three hundred families.

We looked upon it as a calling. The few cents we made, we did doing the hard work. We didn't have any money to pay out for rent or anything, sometimes only enough just to keep our car going. Nobody had anything in those days; they didn't save for the future. You just worked from day to day and hoped that someday it might get better. We thought the photographs could have a hand in it. People could see just how bad it was. Maybe they would build some camp or make it so that they could camp easier and not have to go to an outlying cemetery or a dump, that they could set a little piece aside where these homeless people could set their tents or their wagons. The North Sacramento Hoovervilles eventually got wiped out. The city burned them up and chased the people away.

In the beginning there was no photo market anywhere. Even for two or three dollars you couldn't sell anything except on the California Central Valley cotton strike. Publications would have paid you anything for those photos, but we didn't sell them any. Actually, we didn't know what to do with the photographs we took. I said there might come a time when they would be useful. At the time that we took them there was really no use for them.

We didn't belong to any political organization necessarily. But our world was on one side, and the corporate world was on the other side. I don't know how to explain that. We belonged to the majority of people. We only knew the poor. We didn't have much to do with the rich. They didn't know anything of us, and we wanted nothing of them.

We worked in every valley, from the San Joaquin and Central Valley to whatever valley it was, wherever there was something growing and wherever they needed workers to pick their fruit, whether it was peaches, oranges, pears, apples, potatoes, or peas. There was very little difference. You just let yourself be hired.

Children then were with their parents in the cotton fields. But we had no children to take care of. Most people had a family. Often the children were in the car and had to wait for the parents to come back every so often to the car and give them a drink and let them out and play in the sandbox on the side of the road or on the side of the field.

We had a little car. It had a rumble seat, and out of that we made a grub box, like a kitchen, in the back. We had all the grub. Whatever you needed to put a measly meal together was with us in the car. It took us about fifteen minutes from the time when we opened up a campsite to have water boiling on the tin stove. The tin stove was an old five-gallon tin can cut out so you could make a fire down underneath and boil the water while you were boiling beans and bacon or biscuits.

So many times in the cotton-picking picture, you see me either picking cotton or Otto is doing the work amongst the other people. Or you see me standing out in a picture with the Rolleiflex up in the air to get a better view.

We were part of the people that were working in the fields; they didn't have to give us permission to photograph. It was understood what we were doing and that we were trying to show with our photographs how bad the times were and that they shouldn't get any worse. That if the times ever get better, the photos would be a warning that at any time it could get bad again, and so we should stick together.

When the cotton strike was going on, people we knew were in the strike. Otto went to the field with a truck of strike organizers, and he said let's make a film of what's going on. He thought maybe a film could have given them a little presence and not them individually, but the whole idea, a movement, and show it a little better than in still pictures.

We came home one night, and there was no more camera. We had bought a 16mm camera, and it was missing, and the film was missing, and everything that you needed for the film, everything was missing. And since Otto had left Germany in a hurry when he came here, he did not have any papers. So he couldn't go to the police and ask about it, but I did. I said you took our film away, you smashed our things. The police said they didn't take the film, but we didn't believe them. For years we believed that they did it because they smashed places up, and we were taking pictures of the strike.

Maybe thirty years later we phoned an old colleague from this period in Los Angeles, where he lived, and he said, "My God. Sure. I had the film. I took it with me and all during the war. I had it in my baggage." He explained the whole thing. Because we belonged to the Film and Photo League and he belonged to the Film and Photo League, it was not a matter of swiping it. It was just a matter of if you were in the Film and Photo League, the Film and Photo League owned it. And so he kept it.

Little by little, I eventually got on the WPA [Works Progress Administration] in 1936. I went to the art department with whatever strike pictures I took.

I also had pictures of Chinatown. The young kids didn't have any money, so five or six more Chinese kids usually rented a room, and the bed was in use twenty-four hours a day. It started with one or two men, and after eight hours they got out, and then the next two got to bed. The children didn't have any playgrounds. They played around the narrow Chinatown streets, and I had quite a number of, maybe thirty or forty, prints of that.

I went around with them to the WPA art department, and they looked at them and said, "No, we couldn't employ you. You should not have come to the art department, because what you have here is not art. It is propaganda, strictly propaganda, and we don't deal in that. It has to be art for art's sake. What you have is always dealing with a purpose, and art shouldn't have a purpose like this."

So I went home again and said, well, that was a bummer. But we needed a little extra money, and I had heard of the youth and recreation department, whose headquarters were in the San Francisco Mission district. I went to the director of the project, and he looked at the very same pictures, and he put his arms around me and said, "That's just what I was looking for. Sure you can work for us. But I don't have a photographic project. Why don't you start one?"

So I got three or four people, young photographers like me, and we had a project going. That's when I photographed the boys on the road. I was with all the nationalities in San Francisco who had their headquarters at various places. We did the unemployment situation in San Francisco and all of California. We had an open season. We could photograph what we wanted as far as the director was concerned. Through our project they got a few playgrounds built in Chinatown. They got things organized in the various nationalities, like the International School and the International House. So we really did something.

Time magazine wanted to get some of the pictures. They got to know me through Peter Stackpole [an early *Life* magazine photographer]. I developed some of my pictures in his darkroom, and he showed them to *Life* magazine. Joining up with them maybe wasn't the absolute best thing I did, because I felt I was forsaking my people.

The *Life* man asked me if I wouldn't want to work for them. I said he wouldn't want me because I was not of the very same opinion. He said, "We don't need a bunch of yes-men. I think you will do fine with us. You have a different opinion and don't worry. We'll get along all right." Finally I agreed to do some freelance stuff with them. And they sent me out the rest of the year. That was the end of 1936.

The rest of the year, 1936 and beginning of 1937, I did a number of stories for them. One was on sheep raising in California.

When Gene Smith came to *Life* magazine we understood each other very well. He came out to California a lot, and we talked and talked, and it turned out that what we subscribed to was this responsibility in life. We were born, we have a place in life, and we felt we had a responsibility to give back, to help if we possibly could to move the world a little closer to understanding—one person to the other, against wars and the war industry. Still we were not firebrands of any sort or rushing around rabble-rousing. We just understood our places.

Between Otto and Gene and me in the photo department at *Life* we saw eye to eye. Except Gene had a completely different life. There was no girl who'd live with Gene. He was a wonderful guy, and he was impossible. Even I got tired at times. I told Otto, "You are sitting up all night long, talking, talking, talking, what does it get you?" But with Gene it was all very important.

He had so many fights with *Life* magazine. With Gene, nothing mattered but doing a job well, doing it the way he saw it. "If I can bring just a little glimmer of understanding in the world," he always said, "my job is not lost."

But then he lost their house, and they had to get a divorce. I knew Carmen, his first wife, so well. She was a wonderful girl, a wonderful mother. He didn't make a life for her. With the second wife, he had a child out of wedlock. Some part of his life was completely unrealistic. Not that my life was realistic, but at least I always went back again to where I was born, to what my mother told me.

After a while at *Life,* I couldn't take it anymore. I felt that our marriage—and we weren't really married—was falling apart. That was the first thing. And I could point to so many other marriages that had fallen apart because living had gotten so easy.

There were stories which I just loved doing, and there were stories that I was no good at that I didn't like. But that was not the really bad thing. The really bad thing is the big question of what was I doing? Whom was I helping? You were on expense account; you flew around and took a big room in a train and so on. Your whole life was upside down from where it was before. You looked at the world through the viewfinder lens instead of directly with people, talking with them. And I wanted to go back to where I was before. I wanted to go back to California.

We had come to know most of the West Coast photographers in 1933 and 1934. When you were at demonstrations or were running up and down the sites looking for a picture, usually Dorothea Lange was there with her camera. It was before she had a small camera. She had a big Graflex. Dorothea usually was with a young man, like John Collier Jr., helping her.

Through Dorothea we came to know most of the other photographers. We came to know John, Peter Stackpole, Ansel Adams, and Edward Weston. We even lived with Dorothea and Paul Taylor, her husband, in Berkeley until we found a place of our own.

People like the very early stuff, but we didn't think we were really doing great things. They like that best of all because it came from the heart. The very early stuff I did counts more. It's not just the years; it's not just that collectors go for the thirties. No, it's a type of photograph that grows on you.

We didn't always have a very safe place for the work. While we kept them pretty well—the photographs, the negatives, and the few prints we could make with outdated paper—the thing is that we had to move so often, and Otto and I were not always home together in the same place. He was in Sacramento at one time, and another time he may have been down in the fields, and I was home and during the day I was out working.

I was a salesgirl in a five-and-ten or in a bakery store or in a sewing factory or in an office, and for a while I worked for the forestry department typing. I had so many jobs. Anybody could come in the apartment, so we don't have all the negatives anymore. Quite a few are missing, and I'm sorry about that. I'm looking for stuff that I know I would have wanted very badly that is not there anymore. And then when we moved from Telegraph Hill to another place, Otto had a bench made against the wall that you opened up and the bench was also a box. Somebody got in while we were moving and took quite a few papers, like citizen papers and my photographs. And that never came back.

We have come through so many chapters in my life. In your life you have quite a few chapters that turn what you did before upside down. So it's very hard to say if we were successful. What is success? You cannot buy a cup of coffee with it.

Walter Rosenblum
1919–2000

Lewis Hine, Paul Strand, and the Photo League

W alter Rosenblum's early involvement in photography began before he was twenty when he joined the Photo League, an organization for photographers founded in the Depression era. Later he would serve as its president. The organization nourished many of the generation's most famous photographers, notably Rosenblum's influential mentors Paul Strand and Lewis Hine. Strand contributed to Rosenblum's formal understanding of photography, while Hine opened up the world of social documentation. The Photo League was later accused of communist activity and destroyed during the McCarthyism era.

Rosenblum began work as a freelance photographer in the early 1940s, publishing his pictures in *Life, Survey Graphic,* and *Mademoiselle,* but it was his work as a combat photographer in World War II that brought him wider attention. Rosenblum was among the troops at Omaha Beach on D day; later, he was one of the first army cameramen to film the liberation at Dachau. After the war he photographed Spanish refugees in the south of France and Mexican migrant workers in the Southwest for the Unitarian Service Committee.

In 1948 Rosenblum began teaching photography at Brooklyn College, where he continues to hold the position of professor emeritus. In 1949 he married Naomi Baker, who, writing as Naomi Rosenblum, is the author of important surveys of American photography, including *A World History of Photography.*

Rosenblum has returned several times to the theme of urban New York

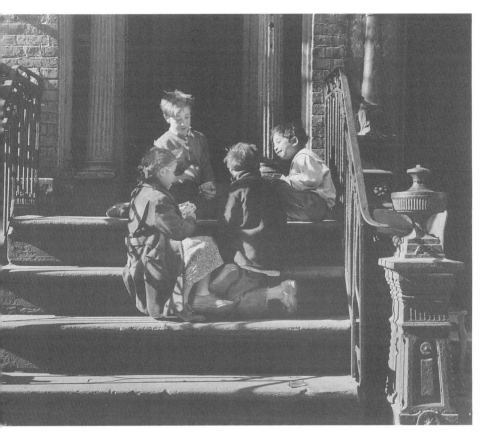

Gypsy children playing cards,
Pitt Street, New York, 1938
(© Walter Rosenblum)

City life, including *People of the South Bronx* (1979) and early work about his childhood neighborhood on the Lower East Side, *Pitt Street* (1938). In 1998 Rosenblum was given the Lifetime Achievement Award by the International Center for Photography in New York and was part of the Whitney Museum of American Art exhibition, "The American Century, Part 1, 1900–1950."

I was born on the Lower East Side of New York City in a neighborhood that provided sustenance for Jewish families recently arrived from Europe. Because my parents were orthodox Jews, my education at home was limited to the study of the Old Testament; art, music, and literature were never subjects for discussion. I knew the inside of my neighborhood synagogue at firsthand, but the Metropolitan Museum of Art was not part of my youthful experience. My introduction to photography was through Gus's Photography Studio, a small store that faced the building in which I lived. Gus used the sidewalk in front of his studio to expose his printing frames to the sun. Had I known how to use a camera then, it would have made for a fascinating photograph.

While in high school, I took a rudimentary photography class taught by a WPA [Works Progress Administration] teacher at the Boys Club of New York. It was a primitive affair. You developed your film by rolling it through a tray filled with developer and then made a contact print in a small printing frame. It was at that time that my mother, whom I dearly loved, died. My mother had been my protector who tried to provide a semblance of reason to my life, but now I was left alone with my father, whose life centered on religion. To assuage my grief, I went for long walks around the Lower East Side. For some reason, which I did not understand, I carried an old roll-film camera that my sister had borrowed from a friend; it turned out to be a true lifesaver. The camera forced me to look more deeply at my environment, and while the photographs I made were of little consequence, I discovered an interest that took me out of myself and into the world that surrounded me.

After graduating from high school I enrolled in the evening session at City College, but my interest in photography continued, so I joined the school's Camera Club. There I met Carroll Siskind, a young man who was sensitive to my needs and who suggested that I take a class at an organization called the Photo League. Tuition was six dollars a semester, which seemed affordable, and there were darkrooms available to members. So one day I found my way to its headquarters at 31 East twenty-first Street in Manhattan. The League opened at noon, and, since I was half an hour early, I decided to sit on the outside stairway until the doors opened. Mike Ehrenberg, a member, quietly joined me, and, when we started to talk, I was impressed to learn that he had photographed the civil war in Spain. Recognizing a beginner, he made every effort to make me feel at home, informing me that the League not only had a school and darkrooms for members, but also sponsored a number of other activities. It issued a mimeographed newsletter called *Photo Notes*, held weekly meetings, and sponsored what were called "feature groups."

The Photo League was housed in a loft on the second floor of an old building of Civil War vintage. An old stone stoop led up to two long flights of rickety wooden stairs and then to a room with a worn wooden floor, an ancient tin ceiling, and decrepit folding chairs set out against the walls. The front of the loft served as an exhibition gallery. Dues at the League were five dollars a year. I later learned that shortly before I joined the Photo League in 1937, it had broken away from the Film and Photo League. The film section had split into two groups, one devoted to what was then called agit-prop film—which meant documenting union activities, strikes, and demonstrations—while the other section thought of itself as an educational study group, where the films of [D. W.] Griffith, [Sergei] Eisenstein, [Vsevolod Illarionovich] Pudovkin, and [Aleksandr] Dovzhenko could be discussed and analyzed. This group, which was first called NYKino, became Frontier Films after Paul Strand joined it as president. During the 1930s, it produced several documentaries including *Heart of Spain*, *People of the Cumberland*, *China Strikes Back*, and, lastly, *Native Land*.

As you entered the loft, you were in a narrow passageway facing the space for the office secretary. At the front was a large area where the school held its classes and the League its membership meetings. In the back were two darkrooms—one for developing film, the other housing five ancient Elwood enlargers. The darkroom fee for one-time use was ten cents, which paid for the developer and hypo, although I never recall paying the fee. The school consisted of three courses:

beginners, advanced, and workshop. On occasion, there was a special advanced class taught by Berenice Abbott. I paid my five-dollar dues and became a member.

Since the school was in midsession, I couldn't register for a class, and so without ever having been in an enlarging room before, I purchased a pack of paper, and decided to try to imitate what others were doing. When a member saw me put my paper into the hypo before the developer, she realized my predicament, and gently showed me how to make an enlargement. I later learned that this generous—and handsome— young woman was the daughter of Robert Flaherty of *Nanook of the North* fame. The members came from all walks of life. There were students, teachers, lawyers, accountants, plumbers, electricians—all interested in photography. It was immediately apparent that members were eager to help one another. I quickly realized that a course of instruction was imperative, and I registered for the beginner's class.

The major figure at the League was Sid Grossman. He was a remarkable person—very bright, mercurial, difficult to deal with on a personal level if he felt you were not serious. Sid was the chairman of the school committee, and the students who had studied with him were his greatest admirers. A few weeks after I joined the League the secretary resigned, and Sid, recognizing my interest in photography, offered me the job. I worked from twelve noon to seven at night, five days a week for ten dollars a week. The ten dollars permitted me to move out of my father's home to a small one-room apartment in New York City. Being secretary provided a wonderful learning experience, because I became involved in everything that was going on at the League. I acted as treasurer, collecting dues; I mailed meeting notices, typed *Photo Notes*, helped to organize and mount exhibitions, arranged for speakers for our weekly meetings, and collected work for the monthly print competitions. The prize was a twenty-five–sheet package of enlarging paper—an important gift in the Depression years.

It was at the League that I met Berenice Abbott, Lewis Hine, Paul Strand, the Newhalls, Ralph Steiner, Leo Hurwitz, Edward Weston, Ansel Adams, Elizabeth McCausland, and many others. I did not realize it at the time, but these individuals were the educational force that prepared me for the path that I was to follow for the rest of my life.

The League provided an environment where I learned about photography's history. When Hine and I were together, I discovered at firsthand what he had contributed to photography as social documentation. From Strand, I learned about David Octavius Hill, Eugène Atget, and Alfred Stieglitz. The League was an exciting place not only because it provided a congenial place to work, but also because interesting people, deeply involved with photography, were happy to help young photographers understand in greater depth the meaning of photography as a fine art.

Aside from my office duties, I spent all of my free time at the League. It became my home. The beginners and advanced classes I attended were well taught and serious in intent, but it was Sid Grossman's workshop class that was of most importance to young photographers. While classes at the League were scheduled from 8 to 10 P.M., Sid held his classes at his home, which permitted us to remain together for a longer period of time. We not only looked at photographs and explored the projects we had chosen as class assignments, but we discussed the many problems that young photographers faced in the Depression years. One's personal growth, the influence of other art forms, our relationship to the world in which we lived—everything was open for discussion. We were free to explore all aspects of photography, as well as our own personal needs and desires. Each session was something to be treasured and remembered.

With the great numbers of photographic books available today, it may be difficult to realize that in 1938 only a handful of books on photography were available for the photographic educator. To fill this void, Sid prepared a series of mimeographed articles on photography that he had collected through the years. His workshop provided the finest training ground for the serious photographer that I have ever experienced. While he paid attention to the technical problems we faced, his primary purpose was to help us to develop as human beings. He recognized that many of us were severely limited by our background and that we would come to his class with little intellectual or aesthetic knowledge, so he endeavored to enlarge our vision and make us more sensitive to life in all of its manifestations.

Sid never received any financial recompense for the time, effort, and love that he gave to students. He worked as a photographer for the Works Progress Administration, which meant that he had to live on a weekly salary of twenty-three dollars. His teeth needed attention that he could not afford, and he suffered terribly from migraine headaches.

But the Photo League was his life and the students his emotional center. Sid was dedicated to photography as a serious means of personal expression, and he communicated this interest to all who studied with him. Besides teaching, he was also the primary guide in seeing that the League played a significant role in the development of photography during the time of its existence.

In 1938 photography was in a state of flux. Even though FSA [Farm Security Administration] documentation and photojournalism were beginning to make their presence felt, among those interested in personal expression, the pictorialist approach to photography seemed predominant. Pictorialist camera clubs throughout the United States were devoted to a kind of psuedoartistic photography, which was featured in many photographic magazines. Their members never seemed to find inspiration in the world in which they lived, but made soft-focus derivative images of nudes, misty landscapes, and individuals posturing in period costumes. In contrast, League members focused on their own environment and dealt with life on the streets in the various working-class and ethnic neighborhoods of New York City. We wanted our photographs to be considered as serious work, but pictorialists were derisively labeling us the "ash can" school of American photography.

A new kind of vitality, exemplified by photojournalists who were exploring the world for *Life, Look, Picture Post,* the *München Illustrierte Zeitung,* and *Vu,* in France, infused the work of League members. The Farm Security Administration group, notably Dorothea Lange, Walker Evans, Ben Shahn, Jack Delano, Russell Lee, and Marion Post Wolcott, also helped us understand a different role for photography.

The League organized a series of "feature groups" where photographers could join together to work on a specific project. Aaron Siskind, Morris Engel, Harold Corsini, Jack Manning, and others were involved in making the "Harlem Document"; Grossman, Sol Libsohn, and Arthur Leipzig worked on a documentation of "Chelsea." "Park Avenue, North and South" proceeded under the leadership of Consuelo Kanaga, while Lewis Hine, who had been brought to the League by Abbott and McCausland, joined with Eliot Elisofon in leading a "Men at Work" project. My self-assigned project for Sid's workshop class was to photograph on "Pitt Street," on New York's Lower East Side, very close to where I had been born.

All of this took place during the depths of the Depression, which served as a motivating force for our work. The League had little in-come—rent was thirty-five dollars a month; the office secretary received ten dollars weekly salary—so all visiting speakers and the school faculty devoted their time without pay. When we ran short of money we organized fund-raising parties and film showings. In retrospect, we recognize that the League produced serious and talented photographers. Dan and Sandra Weiner came out of the League, as did Arthur Leipzig and Max Yavno; Morris Huberland, Rebecca Lepkoff, and Aaron Siskind were nurtured there, as were Sol Libsohn, Rosalie Gwathmey, Vivian Cherry, Elizabeth Timmerman, Harold Corsini, Morris Engel, and Jerry Liebling. Weegee [Arthur Fellig] was a member, and I remember meeting Robert Frank at the League when he had just arrived from Europe.

Unemployment was not easy to deal with in the late 1930s. On graduating high school I had answered an ad for an office boy. When I arrived at the address, there were more then a thousand people jamming the street in the hope of an interview. You learned to live on very little. I had a small one-room apartment; my bed was a mattress on the floor, and my furniture consisted of a table and chair. I ate lettuce-and-tomato sandwiches covered with mayonnaise to give the food some flavor. If I purchased film or enlarging paper it came out of my food budget.

Many of us were motivated also by our political allegiances. The Spanish civil war had ended with a victory for fascism. The Japanese had invaded Manchuria. I may have been about art and culture when I was a teenager, but not about politics, which seemed to be in the air we breathed during the Depression. A close friend, David Alman, whose parents were progressive thinkers, undertook to educate me about social ideas. Knowing of my dislike of my father's orthodox views, he had provided me with a series of pamphlets published by Ralph Ingersoll, which advocated an atheistic view toward religion. The pamphlets were so persuasive that when I was twelve, I felt it necessary to test his thesis by demanding that God end my life to demonstrate His presence. Fortunately nothing happened. As I followed David into new fields of social thought, I came to agree that socialism made much more sense then capitalism.

However, the policy at the League was to keep political beliefs out of official League matters. *Photo Notes*, which documented League activities, bears witness to the fact that League members were never asked to subscribe to any specific political point of view, which were considered personal decisions. Certainly, many League members were politically involved; in the late 1940s they supported Henry Wallace when he ran for president on the Progressive Party ticket. Earlier, others had boycotted Japanese photographic equipment when Japan invaded Manchuria. They might even have wanted to join the Artists Union, but in the mid-1930s the graphic artists who had formed the union refused admission to photographers.

League members usually were called "documentary" photographers, as were the FSA contingent, but over the years I have come to believe that this term was an inaccurate description of what many of us were trying to do. Documentary, which I believe was first used by British filmmaker John Grierson, describes the kind of work done in the nineteenth century to record the buildings, bridges, and roadways and landscape that comprised the physical environment. Later, the term was used to describe work done by Jacob Riis and Lewis Hine, and eventually the Farm Security Administration, to show social conditions that required amelioration. Hine preferred to call his work "social photography," which I believe more accurately reflects our interests at the League.

Many members of the League felt that it was the responsibility of photographers to photograph the social evils that the Depression had brought into being. Elizabeth McCausland, who, as art critic for the newspaper *Springfield Republican,* often wrote about photography, supported this view. In her mind anything outside the range of "documentary photography" was a form of escapism that should not be condoned. Paul Strand presented a different outlook—one which was not always welcomed by members concerned with changing the social scene. As president of Frontier Films, Strand was then primarily involved with motion pictures, but he was on the League's advisory committee and often attended League meetings and joined in print critiques. He felt that so called "documentary photography" often had a tendency to consider only subject matter and pay little attention to basic aesthetic problems such as composition, tonal scale, and print quality—the formal elements important to all enduring works of art. Ignoring these considerations, he claimed, often produced photographs which "exhausted themselves on the first look."

He also felt that we were limiting ourselves in terms of subject matter. The entire visual world was waiting to be explored while we limited ourselves to social themes. Strand never denigrated the work of League members, and for *Photo Notes* he reviewed *An American Exodus* by Dorothea Lange, citing it as a vivid and fruitful influence upon the development of photography as a medium of expression. Nevertheless, there were those within the League who did not look kindly on such an aesthetic overview and let their feelings be known. Of what possible interest could a cobweb in the rain, a church in Taos, or a landscape in New England be to a society faced with the deprivations of a Depression and the horrors of the war in Spain and the rise of fascism in Germany and Italy?

Strand was a mythical figure to most of us. We had heard rumors that he was an important American photographer, but we knew little of his work. We were unfamiliar with the grand photographic tradition of which he had been a part, were ignorant about the Photo-Secession and Alfred Stieglitz, who had by then disappeared into the recesses of his gallery, An American Place. I came to realize that our education, as good as it was, also was limited. I took a class given by Strand, and he remained a friend for more than forty years.

In the late 1930s the photographic scene was enormously different from today. Few books were available; there was one monograph on David Octavius Hill, one book on [Eugène] Atget. *Camera Work* had been forgotten, so it was not available to us. Lewis Hine's *Men at Work* was aimed at young readers, so Margaret Bourke-White's *You Have Seen Their Faces* and Dorothea Lange's *An American Exodus* were considered pioneers in the field of picture books on social issues. The [Beaumont] Newhall history [*The History of Photography*] had just appeared. Picture magazines like *Life* and *Look* were starting to make their presence felt, but there were no commercial galleries devoted exclusively to photographs. An American Place still existed, but Stieglitz showed mainly paintings. I believe that there was a small show at the New York World's Fair of 1939, and in the early 1940s the Museum of Modern Art began to show individual photographers' works—I was part of a group show there called "New Workers One." In fact, aside from the Museum of Modern Art, in the late thirties and up through the forties, the Photo League had the only real photographic gallery in New York City where one could see a range of work by European as well as American photographers.

League photographers worked mostly for themselves, for there was little chance of having their work published. The work of the feature groups received little public attention. In my entire career, all of the work that I did was self-assigned, except for a small number of commissioned jobs for charity groups and a series of photographs of Spanish refugees in France for the Unitarian Service Committee. There were the Guggenheim and Carnegie Foundation grants and, after the Second World War, federal and state grants, which could be very helpful. I was awarded a New York State Fellowship, a National Endowment for the Arts Fellowship, and, later, a Guggenheim Fellowship.

Because there were no commercial assignments available to us, we at the League were able to choose our own way of working. We were fortunate in that there were many outside influences available to us through the speakers who were featured at our Friday-night meetings. We did not recognize it at the time, but a who's who of mainly American photographers appeared at League meetings during the late thirties and forties.

On December 4, 1947, an event occurred which came as a total surprise. The U.S. Attorney General, Tom C. Clark, released to the press a list of over three hundred organizations he deemed "totalitarian, fascist, communist, or subversive," and his list included the Photo League. Forty years later the listing was judged unconstitutional, but by then it had wrecked many lives and done unbelievable damage to the civil liberties of all Americans. None of our members had ever been interviewed or asked for information. Indeed, some of the organizations so listed no longer existed. The League fought back by organizing a meeting at which Strand denounced this unwarranted attack upon our civil liberties. We printed his talk in *Photo Notes*, and asked our membership for their support at this trying moment in the League's history.

W. Eugene Smith, who was a member of the League, was so disturbed by what had happened that he traveled to Washington to personally ask the attorney general why the League had been listed. Unable to gain an audience with Clark, he was shunted off to an assistant who told him that one simply had to trust the government when it listed an organization as being subversive. When Gene responded by saying that if someone called his wife a prostitute, he would like to know why, the young lawyer simply repeated, "You will just have to trust us."

While the listing aroused concern among League members, we went on with our usual affairs. By 1948 our membership list now comprised a very large list of important American photographers and historians. As a result, we had outgrown our small quarters and moved to new space in the basement of the Hotel Albert. Our members—students, plumbers, electricians, and accountants—built walls, installed electrical connections, and fashioned a fine exhibition gallery, classroom space, and an office, constructing a handsome headquarters from what had been a decrepit space.

However, the political temper in Washington had changed. At the trial of the leadership of the Communist Party for conspiring to overthrow the United States by force and violence, Angela Calomiris, a League member who proved to be an FBI spy, named Sid Grossman as a member of the Communist Party. In her book entitled *Red Masquerade,* she continually lied about the political nature of the League. Grossman's career was ruined, and the emotional trauma that resulted ended his relationship with the League. Other members recognized that being associated with a so-called subversive organization affected one's ability to earn a living, so League members had to think carefully about maintaining their membership.

Beaumont and Nancy Newhall, Barbara Morgan, and Ansel Adams were among the first to resign. At first, in answer to the original listing by the attorney general, Nancy Newhall, who had always been a strong supporter of the League, had prepared a booklet entitled "This Is the Photo League" in which she extolled the League's contribution to American photography. She cited the large numbers of lectures by significant photographers and art historians and the exhibitions held at the League, which she said would have done justice to a major museum, and she praised the League school for the way in which it had developed and supported young talent. Later, accepting the generally hysterical political tone of the time, she was quoted as saying that perhaps the attorney general had information proving that the League was subversive, but with which she was not familiar. In support of the League, Gene Smith took over the presidency, and Strand, who was later to have his passport confiscated, maintained his membership, as did Edward Weston, who wrote letters of strong support. We had a loyal contingent of members who tried to continue, but the financial burden became too difficult to bear. We closed our doors in 1952.

Although the League had ceased to exist, a group of us continued to hold meetings at the homes of various members, discussing work and talking about the photographic scene in general. My teaching job at Brooklyn College brought me into contact with many young photographers, whom I introduced to the League. I continued to urge them to attend the monthly meetings that were then taking place, and a group of us later started another organization called the Photographer's Forum, which met monthly at the New School for Social Research. That too dissolved some three years later, because some of us just ran out of steam.

The League played an important role in the history of photography. We rescued photography from the banalities of third-rate pictorialism. We lent support to the Farm Security Administration photographers as they explored the world of the agrarian poor and the dispossessed, and we portrayed the strengths and vitality of the urban poor. We paid homage to Lewis Hine, Paul Strand, and Henri Cartier-Bresson, among others, for their contributions to twentieth-century photography; and we helped many young photographers find their way in a very complicated world. We fought the McCarthyism that was threatening to destroy our democratic heritage.

I would sum up my beliefs and experience as follows: Lewis Hine came into my life when I was nineteen and, by friendship and example, showed me a road I might follow. And then came Paul Strand, who made me see how a simple sheet of photographic paper might become alive with the wonders of the world. From him I learned that anything in the world can be photographed if it has meaning for the photographer, that subject matter is inexhaustible if one is willing to explore its richness, that beauty can be found in a cobweb in the rain, in a bit of sand under a stormy sky, or in the face of someone you love. He made me see that photography must always be treated with respect and given one's best effort. In my philosophy the meaning of life derives from the people one has known and loved, who have made life inexhaustible in its richness. I have met my share of evil people and know what they are capable of—I was at the liberation of the camp in Dachau—but I have always held that evil is not inherent in men and women. Given a caring society, only the best in people will flourish. That is the spirit that has moved me to photograph.

Michelle Vignes

Magnum Photo Agency: The Early Years

Michelle Vignes's formative years were spent in Nazi-occupied France. After completing her education she worked as a secretary at Magnum, the legendary international photo cooperative that was organized at the end of World War II. At Magnum, Vignes was an assistant to Henri Cartier-Bresson and, after Robert Capa's untimely death in Indochina, she took over distribution and sales in Europe for all of Magnum's photographers.

In 1957 Vignes left Magnum and worked in the Paris headquarters of the United Nations Educational, Scientific, and Cultural Organization (UNESCO) as a picture editor assigning and editing stories. She moved to New York City and worked in the photography department at the UN and eventually moved to San Francisco during the height of the "Summer of Love," where she began working as a freelance photographer for the Gamma agency, where she did a series of short, local stories. Her coverage of the Black Panther Party in Oakland and San Francisco brought her a national reputation, and she began to collaborate with *Time, Life, Vogue, Newsweek, Ramparts,* and numerous international publications.

Vignes photographed the American Indian Movement (AIM) occupation of Alcatraz Island in 1969 and AIM's declaration of secession from the United States as an independent Oglala nation at Wounded Knee in 1973. At Wounded Knee the FBI set up roadblocks with tanks, and armed agents policed the area for over three months. Vignes was one of the few photographers to shoot from inside the standoff and created a lasting bond with

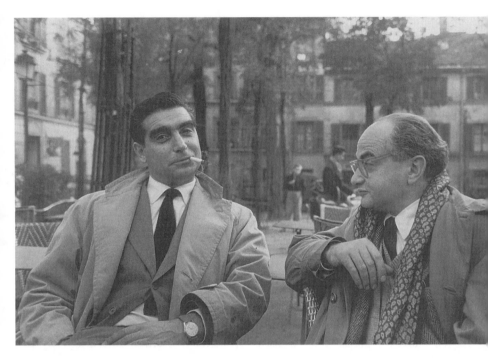

Robert Capa and David Seymour (Chim),
sidewalk café, Paris, 1953
(Collection of Michelle Vignes)

AIM members and the Native American community. Her work as a social documentarian began in earnest with this project.

In the mid-seventies Vignes started a long series on blues musicians, which culminated in the publication of three books: *Oakland Blues, Bay Area Blues,* and *The Blues.* Her more recent work, "The Gospel," flows from her interest in African American music and spiritual traditions in the San Francisco Bay Area.

As a cofounder of the International Fund for Documentary Photography and a respected teacher in the San Francisco Bay Area, she has helped to bridge photographers from different generations and continents. Vignes is currently working on a retrospective book of her decades of personal photographic work.

Her early experiences at Magnum offer a rare look inside the workings of what they called the "Gypsy Factory."

I took a job at Magnum in 1953 not knowing much about photography, just names of well-known photographers like Henri Cartier-Bresson and Robert Capa.

As we had no darkroom, we sent everything to Pierre Gassman, a printer totally dedicated to each one of the photographers. Often I had to send a courier to take the negatives and to bring back the print. I would stay late to send the photos and try to make the deadlines and beat the other agencies.

Henri Cartier-Bresson, or HCB, was scared of keeping his negatives at Magnum because we all smoked, and he was afraid that we would set a fire. His negatives were stored in his studio, which was some distance from Magnum and four flights up. A friend who had been in prison with him in Germany, Claude LeFranc, would pick up the negatives, then bring them to me, and I would register them. Then I had a messenger send them to Gassman and back. I was always worried I'd lose his best negatives.

HCB just cut the frame out of the strip, and put it in a tiny envelope. His work was filed chronologically, in very tight envelopes containing his proofs. On each envelope, there was the list of its contents. In order to know what he had done, you had to have been through all of those, and there were quite a few. I happened to have a good visual memory of his work, and could find anything very fast. I loved it right away.

I put the photo packages together and got them out to the magazines or to our correspondents in other countries. Things were not organized at all, so I created a system to send pictures, go to the train station, or the airport, and give the photos to someone and cable right away to the client that they would arrive via this stranger.

When I made the tour of magazines I would not only sell one story, I'd tell the picture editor, "Oh, listen, Ernst Haas is going to be in Thailand, or in Burma, for these coming weeks," trying to capture an assignment by mentioning a few stories that he could do.

Magnum was born because of the friendship of a few photographers who were involved around the Spanish War—Capa and Cartier-Bresson and George Rodger, who in his way was humanitarian more than political. We had some very political photographers. Magnum followed the intuitive talent of everybody; but each one had his or her different views.

Capa was a real businessman. If there hadn't been the war, he would have been great starting an enterprise of any kind. He was really a dynamo. He also gambled a lot on horses, and when he needed to borrow a little money to go on, he went to our accountant—who automatically would refuse any loan. But if he made a bundle she would accept the whole lot.

Capa had a wonderful sense of journalism. He always had ideas and was throwing people into the work. When I was there, he had started a story, "Generation X," that was the profile of one young person from each of several different countries. Each photographer chose a country. It was for *Holiday* magazine or another big one. After they did it, the magazine turned it down, so Capa recycled it to another one of the leading magazines.

Henri Cartier-Bresson could have become an art photographer. Capa, who had his feet on the earth, directed him, telling him, "No, don't do that mannered thing." Capa was the only one who could say to the photographers this is wrong or this is right. There were around twenty photographers. It was a centering point, where people were dispatched out, where photographers discussed, got the assignments.

Cartier-Bresson was a lot in Paris, but also, in 1954, he spent quite a few months photographing Russia. He was the first photographer to do stories in Russia. George Rodger came in and out, but around that time he had decided to leave *Life* to go and shoot in Africa. With George, we had a regular correspondence.

There were others. Erich Lessing started to photograph still lifes of opera and do portraits. Inge Morath followed Henri Cartier-Bresson on a trip in Europe as his assistant. Inge was married to the picture editor of *Picture Post* at that time.

[Werner] Bischof was a very shy, tall guy. Capa was always joking, and having fun, and drinking, and enjoying life. Bischof was a little straighter, and his sense of humor was so different that it made their communication difficult. The wife of Bischof, Rosellina, a wonderful woman, took care of his work and the work of others.

Magnum was really a turning point among photo agencies, because they had the photographers keep their negatives. They fought for that, that the photographer is the author and keeps his negatives.

After a year I became the picture editor in charge of all the sales in Europe. When Cartier-Bresson came back from Russia we sold his stories. They were divided into thirteen little stories, and I went to *Elle*, *Paris Match*, etc. We went very officially to see Madame and Monsieur Lazareff, the heads of a big chain of leading periodicals, including *Elle* magazine and the newspaper *Francesoir*. With Henri, I had discussed which stories we were going to bring. Those magazines were mostly women's fashion, and for those the editor was Michele Rosier, the daughter of the Lazareffs, a young woman in her twenties. We brought some things that had to do with women and fashion—maybe six of the thirteen stories. She looked at us, and said "Mr. Cartier-Bresson, you are leaving a few drops of your pee pee in each different magazine in Paris." (Laughs)

There was no precedent to establish a price on such a story, so out of the blue, really, I had to find a high price and be firm on it. It was scary. When we went to *Paris Match*, the leading magazine in France, we were asking a high price for each story. I gave them a day to make up their mind. They looked at them, and the next day, returned most of them to me. I think they kept two or three, and we were really disappointed, because we thought that would be our big sale. So right away, I rushed across the street to *Jours de France*, a direct competitor, but who didn't have that much money. They were very impressed, and they said, "Well, maybe yes. Let's consider, you know, the ones that were not chosen by *Match*." I couldn't ask for the same price. I asked a little bit lower.

That next night, around 11 P.M., I received a phone call from Henri Cartier-Bresson, who was at *Paris Match* working with the main editor. I heard the deep voice of the editor saying, "Michelle, we want to buy much more, and we want such and such a story by two days from now, by Wednesday, let's say."

So I said, "Yes, you'll have them," and I didn't sleep at all, because I didn't know if *Jours de France* was still considering them. I got really, really worried. When I called the next day, they said, "No, we're buying a story on Russia from another photographer." I thought, Whew!

The hardest thing was when we heard of the death of Capa, and then Bischof two days later. It was like being totally crushed. Capa didn't want to go on photographing wars, you know, and he wanted to print his new card: PHOTOGRAPHER OUT OF WORK (AU CHOMAGE). He died nonetheless on the last assignment he had accepted to do on war. He stepped on a land mine in Indochina.

Bischof was in a car accident in Peru, in the mountains. We were in shock, in total shock. I thought we were a family, a big loose family. But it wasn't that big, loose family, because right away there was a fight for power. Cartier-Bresson never wanted to have the power, but other people were jealous of him. So, once the magical alliance of HCB-Capa was broken, the others behaved like lost orphans.

After the volcanic and invulnerable Capa came the reign of the least aggressive of the founders: David Seymour or "Chim." He was kind and vulnerable. Here is his portrait by HCB: "He had the intelligence of a chess player with the look of a math teacher. He applied his vast culture to a wide range of subjects. He used his camera like a doctor would use a stethoscope in order to diagnose the state of the heart. He was vulnerable."

So he applied his stethoscope to the wounded Magnum, helping the agency's healing process. Unfortunately he was killed in 1957 in the Suez Canal.

When HCB's book, *The Decisive Moment*, came out, people were amazed with this different form of photography. That's where Cartier-Bresson made his mark. It was a stepping stone, and it has inspired a lot of people.

I think Magnum taught photographers to think in a way that they didn't before. They shot a bit straighter, and it suggested to photographers that you have to have a style, and you have to create an image from life. They taught how to believe in what you do and to live fully, live fully with your little camera. Don't do it just to record.

Magnum wanted everyone to know about the chaos that was going on in the world. George Rodger photographed the Bergen-Belsen concentration camp. Chim photographed prostitutes in Essen. There were Soviet war prisoners that were leaving Germany and many Jewish immigrants who escaped the camps and were never at home anymore. The ghettos where they had lived didn't exist anymore. Thousands went to Palestine, and Capa photographed them. Such was their work and the power of their lives. Their photographs continue to enrich, inform, and move us today.

Wayne Miller

World War II and the Family of Man

After a short stint in art school, Wayne Miller joined the navy and, a few months later, Edward Steichen's World War II photography unit. By the end of the war Miller was working as a freelance photographer for several national magazines and received two consecutive Guggenheim fellowships for the project, "The Way of Life of the Northern Negro," photographed in his hometown of Chicago.

Miller, his wife, Joan, and their three children moved in 1949 to Orinda, California, where he worked as a contract photographer for *Life*. In 1953 Edward Steichen, the director of photography at the Museum of Modern Art in New York City, enlisted him as an assistant curator for the historic "Family of Man" exhibition.

Miller created two books about childhood: *A Baby's First Year* with Dr. Benjamin Spock in 1955 and, after the family returned to California that year, *The World Is Young*. Elected to the Magnum photo agency in 1958, Miller served as its president from 1962 to 1966.

In 1958 he and Joan also purchased a redwood forest and, later, a vineyard, which they continue to manage. After retiring from Magnum and photography in 1977, Miller developed award-winning environmental education programs for the National Park Service. A book of his photographs on Chicago's South Side was published by UC Berkeley's Graduate School of Journalism, Center for Photography and the University of California Press in 2000 to much acclaim. In 2008 a retrospective of Miller's early work was published, *Wayne F. Miller: Photographs 1942–1958*. The book is the

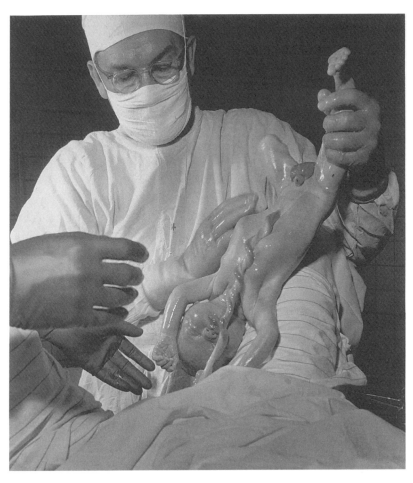

Birth of David B. Miller delivered
by his grandfather, September 19, 1946
(© Wayne Miller/Magnum Photos)

visual chronicle of his evolution as a photographer and includes some of his finest imagery from several classic periods of his oeuvre including his war images and *The World is Young*, which is long out of print.

I was born and raised in Chicago and attended the University of Illinois, where I became photographer for the university's yearbook and newspaper, *The Daily Illini*. I went to the Art Center School in Los Angeles for nine months before I was asked to leave, because I didn't have the proper respect for their curriculum. When World War II came, I joined the navy and became a member of Captain Edward Steichen's special navy photographic unit.

In 1942 I married Joan Baker, which would prove to be the smartest decision I would ever make. In one bold move, I captured exclusive photo rights to her life and those of the four children she eventually produced. (Laughs)

Steichen was an exceptional man. He had been a painter of repute in the early 1900s and had introduced the works of Rodin, Cézanne, Brancusi, and others to the U.S. He was a lieutenant colonel in charge of aerial photography in World War I and, as chief photographer at Condé Nast, had created new standards for fashion and advertising photography between the wars.

I wasn't really a professional photographer. I learned on the job. By chance, I was the first one in the group, and I helped set up the conditions and space and equipment for the others, who came in shortly after I arrived.

I learned because Steichen encouraged me. If he saw something lousy in my work—and there was an awful lot of it—he ignored it and found things good to talk about. I don't ever remember him giving me an assignment, except to photograph the sailors—the "little guys" he felt would win the war. I followed the battle actions around in the Pacific, the Indian Ocean, and southern France. Much of my four years was spent aboard aircraft carriers, where action photography was limited to the occasional times we were attacked by air or torpedo. If you were on the wrong side of the ship, you missed the photograph.

I was excited, ambitious, and afraid all the time. Under similar conditions, anyone who says differently is a liar. Once a navy photographer asked if he could go in my place in a torpedo-bomber mission. When the plane returned, he had been killed by machine gun fire. His last photographs showed a Japanese Zero attacking his plane.

Often when I got into landing craft, I would get seasick. Off Italy, while waiting for the invasion of southern France, I went ashore out of boredom and photographed the children of Naples. Later I learned that these hungry, ragged children were not necessarily a reflection of the war, but of normal conditions in Naples. Gene Smith, who saw the photos at *Life* with only the traditional credit line, "Photo by U.S. Navy," sent me a telegram that said, "Congratulations. I knew that these were yours."

Toward the end of the war in Japan, I traveled with a task force whose job was to liberate the prisoner-of-war camps. Unlike in Europe, the Japanese often put POWs in hotels. In one case, an American prisoner who had liberated himself was soaking in a bath while one of his former guards served him a cold beer.

I was also in Japan for the securing of Tokyo Bay harbor, then I left immediately with photographer Jay Eyerman of *Life* magazine for an eight-to-ten hour train ride to Hiroshima where the United States had dropped the atomic bomb. *Life* magazine had found us a nisei to act as an interpreter. He had been trapped in Tokyo at the beginning of the war and was a hot trumpet player at Radio Tokyo. Later I learned that—even though we were grimy and unshaven—he was passing us off as generals investigating the war damage.

The people with whom we had been at sword points for four years completely ignored us. They didn't push us or swear at us. They acted as though we weren't there. The emperor said the war was over and they were going home. We were in Hiroshima for only a day. We had no food or blankets. And we didn't know what we were walking into. Hiroshima was a horror, the ultimate denial of sanity.

I could have attended the surrender ceremonies, but I didn't. I was just tired of it all. During my four years, I'd seen an incredible waste of lives and resources. One evening toward the end, I drifted out on deck and joined a group of my shipmates. We swapped jokes for awhile, but then our mood shifted, and we began to discuss the blind futility of war. Many of us felt we were fighting in the dark against enemies we didn't know and who didn't know us. Guns and bombs might win the war, but ignorance would surely lose the peace.

I never forgot that conversation. It helped convince me to document the things that make the human race a family. We may differ in race, religion, language, wealth, and politics, but look what we have in common—dreams, the comforts of home, the hunger for love. With photographs, I thought I might help some of us better understand the strangers who live on the other side of the world—and on the other side of town.

Not long before the war ended I received a grant from the Guggenheim Foundation to photograph "The Way of Life of the Northern Negro." I went back to Chicago, where there was a large black population on the south side, many of whom moved there during the war.

Getting started was my biggest problem. After two months of stewing and stalling, I slung my Rollie around my neck and went to meet the people of south Chicago.

I had good luck almost from the start. At the South Parkway Community Center, I met Horace Cayton, the coauthor, with St. Clair Drake, of the sociological study, *Black Metropolis*. He knew everyone and was most generous in sharing his immense knowledge and contacts. Interracial groups of artists, activists, social service personnel, and society leaders often gathered at the center. It was always exciting. Once, I made a picture of a young white woman hanging a picture by hammering a nail into the wall with the butt of a revolver.

A struggling new magazine called *Ebony* occupied an office at the rear. Horace introduced me to its editor, Ben Burns, who promptly gave me photographic assignments, including stories I could never have discovered on my own.

While working on the grant, curious South Siders only challenged me a few times. So I'd cheat a little and answer, "Oh, I'm with *Ebony* magazine." As a rule, though, those black men and women of Chicago were gracious and generous. Conversation was easy; doors were opened and invitations offered.

When I spotted an interesting situation, I didn't hide my camera or myself. Instead, I often approached and said, "Please, pay no attention to me." I think that I somehow created good vibes. I was trying to tell their story. I was trying to respect their lives. That was my only reason for being in the streets and the homes of south Chicago.

I gravitated to places where people were having fun, raising hell, or trying to raise money. Once I photographed a veteran prostitute on the job with one of her regulars. Afterward, he asked me if I'd gotten the pictures I wanted, and, when I said it happened pretty fast, he invited me to come back next Tuesday for me to have more time.

One of my favorite haunts, a bar on Forty-fifth Street, had a lurid reputation. Its clientele were stockyard workers, day laborers, and a few unattached women. Some passersby would step into the street rather than stroll by its open door. True, the crowd was a bit noisy and uninhibited. But, although I never saw another white face there, whenever I stopped in to make photographs or drink a beer, I was welcomed. Every summer the owners threw a big picnic for their friends and favored customers. I was invited, too, a gesture I'll never forget.

In addition to the thousands of photographs I made, there were thousands I didn't because my eyes and instincts weren't good enough. When I think of what I missed, it makes me want to cry. That I had the arrogance to even attempt such a grand concept now makes me uncomfortable.

It was a marvelous time. Magazines were hungry for photographers. I worked for *Life* on assignments, and for *Collier's,* and *Fortune.* I had more work than I could handle. I was also teaching at the Institute of Design in Chicago for one day a week. But after a while, it gets a little repetitious. I wanted bigger challenges.

I began to photograph my family in a documentary fashion. I did an assignment for *Ladies' Home Journal*—"Baby's First Year." I did two pages every month, photographing the changes within this baby's life. Later, with Dr. Spock, I made a book of these photographs.

In 1949 we decided to move either to the East Coast or the West Coast. The East seemed too much like Chicago. The sense of growth and movement in the West was more appealing, so I got a contract from *Life* in their San Francisco bureau and worked there four years.

I had met Dorothea Lange during World War II when I was going from Washington, D.C., to the Pacific—just an afternoon with her with warm pie and coffee in her garden. That was Dori. Dorothea was the reason I came out here. She was the only person I knew. She became a very close friend of the family, and she and Paul, her husband, invited us into their family lives. That quality she had was the quality she got in her photographs.

After the war Steichen had become director of photography for the Museum of Modern Art in New York. During the war, he told me of a dream that he had had in the 1930s of a massive photographic exhibition, a Walt Whitman–like hymn to America—photographs two or three stories high, to be hung in New York's Grand Central Station.

This dream was interrupted by the war. But Carl Sandburg, Steichen's brother-in-law and Lincoln's biographer, spoke during that time of Lincoln's use of the phrase, "The Family of Man," and Steichen realized that his project should not be limited to America, but worldwide. In 1952 he traveled to eleven countries and twenty-nine cities in search of material.

He felt that people the world over had a lot in common. And he wanted to show there was more love than hate in the world, and more goodness than there was badness. He felt that without a greater amount of love in the world, we would destroy ourselves.

In 1953 he called to say he wanted to meet California photographers. Dorothea Lange, Joan, and I organized a meeting at our Orinda home. The next day Steichen asked me to assist him, and I couldn't say no. Joan and I and our four children moved from California to New York City.

The "Family of Man" was a big idea, and we needed to find the photographs to convey it. I looked through the Time-Life files, where there were three-and-a-half million pictures, all in different file cases. In addition to the work of *Life* photographers, the file contained pictures collected by Time-Life from photographers all over the world. I'd make a pile of selections and take them back to the Museum of Modern Art. Steichen and I looked through them again. I spent five months there, and I put my hands on every one of those prints.

We also announced what we were trying to do and asked photographers who were interested to send material to us. We received pictures from all over the world—bags of mail filled with both snapshots and large prints.

We got some from a Russian photographers' association in Moscow —great big prints, images of factories, and fellows wearing suits. From China we received pictures of farming successes. The farmers were nicely dressed in peasant costumes and invariably wearing medals. One of them is in the book.

In addition, I visited picture agencies, corporate collections, and looked at the personal collections of photographers in New York City. We must have looked at four million or more photographs. Steichen said, "No one will believe four million. Let's say two million."

Our workspace was a loft over a striptease joint in New York City. We gathered the photographs there, and a couple assistants would log them in. We were never concerned about who made the pictures. We dealt with the pictures on the basis of their value to the core concept. We ended up with about ten thousand pictures. When we started working with these photographs they began to sort themselves out into certain categories. An obvious one would be "mother and child." Another would be "work." Another would be "play."

The assistants pinned them up on four-by-eight panels. We moved them around to relate one picture to another. As we got them up on these panels, obviously some of these things just didn't have any electricity to them. We continually questioned our values. Steichen also invited critics to come see the work in progress—photographers like Dorothea, some anthropologists and sociologists, the museum's director and his staff.

We created new categories, and we destroyed other ones, and, eventually, these categories began to create sequences. This is the way the exhibit was developed. I think you could say the photographs created the exhibit rather than Steichen and myself.

This was not an exhibit of fine photographs. This was an exhibit of photographs that expressed this common theme of the oneness of man. Most of the photographs had a relationship to another photograph. So the photograph itself was not necessarily complete in itself. It depended on the other member of the family to give it meaning. The idea of joining different photographers' work was unique. It was hard for some photographers to want to be involved in something like this because in the past it always had been the individual on the wall.

When it came to making of prints for the exhibition, we were dealing with concepts of communication that depended upon size, juxtapositions, and sequences. Some of the photographs were quite large—ceiling to floor. The largest one was of Mt. Williamson by Ansel Adams. It was about 10 feet high and 12 feet wide. We used an English paper that came in 40-inch-wide rolls. We had to make it in four panels, and it was quite a trick to match the quality of each panel.

Wherever the show went, it broke attendance records in major museums. The original exhibition made for the Museum of Modern Art in New York was hung on walls that were specially designed for them. Months later the U.S. Information Agency replicated the show and distributed it overseas. They were not involved in the creation of this show, but expressed their desire to distribute it. First it went to the world's fair in Moscow. In all, ten copies of the show were seen in sixty-nine countries by more than nine million people. The book was a best-seller and is still being published.

There were criticisms. At the time, we were dealing with Senator Joe McCarthy's communist hearings. McCarthy suspected physicist Robert Oppenheimer of being a red sympathizer, and we had a picture in the show of Oppenheimer conducting a seminar with graduate students. We talked about it, and Steichen said the hell with it, this is a good picture. Let's use it.

After I returned to California from New York and the "Family of Man," I realized that not one of all the pictures I'd seen had photographed childhood. Sure, we all make pictures of kids, but no one had really made an in-depth effort to photograph that world of childhood. I decided I wanted to do that. I wanted to come back to what was me. I loved news stories, and I was pretty good at them. But those things were like a skyrocket. You'd grab hold of it and ride it to the top, and, after it was over with, you'd come back to earth.

I really enjoyed photographing those closest to me. Edward Weston photographed his backyard because it was as important to him as the migrant worker was to Dorothea. Well, that's what my family was. And is.

I got an advance from the publisher of the "Family of Man" book, and I did it. I photographed my own family, and as the children played with the neighborhood children, their own friends, neighborhood friends. Then they went to school, so I followed them to school, until they became young adults. I was trying to show how the world appeared to them.

They seemed to be pleased with the book when it was published. About seven or eight years later, when Jeanette was a beginning college student, she paid me a compliment that I shall never forget: "Dad, why don't you do another book about my age group? People don't understand who we are or how we feel."

The World Is Young sold about eighty thousand copies and was one of the first Reader's Digest Condensed Books. Unfortunately, it didn't go back to press. I don't know why. Publishers are timid souls. After the publication of *The World Is Young* in 1958, I returned to magazine photography, then I retired from active photography in the mid-seventies.

I was asked, "Why did you quit?" For many years, I had been a spectator, an observer of other peoples' lives. I wanted to be a more active participant in the world, no longer just a fly on the wall watching the world through my viewfinder. When I mentioned this to my photographer friend Eve Arnold, she said, "I know exactly what you mean."

Peter Magubane

A Black Photographer in Apartheid South Africa

Born in Johannesburg in 1932, photojournalist Peter Magubane has helped expose South Africa's humanitarian crimes to the West. Magubane began at *Drum*, one of the only magazines dedicated to the anti-apartheid cause in the 1950s, first as a "tea-boy" and then a driver. He joined the photographic staff in 1954. The magazine was later syndicated, and, during the uprisings of the 1960s when other magazines such as *Time* and *Life* were forced to shut down, *Drum* was the world's primary source of photographs of apartheid.

Since Magubane is a black photographer, his work put his life in danger. The police broke his nose, and he has suffered multiple gunshot wounds. In 1970 he was accused by the government of being a communist and a terrorist. Imprisoned, he spent almost six hundred days in solitary confinement and was repeatedly and savagely beaten by guards. After his release the government "banned" Magubane, which prevented him from working as a photographer for five more years—a punishment he says was the most painful of all. In 1976, after the Soweto uprising, Magubane was able to resume work as a photojournalist for the *Rand Daily Mail* and covered the events that finally ended apartheid.

Magubane's work, much of which has been collected into the books *Magubane South Africa* (1978), *Soweto* (1979), *Black Child* (1982), *June 16, 1976* (1986), *Portrait of a City* (1990), and *Women of South Africa* (1993), provides a visual history of apartheid and the movement against it. With the end of apartheid and the election of his friend, Nelson Mandela, as presi-

Soccer fans go wild and police use dogs
to control the crowd, South Africa
(© Peter Magubane)

dent, Magubane turned to documenting native South African culture and traditions. *Vanishing Cultures of South Africa*, published in 1998, celebrates the rituals of ten major South African ethnic groups and contains a preface by Mandela. Peter was awarded a Leica Medal of Excellence for Lifetime Achievement in 1997. Recently he gave up photojournalism and to concentrate on art photography. His work documents the surviving tribal ways in post-apartheid South Africa in color. These photographs have been published in the *African Heritage Series* by Struik Publishers.

In 1956, when the "Family of Man" exhibition came to Johannesburg, I looked, and I said, "These are great pictures. If these photographers who took these pictures can do this, why shouldn't I?" I began working very, very hard to try and reach the standard of those pictures that I saw.

I was able to understand and make the world understand what was going on in South Africa because of *Drum*, a magazine that dealt with social issues affecting black people. I had to say to myself, "Here, I'm a black person. I have to liberate myself through the medium of the camera. I have to liberate the oppressor through the medium of the camera. I have to liberate my people through the medium of the camera." If you liberate yourself and you leave out the oppressor, you have not liberated your country at all.

I did all I could, truthfully. I recorded everything that happened, even if I found a white person being molested by black people. I would not turn around and face the other direction and say it has nothing to do with black people. I photographed that as well.

Drum magazine had a circulation of about 120,000 readers. Its audience was black people and liberal whites. It was a magazine that dealt with social issues—issues that were affecting black people. We did stories such as how prisoners were treated, how farm workers were treated, the prisoners that were sold to farmers who died while working—they would be buried on the same grounds, and the work force would carry on—child labor in South Africa, the Morality Act, the pass, the carrying of passes. You name it.

Anything that affected black people, we, as *Drum* magazine, were involved in. We were able to expose and show the world what South Africa was about. It was the only publication that told the truth about South Africa.

In the beginning there was no pressure from the outside. The authorities didn't deem it necessary that they should be raiding the paper. It was only in the 1960s and 1970s that you couldn't publish what you wanted to publish. Especially, there was a story that we did in the 1960s on prisons. Newspapers were no longer allowed to photograph prisons or to say anything, whether good or bad, about prisons. Anything that involved police, you had to get it clarified first.

Of course, you know you would never be given permission to run it, but, in some cases, we did, hoping that we would not be prosecuted. When things began to be tougher is when the world put pressure on South Africa through the writings and photographs that were taken in the country about how black people were treated—what apartheid was about.

As a black person in South Africa in the fifties, sixties, and up to the seventies, it was a very difficult period. You had to carry a pass. Without a pass you did not exist. You could be stopped, arrested, and sent to prison. You couldn't even work. You couldn't even get a house. You couldn't be in a city. You had to be in a rural area. You could go into a camera store, and buy a camera, and photograph, but it would not be photographing, like an exposé. You would be probably doing portraits and have a studio.

But I said to myself, "You are here with a camera. Do you allow yourself to be dictated to by the system or by anybody?" Answering myself, I said no. That put me in a fix. I was arrested.

Before the arrest came, I was refused a press card, because I was black and because of the magazine that I was working for. No black person in that magazine had a press card, because the commissioner of the police signed the press card, and, therefore, you had to be very good to be able to get a press card. Well, I was one of the bad boys, but I didn't care at all, as long as my editors liked what I was doing, and the world was able to see what the oppression was like in South Africa.

In 1960, during the Sharpsville massacre, I had never seen so many people dead. There were about sixty-nine people who were shot by the police and over two hundred that were injured. I got to the scene. I was just shocked, didn't move for five minutes. When I moved, I took pictures from a distance. I was happy I had pictures. But my editor wasn't. He wanted a close-up picture, a picture that would make you cry if you looked at it, a picture that would sell the newspaper or magazine, as he put it to me.

I apologized profusely. I said, "I'm sorry. I got shocked." He said, "In this game, you don't get shocked. If I didn't think you had a potential of making a good photographer, I would fire you."

And the man was serious. I said to him, "Sir, thank you." I left the office. I searched myself. I began to page through pages of *Life* magazine and other magazines. The man was right. You know, here when you deal with events like this, you really have to do long, middle, and close-ups so that he has a choice. Then I said, "Well, I have to prove myself now." From that day, I wasn't going to be shocked by anything. I wasn't going to get emotionally involved. When I get into a scene, I just have to think about me, think about the reader, and think about the magazine.

That's exactly what I began doing. I knew very well that things might be different in the future. One will probably have to lay his head on the block whilst you're doing the work, but I would not be sorry if I died doing this. I would be dying for the cause. I would be dying trying to liberate my country and myself.

As a result, I had narrow escapes. I was detained for 586 days in solitary confinement. I was banned for five years, which meant I lost seven years of my photographic career.

In 1985 I was shot below my waist, seventeen buckshots, which are still embedded in my body. The community looked after me. They dragged me into the house. I could have died. The police would have finished me up, but the people dragged me into the house and kept me in the house until such time that things cooled down, and they took me to the hospital. I must say I'm very grateful to the treatment that I've gotten in all these years from my community. Because without them, without their patience, I would not have operated freely. They did understand the work that I was doing. They knew that it was not for me only, even though I was being paid for doing that. It was for the sake of the country that I was doing this. Of course, you had to be with the people who are demonstrating against the system. You could not be on the other side. You couldn't be with the police. Now today, things have changed. You don't have to be on this side. You can mingle with the police, because the laws have changed.

In 1976 the police bashed my nose, and then I fell and got up. This captain said, "Take out the film."

I said, "no."

He said, "I repeat. Take out the film. If you don't, I'm going to hit you harder than I did."

I realized the man meant business. I took out the film, and he said, "Expose it."

The pain! The pain that I got with the hits on my nose was not as serious as the pain I got when I was made to pull out and expose these images that I knew I had. It was more painful to me to be made to destroy these images. I still say today that the policeman was a fool to have made me do that, because if he knew what photography was, he would have probably taken the film, and took it to the police archives. But he was a damn fool!

I was banned and not allowed to talk to more than one person at once or to attend gatherings. There's no way I could work as a newspaper photographer, because, if you have to photograph two people there's no way that you can do that. You can't go to a wedding. That's a group of people.

I broke my banning orders. I was arrested. I was sentenced to six months in prison, no fine. I went to prison, served the six months. I came back. In 1976 I was arrested again, detained for another 123 days. I had my nose fractured, and I was hospitalized for five days.

I was prepared to face the music. I did not use any pseudonyms. I used my own name under my pictures, and I had exhibitions all over the world. I wasn't afraid to speak out. They could not refuse me a passport, because I didn't apply personally. My first passport was through a mining magnate who was Anglo-American. They made the application. They had given me money to come overseas and exhibit my pictures.

What it meant was that when I came back, I had to return the passport. So, if I want another passport, I should reapply. The only other time I was able to leave the country was in 1977, when I won the major South African photographic prize for distinguished journalism. They couldn't refuse me a passport.

It would not have paid me had I left my country. I think I have gained more, because I have helped liberate my country with my pictures. It was more important to work in my country, to get as much material out of the country for the world to see, than to work in other parts of the world.

One time when I was in one of these farms, the police came and arrested us. I was with a writer. They took us to the police station. When we got to the police station, they were using abusive words. I realized, hey, we're in danger here. I had a Weston Master III light meter. I took it out of my pocket. As this guy was talking, I opened the back. You know, when you open the back, it goes, "Wiing!"

So I open the back. It goes, "Wiing!"

The guy says, "What are you doing?"

I say I'm communicating with my office. I'm telling them that you are using abusive words and you are threatening us with beatings. So you can carry on now. If you want to beat us, you can carry on. And the guy called his superior. His superior came, and I did the same thing. When he started talking, I opened the back. So the needle's moving back and forth, and they think I'm talking to someone.

So, I said to him, "Well, if you want to beat us up you can." Then, I held the light meter, and I said, "Well, is this my editor there? We are still having a problem, which we are now discussing with these officers here. It looks like they're going to let us go. Okay, bye." And I closed the meter.

These guys did believe. They said, "Take your fucking car out of here and move," and we really got into our car and we drove off! And I said, well, you know, it worked. (Laughs) They were not that sophisticated because, those days, they used to take them raw, from the farms. They didn't understand what was going on. One had to use one's brain to play with the system, to beat the system.

One time this policeman came and asked for my pass. I gave it to him. It was not signed. By rule the pass has to be signed every month by your employer. And he said, "Well, it was not signed. I'm arresting you."

I said, "No, bring it here, bring it here." He gave it back to me. I said, "Could I have your pen?" I signed it, and I gave it to him.

He said, "Well, this is fine. Now you can go." (Laughs)

There are projects that I'm working on now. People need to know how we lived in the country for all these years to deal with things like the vanishing tribes. That is important to document, not leave it to Europeans to come down to South Africa and photograph this and have books made like they have done with other parts in Africa. It is important that one deals with these subjects, especially the street children and the children working, so that the government can do something about the plight of these children.

I introduce myself to these children, tell them what I'm doing. I become their friend and stick around without taking pictures. After a week, when they trust me and I trust them, I begin to work, and they don't see me as a stranger. It's only if someone else comes whilst I'm working, and if that person tries to photograph, then they go to this person. They say, "Uh uh, we don't want you to take our pictures."

The same applies to the children working. If there are any objections from whoever is the supervisor, I go to him, I tell him what I'm doing. And if he doesn't approve of what I'm doing, I carry on. If he wants to pick a fight, I say, "Well, if you want to pick a fight, I will fight as well." But first, my approach is very humble. I make them understand that I'm here to work, but if someone wants to pick a fight, I put my cameras down. I say, "Don't interfere with my work. Don't come between me and my camera."

Even though I suffered pain, that loss of images, today I still don't have any hatred whatsoever. I know that it will not help me. In fact, it will destroy me. I am not going to be thinking about what happened yesterday. I have to think about today and tomorrow. Revenge does not pay. Even though seven years of my photographic career was taken away by the South African police and the government, I will be able to make amends. Who am I to refuse to accept people of all colors and embrace them so that we can live peacefully in our country?

Matt Herron

The Civil Rights Movement and the
Southern Documentary Project

I n 1962 Matt Herron, his wife, Jeannine, and their children moved to Jackson, Mississippi, and began the Southern Documentary Project, which he hoped would document the Civil Rights movement in the same spirit that the Farm Security Administration had covered the Depression. His project's eight photographers traveled through Mississippi, Alabama, and Georgia to document rural and small-town life in the summer of 1964.

More than thirty years later Herron's project has become one of the more important bodies of visual documentary on the Civil Rights movement. Photographs from the project have contributed to exhibits, documentaries, and books, among them *Eyes on the Prize* (1987), *The Movement* (1964), *Appeal to This Age: Photography of the Civil Rights Movement* (1994), and the *Civil Rights Movement: A Photographic History, 1954–1968* (1996). Herron continues to collect and archive photographs of the movement and has helped to establish an online database, at www.TakeStock.org, that displays digitized photographs, captions, biographies, and interviews with photographers.

Herron worked with Greenpeace to report on whaling voyages and the seal hunt protest at the mouth of the St. Lawrence in 1979. He is also a past president and a national board member of the American Society of Media Photographers. His photographs are in the Smithsonian Institution exhibit, "We Shall Overcome: Photographs from the American Civil Rights Era," which is traveling throughout the United States and abroad.

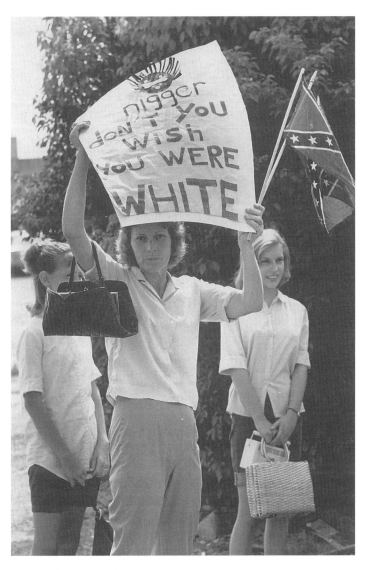

"Nigger don't you wish"
(© 1976 Matt Herron/Take Stock)

In 1962 and 1963 I was photographing in three different capacities. First, I was a photojournalist on assignment in the South. My hope was that by being in the South I could send better story suggestions to editors I worked with in New York. With a closer connection to what was happening, I hoped my suggestions would allow the magazines to do better journalism. What I learned was that basically the editors didn't care. They were interested in having somebody on the spot when the riots broke out. I got a lot of that type of assignment, and I have to admit that some of it was pretty interesting and led me into situations I might not have had access to otherwise.

Second, I went South to work with the Civil Rights movement, and in Mississippi that meant SNCC [The Student Nonviolent Coordinating Committee]. Although I was never a formal member of SNCC, I did some movement photography—demonstrations, jailings, marches, coverage of SNCC workers and activities.

Third, I tried to work as a social documentarian. I had met Dorothea Lange a couple of times in the fifties and sixties and had shown her work. Although [photographer] Minor White was my teacher, Dorothea was in many ways my mentor. She represented the direction I wanted to go. So, in Mississippi I was trying to document a manner of life; I was interested in Southern culture, black and white, and Southern institutions. Often, I would use assignments as a vehicle and a cover to do documentary photography. As social activist I was probably looking at what was going on in the country in a slightly different way. I had discovered a strong affinity for history courses at Princeton, and now I had a conviction that what I was witnessing was history, that things which people saw as everyday events were in fact special and unique.

For example, in 1963 *Time* assigned me to cover the inauguration of Mississippi governor Paul Johnson. It was a one-day shoot, but I felt like I was walking on another planet. The dress, the mannerisms, the folkways of southern politicians, including George Wallace and Ross Barnett, were extremely normal to them, but to me they looked like a scene straight from Mars, and that's the way I photographed it. There were newspaper and wire service guys and other photojournalists present who probably did not see it the same way I did. *Time* ran an extremely ordinary head shot of Johnson, but I came away with some real treasures.

These were the three modes of photography that I juggled, and in this I was probably unique among civil rights photographers. People tended to be movement photographers like Danny Lyon, or photojournalists like Charles Moore and Flip Schulke. The juggling wasn't always easy. Sometimes movement people didn't trust my press connections—it was the mark of an outsider. And journalists would sometimes imply that I was not "objective" enough, meaning that I had ties to the movement. But it all worked for me.

Danny Lyon was actually finishing up in the South when I came to Mississippi. He had been photographing in 1961, 1962, into 1963 and was thought of as *the* SNCC photographer. Danny distrusted journalistic media and didn't want to have much to do with it. I don't know how he felt about me doing assignments, but we were friends and got along.

I believe SNCC was the first social activist group that understood the press could be an instrument they could use to promote social change. The press wouldn't necessarily be on their side, but they could be used to get the story out. This was essentially the vision of James Forman, the chairman of SNCC, who had been a schoolteacher in Chicago and had a more sophisticated understanding of media than more young activists. Forman invested scarce funds to set up a communications office in Atlanta, employ photographers, and create a darkroom. Julian Bond was his first director of communications. Although I was working independently, I cooperated with them. I trained some of the SNCC photographers, and there were times when Forman would call me, and I'd go shoot something.

In 1963 I photographed the riots in Birmingham [Alabama] following the Klan church bombing that killed three little girls and various news assignments into 1964. But it became clear in early '64 that the summer would produce a major confrontation between SNCC and the forces of segregation in Mississippi, as SNCC leaders prepared to recruit one thousand students from mostly white, Ivy League colleges to move into the state to teach and do voter registration. All of us were thinking how to prepare for it, and I could see that by then SNCC would have a team of photographers that could probably handle the movement's stuff pretty well.

I decided that what I wanted to do was set up a team of documentary photographers who could photograph white and black Southern society in transition. I put together a position paper and talked to people about it, and I suggested to SNCC that we work in cooperation.

I got in touch once again with Dorothea Lange. She was interested in my plan but felt that I was too politically motivated to generate true, objective documentary photography. Dorothea was always very concerned that a documentary photographer should have no political bias whatsoever. I'm not sure she herself always practiced this, but that's the way she preached.

I asked her to become our official adviser. She thought about it quite a while and finally decided she could not lend her name to the project, because she perceived my heat and felt I could not be objective enough for her. But she agreed to be an informal adviser.

Then I went North to raise money, and I failed utterly. I called Eastman Kodak and suggested they might want to donate film. Instead, I got a lecture from this Kodak vice president: Why didn't I stay North and mind my own business?

I was then in my early thirties and older than most people I was working with. I had a formal relationship with the Black Star Photo Agency, but for some reason I never thought to tell Black Star about the project.

One day, I was in the office of Howard Chapnick, the president of Black Star, and I told him about the plan, and he loved it. He asked how much money I needed. I said well, about $10,000. He got on the phone and in about fifteen minutes raised the money. He worked out a guarantee from *Life*, where *Life* would have access to us if they needed a photographer on site, in return for which they would give us a retainer. A union and Black Star also put up some money.

I turned to recruiting photographers. I wanted to get the best talent I could. Danny Lyon had left the South by now, but I made a trip to New York to enlist him. We had lunch together, and I twisted his arm and more or less dragged him back South. He said he would not have returned except for this project.

Eventually I had eight photographers, mostly unknown. George Ballis came from California where he had been covering the migrant farm worker movement and did marvelous work for us. George and I were the only ones who were married with kids. Norris McNamara was a SNCC photographer who gravitated to our group. There was also a black photographer named Fred Devan and a student who came down from Antioch College, Dave Prince. Dave is now a video filmmaker working in Africa.

Halfway through the summer I recruited another photographer, Nick Lawrence, who was touring the South with his wife. Nick worked about a month photographing white planter culture in Ruleville, Mississippi. All together the project ran about two months. It was a very chaotic time. Mostly we were on the road, living out of the trunks of our cars, operating on about $30 a week. I was shooting and running the project, calling clients, assigning photographers, negotiating with *Life*, and trying to keep in touch with my family. We shared some facilities and funds with SNCC.

By summer Jeannine and I had blown our cover in Jackson, Mississippi, where we lived incognito in a white neighborhood, and had been forced to leave our house. Jeannine moved to Atlanta with the kids and worked with Julian Bond in SNCC communication, running the darkroom. The darkroom processed film for both the Southern Documentary photographers and the SNCC photographers—ten or twelve all together.

I had phone conversations everyday or so with my photographers. George was particularly good. He would call and say, "I'm finished here; what do you want me to do next?" And he'd go off on some other mission. He went to Atlantic City to cover the Democratic Convention and came back with a wonderful collection of images. George and I probably produced the most consistent work.

Danny was pretty independent. He roved around, and he didn't shoot a lot, but what he did was lovely. He did some beautiful stuff at the Nashoba County Fair. Danny had begun as a movement partisan but was now burning out on civil rights and was beginning to be more concerned about following his own personal directions.

Dave Prince was just beginning his career and was still quite green. He got beat up in Selma, a very scary place, and ended up in the hospital. I followed him in the next day and found myself that evening photographing a meeting at the same church where sheriff's deputies had worked Prince over, but I managed to get out intact.

Later in the summer Prince photographed the funeral of James Chaney, one of the three civil rights' workers murdered in Nashoba County, and he spent a week with the Chaney family. He followed James's younger brother, Ben, in a moving series of photographs as he tried to cope with his brother's death. It could have been published as a very good magazine essay, but nobody would buy it. I spent a lot of time in the Mississippi Delta in one particular community of independent black farmers. Norris and Fred had a dispute with me and left the project early.

The whole thing happened so fast. It really required three months of preparation: interviews with photographers, looking at portfolios, and so on. Instead we did it in weeks. The model was clear, but the project suffered from its hasty inception. Insofar as I understood how the FSA [Farm Security Administration] worked, I tried to work that same way. I made suggestions to photographers, I gave assignments, and I gave people lots of freedom and latitude. And they had film and cars and a little bit of expense money.

It was really a little experiment that should have grown and developed for another two years. We might have produced a real body of work had we done that. I always regretted that I was not able to raise more money and continue it, and I used to reproach myself with that, but in fact I didn't have the organizational skills at that time to pull it off.

Most of the film went to Black Star, which held the collection in New York and published a good deal of it. I had assumed we would have a show and book that would allow the project to go on from there. I showed the work to John Szarkowski at the Museum of Modern Art [MOMA]. John was intrigued with the project, and he began to talk about doing a show. He asked me to put something together, so I went out to Ohio, and Dave Prince and I put a set of work prints up in a gallery and pushed them around until they began to make sense. But that was as far as it went. John became less responsive, and finally I couldn't get him to return calls.

Later I learned that Danny Lyon had been to MOMA to see John, and, when John asked him what he thought of the project, Danny said the pictures were all terrible. And that was the end of it.

I think that to a certain extent Dorothea was right. It was extremely difficult in that pressure cooker to work in an objective fashion as a social documentarian. One could not travel the highways in Mississippi with cameras without being stopped and questioned. The pressures were intense. We were chased, and we had frequent dealings with police.

In the fall of 1964 there was a general ebbing of energy in the movement and a critical change of direction. The big push had been to send an alternative black delegation to the Democratic Convention in Atlantic City under the auspices of the Mississippi Freedom Democratic Party. That effort ultimately failed. Lyndon Johnson, aided by some prominent party liberals, put great pressure on the Democrats not to seat the black Mississippi delegates, and there was great anger and disillusionment among movement people following that.

SNCC's strategy had been to shame the liberal establishment into forcing social change by confronting it with the disparity between liberal aspirations and actual practice. With the failure in Atlantic City, people began to lose faith in that strategy and to consider more radical measures.

Blacks were beginning to realize they were losing control of their movement. More and more SNCC offices were being run by white kids with typing and filing skills, and there was a growing sense that it was time for whites to get out of the way and let black people run their own affairs. We parted with hugs and tears. The only truly integrated, beloved community I had ever known was breaking up. Money also began to dry up as SNCC grew more militant. By the winter of 1964 people were living in freedom houses in the Delta on bread and peanut butter—that was all they had.

That winter I went to Mexico with a huge suitcase filled with Southern Documentary prints, intending to organize a show and a book. One night in Mexico City my van was broken into and everything was pulled out and taken away, including that suitcase. I don't know how many prints were lost—essentially the core of the show.

In the fall of 1964 we moved to New Orleans. We needed to put our kids in school and wanted something better than a Mississippi education. I established a darkroom with the idea that I would carry on the Southern Documentary Project from New Orleans. The Free Southern Theater also moved to New Orleans along with some movement writers and poets. Our intention was to start an arts movement based on our civil rights experience. But, in fact, everybody was very volatile, pretty shell-shocked from the fear and tension of working in Mississippi. Some people simply burned out, turned to religious orders or drink and drugs.

In a year our movement had boiled down to the Free Southern Theater and myself. But, during the next two years, movement people, especially photographers, cycled through our New Orleans apartment in a steady stream. They would sleep on our floors and use the darkroom. Danny was among them. Those who were learning photography would show me work, and I would say, "I think you should do this" or "Why don't you go out and shoot that?" And they would shoot, come back, develop, print, and show me more work. Without planning to, I had established a kind of a center.

When the Smithsonian [Institution] came to do their first civil rights show about fifteen years back, and they interviewed me, they said, "Let's talk about your role as a teacher. Every movement photographer we've talked to speaks of you as their teacher." This was a huge surprise to me. I began to think back on those times and realized I probably had been teaching, but it was all so informal I never thought of it as such.

Sometime in the mid-sixties the Southern Documentary Project images disappeared for twenty-five years. Black Star told me that everything in their files had been returned and was probably lost in the mail. But when Black Star moved their offices about ten years ago, I discovered a huge carton left on my front porch by UPS. In it somebody had dumped hundreds of negative sleeves, contact sheets, and prints: the majority of my civil rights files and a good deal of Southern Documentary work as well. Apparently it had been sitting in a file drawer that nobody opened for twenty-five years—unused, unsold, and unutilized. There were five or six thousand negatives, mostly my own work but also images belonging to other photographers. Both outraged by the neglect and thrilled to get my work back, I sorted out Danny's stuff and mailed it to him.

As I began going through the files, I discovered work and visual threads I had long forgotten. It's hard to describe the experience—it was like getting a piece of my life back. I began to realize that the important pictures had never been printed. With the work already in my files I now possessed a coherent body of work, and that's when I decided to start my own stock agency.

That's the story of the Southern Documentary Project. Looking back, I think I share the feelings of most people in the Civil Rights movement: those were the most significant years of my life.

There is a coda to this. Among the Southern Documentary pictures I put together in the sixties was a set of slides of the best work. At one point, probably a year or more after the project folded, I was in California and I phoned Dorothea Lange. I said I would like to show her the work, and she said she would like to see it. I did not know that Dorothea was dying of cancer. I went to Berkeley, and I projected the images on her bedroom wall. She was, I'd say, within a week or ten days of the end. She looked like a skeleton. I was probably there an hour, an hour and a half, throwing these pictures on her wall. Her husband and collaborator, Paul Taylor, was there as well.

Dorothea and I talked about the work, and, when I was ready to leave, she turned to Paul and said, "Now would you get the medication, Paul," and I realized that she had forgone morphine in order to be clearheaded for the showing. Then she said, "I want to give you a book." She sent Paul off to get their last copy of *An American Exodus,* the first book they did together on migrants in the Central Valley of California, and she signed it. It's probably my most precious possession. That was the last time the Southern Documentary Project was ever shown as a body of work.

Jill Freedman

Resurrection City

Jill Freedman, born in 1939, worked as a cabaret dancer and as an advertising copywriter before becoming a photographer. Upset by the 1968 assassination of Martin Luther King Jr., Freedman went to Washington, D.C., to photograph Resurrection City, the conclusion of King's Poor People's March. Thousands traveled from all over the United States to camp on the Washington Mall in flimsy plywood shacks and protest the squalid conditions of the poor.

Freedman then spent two years traveling with the Beaty-Cole Circus, paying tribute to a "dying way of life." In the preface of her critically acclaimed book, *Circus Days* (1975), Freedman wrote, "I was the kind of kid that always wanted to be carried off by the gypsies."

Freedman, who has freelanced for *Time, Life*, German *Geo*, and the *New York Times Magazine*, is known for her sharp sense of humor, which she displayed in books like *Street Cops* (1982), *Firehouse* (1977), and *A Time that Was: Irish Moments* (1987). In 2004 Freedman published *Ireland Ever*, which commemorates the traditional life of Ireland in bygone days, just as the modern world began to creep up on it. Her photographic style shares the conviviality, the sharp wit and black moods, and the kindness of the old country.

The Holocaust had affected me deeply. I was born during the war, and when I was seven I found old *Life* magazines in the attic. I saw the pictures—a burnt head under the door, the beautiful face on the skeleton on the pile of bodies.

Old news; Resurrection City
(© Jill Freedman, Grossman Publishers,
1970, cover)

I was a normal kid, a tomboy. I used to come home, go up to the attic, look at the pictures, cry for an hour, then go out and play softball. After a year my parents discovered that. Burned the magazines. I'm sure that's why I was a photojournalist.

I lived in Europe after college a few years, and when I came back I didn't know what I was going to do, and one day I woke up, wanted a camera, borrowed a friend's, ran out into the street, shot two rolls. I didn't even know what a contact sheet was. I looked at it, I said "That's it, I'm a photographer." Pretty funny. I decided just to teach myself.

I got a job as a copywriter at an ad agency. Every paycheck, I bought my equipment, built my darkroom. I learned to print by reading books and watching a few people print. I went and looked at Gene Smith's prints at the library. I found a book of [Robert] Doisneau, with the cover ripped off, for $2.50. I'd never heard of him. Right away it was documentary photojournalism for me.

There were a couple pictures that really hit me. One that was a very small book that *Life* put out of memorable pictures of the war with that picture of Smith's where soldiers found the baby on that island. This friend said, "Oh, you could blow that up." I had that on my wall. I mean, talk about masochism. I lived with that.

When they killed Martin Luther King, I was so enraged. I just quit and joined the Poor People's campaign. We went through a different town each day and then slept in people's homes and churches. Wilmington, Philadelphia, Paterson, Newark. Chemical toilets, no chemicals. Bologna sandwiches on white bread every day. We marched through different cities and towns for a week and then lived in the mud next to the Reflecting Pool between Abraham Lincoln and the Washington Monument, which we called the Klansman because at night there was the pointed head and the red eyes.

I felt it was going to be the last big, nonviolent demonstration, and I wanted to be there. By then I believed in nonviolence; I saw it worked. In my heart I'm a killer—there are people I could absolutely kill with joy, and I'm sure not feel a thing about it—but I know that nonviolence is the only way to go.

My tent was right next to the Georgia Sea Island Singers. It was fabulous. The first night my boots and sleeping bag were stolen. It was freezing. It rained every day. Every day. So we sang—I played a really good kazoo and spoons—and we demonstrated every day.

That was six weeks, demonstrating every day, and I was loading my film into cassettes from 100-foot rolls of Tri-X. I always thought that the day I could buy it ready-rolled I'd know I had arrived. I still feel that way.

I had my two little Nikons; I was working blind. One day a *Life* reporter was down there, and I got to talking with him in the food tent. He looked at them and he said, "Why don't you give me your film? Even if *Life* doesn't use it, at least they'll develop and contact it for you." My first published pictures were six in *Life* magazine for which I got $600.

I shot everything going on around me; it was like another American city. We had the first Black Panthers come from Oakland. I've always wanted to go to Marks, Mississippi, because I'll never forget those old ladies, when they came up with the mule train. I met some of the greatest people I ever met in my life.

After it was all done I looked at the stuff, I said, "This is a book." A couple years later I took them to Grossman, who published them. It was a great experience. It was the first story that I'd photographed and written. It set my way of working.

I try not to preconceive anything. Before I went to do *Circus Days,* [Federico] Fellini's clowns film was out. I adored Fellini, but I purposely didn't see it until afterward. I just go, and I immerse. I'm just like an antenna, an instrument. I like to feel it, absorb it into the skin. When I taught myself photography, I was very strict about composing in the viewfinder. I could only afford one lens, so I moved up for telephoto, moved back for wide. That freed me to just think of the pictures without much conscious thought. I work by feeling. I'd been a musician, and I think of photos like music. When I put together a book, I think in terms of a symphony—the rhythm, the beginning. Above all, I try never to preconceive until I'm faced with actually laying out and writing the book.

It's a very great honor and a privilege to be able to enter people's lives. It's very humbling. The most important thing which sets photography I like against most of which I hate is respect. You don't get anything decent unless you have the respect. When you're sincere, then people will work with you. If you put in enough time, you can be invisible. It used to amaze me what people would do in front of me, and what people would say—to the point where sometimes I would say,

"Remember, I'm a reporter; do you want to say that?" Documentary is a pure form. Certainly the photography turned me on, those moments, catching the moments, but unless it has the heart, to me it's nothing.

In 1971, after my first book, *Old News,* came out, I sent it to my heroes, people in the antiwar movement. I sent one to Walter Cronkite, and I got a note—"would I like to come see him"—and I did. I told him how I always wanted to do photography for TV, for news: stills, which you could animate, like that great Civil War series by Ken Burns. Uncle Walter said, "The time is right now, they're gonna have to let a woman into the union, and you could be the first woman."

I've gone over this at three in the morning with myself for years since. He had his hand on the phone. Without even thinking I said, "No, I want to be a photographer." I put myself down for years, saying well, I could have done that, earned a great living, met people, maybe even my true love, have people to work with so you're not out there alone in those hotels. Then I realized, well if I had, I wouldn't have done these projects.

The point is just to stay alive. I really didn't have much money, but I sold a couple of portfolios to magazines. A friend gave me his Volkswagen bus, and I got some film from one of the magazines. That's how I did *Circus Days,* on a shoestring, of course. I met the lead clown, and I was under his wings. It was seven weeks of one-night stands—two shows a day, one on Sunday, tent up every morning, down at night, drive to the next town.

I shot one roll of color. It took me months to talk my favorite clown into lying on the fur rug in the middle of this field next to a burnt-out house—the naked, round, pink clown, like a baby picture, a clown baby picture. That was the whole color roll.

I didn't have the money to develop as I went along, and I'm thinking, what an idiot, I mean if one of those cameras had been broken. But thank god. They say He watches over drunks and idiots. The cameras worked, and when I came back I had all the film. Arthur Rothstein was at *Look,* and he was wonderful. He had them developed and contacted. It was like a birthday present, like Hanukkah morning, you wake up and there are these presents, glistening contact sheets. I shot everything. It was only afterward that I saw I was only interested in the backstage life, the life of the circus.

We're storytellers, really. I consider myself a documentarian, in the sense that I try to show—of course from my point of view always. Otherwise, what am I, a machine? I try to show what's going on. I try to, as much as possible, keep myself out of the focus. I hate photographers who act like big stars. Somebody did a thing that's famous on Harlem, and he talked about the hardship. Well he had a bodyguard with him. He set up every picture.

I like to work to try to tell the story of the lives that I'm trying to show, from their point of view. Like *Street Cops*. When I was doing *Firemen*, someone asked, "Well, are you going to do cops next?" I said, "Get outa here; I hate cops." Because of Vietnam. And then I thought, what do you mean you hate cops? You don't even know one. I'd only seen books about bad cops. What I wanted to do was to show the job, and show a good cop, my definition. Compassion, humor, street smart, tough.

I get to identify deeply with the subjects. I've always felt like an actress. You live your role; you immerse yourself in your role, and that's what I do with the photography. I absorb it; I just become part of it. I'm not thinking of anything else. I have one rule: I never sleep with people I'm working with.

Sometimes I feel I don't have a real life at all. You always assume you'll have kids, but I think I really didn't want to, because I knew I just wanted to be free. I wanted to just go and take pictures.

I love my work. I love my books. It's important to love your work. But have the decency not to inflict it. There are far too many images, which has cheapened the sublimity of great photography. If you're gonna do it, have the respect to learn the craft, the decency not to bore or show mediocre stuff, and go and follow your bliss. For me it was a passion from the minute I picked the camera up. A lot of people, all they're interested in is exhibiting, being stars, and going to all those stupid openings. There may be technical competence and all kinds of machines, but without that heart, so what? There's all this cold, heartless stuff and without the craft. I don't care about snapshots of junkies. I like cocks, but I don't need to see a big old hard-on beautifully printed.

We still have the idea that we're gonna help somehow. I'm gonna have a big show in the Miami public library in January. I took them the book, and I said, "You should do this for Black History Week," and they agreed. A few people on the committee were worried. They said, "I don't know; she's white." But I said, "Hey, I was there." So that's gonna happen, and I said to the director, "Look, get some of those people who were involved. Get them to sing those songs. Get these older people to talk about the experience so these kids know where they're coming from. Let them see the greatness of these people."

Even my last book, *Jill's Dogs,* is about love. I truly feel that even if you don't love dogs or animals, there will be some people who will see the book and maybe they will be nicer to animals. Maybe it will make them treat everything nicer. There's not enough love, you know?

Mary Ellen Mark

Streetwise Photographer

The curator at the George Eastman House in Rochester, New York, Marianne Fulton, describes Mary Ellen Mark as a "woman possessed—possessed of great talent, conviction, strength, and continuity. A person obsessed with photography, it is the center of her life, of who she is."

Mark studied art history and painting as an undergraduate at the University of Pennsylvania. Her "obsession" began in 1962 during her graduate studies at the university's Annenberg School for Communication when, on a whim, she took a course in photography.

In 1965, with a Fulbright scholarship, she began a two-year project in Turkey, which was later published by Ralph Gibson as her first book, *Passport*. As a freelancer, she photographed for several national and international magazines. An assignment from *Look* in 1970 on heroin addicts in England helped cement her reputation as a social documentarian.

While working as a still photographer on the set of *One Flew over the Cuckoo's Nest*, Mark became interested in the mentally ill. In 1979 she spent thirty-six days photographing women in a maximum security mental hospital and produced the book *Ward 81* (1979). Other major books include *Mother Teresa's Missions of Charity in Calcutta* (1985); *Falkand Road* (1982), on prostitution in Bombay; and *Streetwise*, documenting homeless teenagers in Seattle. Mark and her husband, Martin Bell, later developed it into the film *Streetwise*, which was nominated for an Academy Award.

In the 1990s she pursued a long-term project on Indian circuses. Mark has also worked as a portrait photographer for *Rolling Stone*, *People*, the *New Yorker*, and numerous other publications.

Lauri in the Ward 81 tub,
Oregon State Hospital,
Salem, Oregon, 1976
(© Mary Ellen Mark)

Mark has continued to prolifically publish books including Aperture's publication of her portraits of twins, a retrospective, *Exposure* (2005), and her movie stills, *Seen behind the Scene* (2009). Her most recent book and exhibition project, *Extraordinary Child*, was commissioned by the National Museum of Iceland and features photographs of children at two schools for the disabled in Reykjavik. Retrospectives of her work include "Mary Ellen Mark: 25 Years," organized by the International Museum of Photography at the George Eastman House and "Mary Ellen Mark: American Odyssey." Her photographs have been exhibited worldwide.

When I started to take pictures in the early sixties, I chose the path of magazine photography. At that time it was exactly the right choice for me, because magazines loved and supported documentary photography. Unfortunately, today most magazines are no longer interested in documentary photography.

This shift has occurred because now advertising has much more control of magazine content. There are still a lot of editors that would really love to have great documentary pictures in their magazines. But the advertising and business side is very powerful, and they want photographs that are more commercial and will sell the magazine.

Great documentary photographs are powerful and memorable. The fact that they no longer fit the economic needs of magazines is a tragedy. Because of this, the public is missing the experience of seeing many great images. It's especially a loss to young photography students who miss the opportunity of being inspired by the work of excellent documentary photographers. It is also very difficult for the seasoned documentary photographers who are at their prime and ready to do their greatest work, because they have a very hard time financing and publishing their work.

Still photographs do something very different than television. Still pictures exist forever. If they are really exceptional they can become icons. We see powerful video footage on CNN, but we see it only once. Great photographs become locked in our minds. For example, Larry Burrows's Vietnam photographs are stamped in our memories. Don McCullin's pictures in the seventies of the war in Bangladesh are also unforgettable, and the perfect decisive moments of Henri Cartier-Bresson are part of our lives.

All photographers have certain images that they are more known for. It is mysterious what makes a photograph an icon. Sometimes I think these icons are the photographs that are most easily understood by all people and all cultures. They are graphic, emotional, they cross cultural boundaries and touch us, and we remember them. When I see a great frame on a contact sheet I am not always sure; I say to myself, "Well, maybe that could be a really fine picture," but I don't always know. I have to live with the picture for awhile to see if it survives time.

I have completed a book called *Mary Ellen Mark: American Odyssey* published in fall 1999 by Aperture. The book consists of my American pictures dating back to the early sixties, when I first started to photograph and ending in May 1999. During the last three years, I edited hundreds of pictures from my thirty-five years of work. I would select images, scan them, and then leave them in a folder. I would look at the pictures several months later and ask myself, "Are they really good?" The pictures I selected for my book were the ones that were still strong after looking at them again and again.

In order to survive as a magazine photographer, I've had to learn how to do magazine portraiture. I had to learn to do lighting and to work under time restraints. This has been both challenging and interesting. But, every once in a while I still do get a chance to do real documentary work for magazines, and I am always thinking of the different ways that I can finance my own work. Because without personal projects, what's the point? The self-assigned subject is your heart and soul.

With both magazine assignments and personal work I am really putting myself on the line. In magazine assignments I work hard to figure out how to achieve a great image with the added difficulties of limited time and limited access. The ideal situation is when a magazine assignment overlaps with your own body of personal work.

I have several subjects that I have slowly been photographing over the years. One subject is the circus. I'm obsessed with circuses. I made a book on the Indian circus. Two years ago, I went to Mexico to photograph circuses. I would love to photograph circuses all over the world, but it's really financially difficult to put that kind of project together. I financed the trip to Mexico with the help of *Texas Monthly* and some European magazines. I called and faxed magazines all over the world and got a little bit of money here and there. I made no money on the project but for me this was absolutely fine, because it gave me the opportunity to continue my circus work.

One of Mark's early stories was of heroin addicts.

It's horrible to be an addict—a terrible life. I photographed that story to show just how tragic the lives of the young people were. I wanted the people who saw the pictures to enter that world and to better understand the plight of those kids. I hate fashion pictures that glamorize drug addiction to sell clothes. It's very tasteless and empty to commercialize social situations that are very serious and very unfortunate.

Years ago I got a call from a big Hollywood producer. He wanted me to do the title stills for the film *Mr. Goodbar*. He told me that he wanted me to take pictures in bars that were honest, tough, real. I went out every night from 11 P.M. until 6 A.M. for six weeks and photographed. I met all different sorts of people that were a part of the late-night bar culture. I worked intensely and made some good pictures. They were also very real and very strong pictures. I was so excited. I edited my contact sheets, made work prints, and sent them to the producer.

A few days later he called and said, "These are the most depressing pictures I've ever seen. We're not going to use them." He even went so far as to say that I would never work in Hollywood again. My pictures were too tough for him to understand. I guess he just wanted something much more commercial. The nightlife in bars is often strange and desperate. Anyhow, that was how I saw it. That was my reality. Even though those pictures were not used in the film, I still had the opportunity to make them. That was by far the most important thing for me. Some of those pictures are in *American Odyssey*.

Documentary photography is about reality, both in it's authentic sense and it's surreal sense. For me, nothing is more imaginative, or fascinating, than reality. Great pictures are the images that transcend time and content. That's what all of us strive for.

The best documentary images, like all great photographs, have always had a place in the world of fine art. This is very important, especially now when we no longer have the opportunity to see these pictures in magazines. Exhibitions and books are the primary way to be aware of documentary work. When I began to take pictures, my inspirations were the many memorable documentary essays I saw in magazines. Now we all must work more independently to produce books and exhibitions. We must never give up.

Earl Dotter

The United Mine Workers

Earl Dotter follows in the tradition of Lewis Hine, who documented the dangerous working conditions of the coal-breaker boys in the early twentieth century. Hine's photographs helped spark legislation against industrial child labor. In the 1960s, when Dotter began his work, another series of egregious events were under way in America's coal mines. Black lung, a disease caused by work in the coal mines, was widespread, and there were a series of disastrous mine accidents, such as those in Buffalo Creek and Farmington, West Virginia.

Dotter joined Volunteers in Service to America (VISTA) in 1969 and went to the Cumberland Plateau region of Tennessee during a volatile period. Jock Yablonski, the leader of a democracy movement within the United Mine Workers of America, had been brutally murdered by union thugs. The union president, Tony Boyle, was found guilty of the crime and was eventually ousted.

Dotter joined the democracy movement, and, when their slate was elected, he joined the new staff of the *United Mine Workers Journal*. His powerful photos, published in *Life* and other magazines, brought public attention to the mine workers' concerns, especially issues of safety. Dotter's work was later honored with a National Magazine Award.

Dotter remained dedicated to exposing occupational health hazards in several industries. In 1998 he assembled a collection of twenty-five years of work in *The Quiet Sickness: A Photographic Chronicle of Hazardous Work in America.*

Coal miner setting temporary supports,
Clearfield County, Pennsylvania, 1976
(Earl Dotter/UMWA Journal)

I was a photographer fresh out of the School of Visual Arts [New York City]. My background was in advertising design, and I had one course in photography. This was 1968. Martin Luther King Jr. had been assassinated while I was still in school and Bobby Kennedy soon after. The cities were up in flames. An advertising career didn't seem appropriate at that time. The minute I picked up the camera, there was an opportunity for me, a rather shy individual, to reach out into the community where I lived in the Lower East Side. It gave me the greatest excuse to poke into other people's business and really helped me overcome a great personal timidity in relating to people.

I was 1-A and readily draftable in 1969, so I chose to join VISTA as an alternative and ended up in the Cumberland Plateau region of Tennessee.

I had become acquainted with a lot of disabled and elderly coal miners who were quite upset with their union, the United Mine Workers of America [UMWA], because of its position on the question of mine health and safety and the Farmington mine explosion. Seventy-eight miners had been entombed in a mine that had exploded, and the mine had to be sealed with the miners inside.

Jock Yablonski, a reform candidate for UMWA presidency, and his wife and daughter had been murdered for opposing Tony Boyle, who was the union president. There were other factors too. The union was not aggressively pursuing black-lung claims. Despite all these problems, the Mine Workers was an institution as close to miners as God is to religious folk.

Initially, my pictures were war-on-poverty oriented, but I became acquainted with the dissidents in the coalfield who were attempting to organize a mass movement to democratize and reform the UMWA. There was a publication called the *Miner's Voice*, that Don Stillman out of Charleston, West Virginia, was publishing. I was invited to join the UMWA reform campaign because I had multiple skills. I would take the photographs for the literature in the campaign and then design it. This enabled me to become a full-time staffer on the six-month campaign at $50 a week.

I managed to photograph in the coalfields, which was a bit dangerous, given the history of violence within the union. It was a remarkable experience. I began to get my first access to coal mines, and coal miners, and, in particular, miners who had accidents, who had become disabled, who had contracted black lung, but nonetheless were very active in the effort to repair their union. During the course of the campaign, I took one hundred rolls of film.

Once the reform candidate, Arnold Miller, was successfully elected and Don Stillman had become the editor of the *United Mine Workers Journal*, I was invited to do the first redesign of the *Journal*, as well as become its photographer—an opportunity I jumped at. After a period of time I passed the design work on to someone else and worked exclusively as a photographer for the *Journal* from 1973–77. It enabled me to develop or prepare a body of work that, as far as my own twenty-five-year history of photography, is still hard to beat.

As a representative of the *Journal* I was made welcome into the homes of mining families. I've learned that before I ever bring my camera out of the bag, the first thing I try to do is to let folks know who I am, why I want to take their picture. Then, if they are satisfied with what I'm up to, they are better able to respond and live out their life in front of the camera rather than act it out.

You are essentially a stranger. If you can connect on an emotional level, you really will get back so much more. I'm reminded of Robert Capa's saying "If your pictures aren't good enough, you're not close enough." I don't think he was talking about physical distance as much as emotional distance. Often, I would have dinner with the miner and his family the night before. Perhaps some other miners in the same section would join us, and we'd talk about how I would take the pictures, and the kinds of things they thought were important to record.

A picture-taking and editorial strategy was developed fairly early on by the four-person staff of the *Journal* to highlight individuals and community people who were doing exemplary work within their union and their communities on a wide range of issues. It became fairly easy to figure out what kinds of subjects were worthy of treatment.

Miners love to hear about some of the good things that their union was accomplishing after a period of so much violence and corruption. The doors just opened to us. The company wasn't so hot on us coming to a mine, but, because the union was together, and the local union was behind it, they were hard put to resist our access.

After our new editorial philosophy had been put together and a few issues of the *Journal* had shown evidence of this new philosophy, we began to hear from miners themselves about somebody doing something that was extra special, like developing a community garden for everybody prior to a strike so they'd have food. The administration was filled with people who had just arrived after the struggle to reform the union and folks in the safety division of the union. We were really interested in hitting very hard on key issues where past activity within the union had allowed problems to get to such a difficult level that coal mining had become the most dangerous occupation in the country.

The *Journal* had been reestablished under the Miners for Democracy administration with independence. The *Journal* wasn't reviewed in the process of editorial decisions; occasionally there were some modifications, but generally it was not interfered with.

I do recall the controversy when women entered the mines. I had taken a photo of three women who had just emerged from the mine, and it has since become one of my most popular photos. I had taken it with the idea of it being on the cover of the *Miners Journal*.

Well, male coal miners had resisted the arrival of women in the pits with a great deal of fear, harassment, entrenched superstitions—they said it was bad luck. I was disappointed when the decision was made not to use this photo on the cover. It was used inside, and an illustration of Mother Jones [Mary Harris Jones], the organizer, was used in its place on the cover.

When Dotter was photographing in the mid-seventies, fast-speed films, such as T-max 3200, had not been invented.

I approached everything with pretty much a blunt-force technique. Rather than trying to do sophisticated lighting underground, I used direct strobe, and I was disturbed with the shadow direct strobe created and developed the technique of getting a very small Vivitar strobe that I could hold right against the lens barrel. So if there was a shadow it was just a pencil-thin line of shadow. It was just a blunt-force light, and the blacks and the highlights would kind of fight each other to some extent and create a very graphic rendition. The starkness of the subject really lent itself to this kind of treatment.

I've always developed and printed my own black and white negatives, and the darkroom side informs your shooting. You learn to not shoot things that are unphotographable. You learn to burn and dodge—with direct strobe you have things that are washed out in the foreground and need to be adjusted.

The most difficult obstacle with underground photography was the dust and the frame. My mine light would poke a doughnut hole–size shape of light into the dim, and you would see the character by moving your head in such a way that you could see the shape and where his body began and ended. Well, when you began to frame a picture—and this is a subject that's moving—it became very hard to crop the pictures in a way that you didn't end up amputating some essential element of the subject.

The other thing was that in a dusty atmosphere, if you are using a strobe that automatically shuts down after the proper exposure has been achieved, all this ambient dust will tend to shut your strobe down prematurely. So, in real dusty situations I learned to just shoot on manual, and this was tough because you had a subject that was coming at you and moving away from you. Zone focusing became the rule for me, judging the distance and adjusting the lens barrel appropriately.

The consequence of all these difficulties was a lower success rate, but if your access was good, you were compensated by the fact that you had more time to spend and that you had a subject who wanted you to succeed. That was critical.

Photographing underground is sort of analogous to taking pictures from the moon. It's a subject we don't regularly see. Very few of us have been in a coal mine. It's a subject of great fascination because you don't get to see it everyday.

There was a lot of interest in this material. I never became a full-time employee of the *Journal* so that I would own my own negatives. This benefited the union, because outside publications would come to me directly for photographs, and I owned the rights to republish the work. *Time* magazine came to me for pictures that related to a strike that occurred in the mid-seventies.

After I left the UMWA in 1977, I started becoming interested in the problems of textile workers and brown-lung disease. That was concurrent with the effort to organize the J. P. Stevens textile mills. After that experience I really started to look at occupational health and safety in general and went into auto plants, and chemical plants, and all different kinds of occupations.

It became very apparent to me that in photographs of someone who has been victimized, about the only element the viewer of this kind of photograph can relate to is in an individual's desire for self-respect and dignity. So, when I photograph I'm always looking for the common ground between my subject and the viewer of my photographs. If you can attract their interest initially by your artistry and lead them into confronting the issues your subject matter raises, then you've gone a long way toward at least presenting material that they can think about.

Eugene Richards

Americans We

Eugene Richards has repeatedly returned to themes of tragedy and renewal in difficult or extreme circumstances. He has extensively documented American poverty in books such as *Below the Line, Few Comforts or Surprises: The Arkansas Delta, Americans We,* and an urban emergency room in *The Knife and Gun Club.* His book *Cocaine True, Cocaine Blue* created controversy for its unflinching depiction of inner-city neighborhoods destroyed by drugs.

Richards began his career as a Volunteers in Service to America (VISTA) worker in eastern Arkansas in 1968. After several dangerous run-ins with the Ku Klux Klan and local police, he was forced to "sort of limp home."

In 1978 he founded Many Voices Press, which published his books *Dorchester Days* and *50 Hours.* In the acclaimed book, *Exploding into Life,* Richards and his first wife, the writer Dorothea Lynch, chronicled her experience with breast cancer until her death from the disease.

A former member of the Magnum and VII photo agencies, Richards has won numerous photojournalism awards and prizes for work that has appeared in *Life,* the *New York Times Magazine,* and other publications. After 9/11 Richards created an elegy, *Stepping through the Ashes,* to those who lost their lives in New York that day.

His most recent book, *The Blue Room,* is his first color book, and brings together the themes of his work in a beautiful, moving series of pictures of the landscape and abandoned houses of the American Plains. Richards lives in Brooklyn, New York, with his wife, Janine.

Maniella, East New York, 1992
(© Eugene Richards)

I was influenced growing up working class, with a mother who once worked as a domestic and a father who perhaps never got over the years his family had to struggle during the Depression. I was also profoundly influenced by the Vietnam War. I protested, draft resisted, finally didn't go, and always felt very fortunate, but very conflicted by my decision. I might have gone to prison, but other young men went to war.

When I was young, I never thought about being an artist. I had my viewpoints—I was writing poetry, I was doing things confusedly—and then I met a teacher at Northeastern University named Robert Wells, who got massively excited about painting and sculpture, its history and its influence on world events. He'd inform his students about the life of the painter, where he or she came from, and the great pains that come from doing something personally and socially creative. Most people don't care about the painter's processes, but they're important. Art is a crucible, the means to express what we're feeling, what we care about, providing we care about anything.

The photographer who caused me to recognize how wonderfully photography could define an era was Robert Frank. I looked at books of America that were being done then. Most were flag-waving books. Then I saw *The Americans*. Frank looked at this country in the fifties and saw a malaise underneath all the patriotism. I felt, after seeing this work, a pat on the back from someone I never knew. I felt freer to express my own feelings about this country.

My father and I have had a series of running arguments about politics my whole life. My father, who never went to high school, said the single thing he was proudest of himself was that he worked hard enough to support his family. Now the thing I'm proudest of is the ability to support my family with my work, that now I'm a working man.

My job is to get my worldview out there, to get what I see published. I'm a photojournalist as opposed to what some might call an art photographer, because I like to tell stories. Probably in the next life I'd be a writer. But I was driven by early events in my life to be a photographer, so I try to tell stories mainly through pictures.

If there's any philosophy that I have that I could put into words—and it's not particularly new or deep—it's that when you say you're a photojournalist, you attempt to tell the truth. After you become aware of a person's life or a human situation, you try to find the tools, the metaphors, the shapes, the shadows to translate the event or personality as truthfully as possible.

Most documentary work is concerned with what's past—trying to preserve something, trying to record for posterity. That's why I call myself a photojournalist. It's about now. You have to go out and capture the spirit of the events or the environment today. Our society is changing and becoming more insular in terms of what we're willing to see beyond our own lives. Such insularity comes with being more successful, making more money. And we don't want to rock the boat.

Problems, of course, do exist. The labor camps are still here, the coke ghettoes are still here, the isolated people living along the delta regions of the South are still here. The people that I met up in the mountains of Tennessee are possibly in worse shape than before because the mines are closed.

So it's left to TV and the magazines to inform us. And we don't do our job. We ought to look at stories more deeply. Our work has to be closer to psychological dramas than literal dramas. We have to go inside the house instead of standing outside, because little is showing on the streets the way it used to.

I always felt I was part of a way of life, lived by a number of artists who came together in the age of the Vietnam War. A lot of people came out of the sixties and seventies with a lot of questions, not only about the war, but about class and where we personally fit into our society, about our lack of social balance, our nation's economic situation, what was causing the dire poverty and racism that was racking the country at that time. And many times, more often than not, we were full of anger. We were pissed-off photographers, and sometimes we pissed off the general population.

We pushed ourselves out there—sometimes in arrogant ways—into societies we weren't initially comfortable in. We weren't born into them. Some people went in to cover the war. Some people went to the South. I was a white guy going south, documenting the lives of sharecroppers, the Klan, the last of the Civil Rights movement. Other photojournalists covered the [Black] Panthers, joined motorcycle gangs. Everybody was pushing outside of themselves. Anger was probably the one thing I shared with other photographers of my generation. And now for many that's gone, displaced by other drives and concerns.

It's hard to sustain the vigor of youth. There are certain art forms of expression that improve with age. Very often musicians don't mature until late in life. Same with writers. Dance we know is a killer; you have it when you're young, then it's pretty much over. So it varies. Photography is tough. With photojournalism, your ass has to be on the street. And as you get older, there's no doubt about it, a certain physical energy fades, and it becomes tougher physically to do the job. Financial concerns also multiply; photo markets are declining. So the result is that not many social photographers after the age of fifty are still social photographers. At some point, some need the money, so they become advertising photographers, need steady work, so they become teachers. You get really weary of being pushed away, and weary of not making a living, and weary of not getting published. So it's a rare person that, for lots of reasons, can keep it up.

Also if you throw out something that is socially critical—especially about issues of race and class—no one is going to pat you on the head. Ultimately, few people, those with money, are going to buy your photographs. No one is going to give you exhibitions, except many, many years later, when you are old as hell.

In 1978 Richards's first wife, Dorothea Lynch, was diagnosed with breast cancer. Lynch wrote about her experience, while Richards photographed it. Their book, *Exploding into Life*, was published in 1986, after Lynch's death.

The photographers who worked in Central America in the 1980s got pushed around because they were reporting on wars that our government claimed we were not supporting. But who would have thought that a book on breast cancer would upset so many people? Perhaps it was the medical establishment that didn't care for any criticism of its methods. Perhaps it was the American obsession with the breast. Perhaps it was a fear of our bodies aging.

The truth is, after Dorothea kept a diary of her cancer experience, after I took the pictures, it required a personal subsidy before the book was published. Now this was after doctors had forced Dorothea to leave the hospital, where she was reporting on the lives of cancer patients. When the book was finally published after Dorothea's death, it was criticized at a meeting of the American Cancer Society and, if you can believe this, ostracized in effect by the Boston Women's Health Collective for having a male coauthor. This group, publisher of *Our Bod-*

ies, Ourselves, said they wouldn't sell *Exploding into Life* in their bookstore.

If you comment on women's lives, you're asked why you, a male, dare do that. Now, if you do a book on poverty, people ask, "Are you poor yourself? I see that you live in a nice house." No kidding. People have come to my house, and it bothers them that I don't live in a sty. My book, *Cocaine True, Cocaine Blue,* showed people shooting drugs and dying of gunshots, overdoses, and AIDS. There were young girls prostituting themselves. And what was the primary criticism of my four years of work? If you cut through all the bullshit, critics were saying that I was racist, a white guy who had the audacity to look at the lives of poor black and Hispanic addicts. I was also accused of giving clean needles to addicts, which I did, of setting up pictures and paying addicts to model, which I didn't. But it was the racism charge that hurt, mainly because only a very few photographers came to my defense. Not surprisingly, most of those who did were black photographers. Almost all the others, who knew me, knew my past work, knew something about the nature of addiction, said nothing. This included major magazine photo editors, my own agency's director, and a renowned museum curator, who wished to maintain their privileged status among the politically correct.

The drug project that ultimately became a book began in Detroit. I went out with narcotics cops in Detroit and saw a pantheon of dying. There were kids in the morgue who were being killed by dealers after selling drugs for them. There were drive-by shootings; drug gangs were shooting up funerals. And all I could get was the cop work and some pictures of people tearfully holding their children's pictures.

I wanted to go out and do more, but no magazine would permit me to do more, and without an assignment I couldn't pay my bills. Then I talked to a reporter at *Life* named Ed Barnes, a really fine reporter, and he wanted to do the same thing. We honestly didn't know if we could. There were things done in the past by great photographers. Bill Eppridge did a piece on a couple in Needle Park, but it was somewhat acceptable, because it was a couple of young, attractive people who did the suffering. Could we do anything like that in the more complex, violent, interracial Brooklyn neighborhood close to where we live?

So Ed and I went down to Red Hook housing project—it was Ed's idea and it was the right idea. He found, after some research, a flag pole around which people sold and bought drugs. We had an assignment from *Life*. We went down there for three weeks and initially got nowhere. We were a nuisance to the dealers.

Among other things, they thought we were police officers. That waiting period was nothing more than an exaggeration of what we all go through as journalists. You just grit your teeth and bitch and moan and call home all the time and complain and try to keep away from the alcohol and don't get too depressed and go back the next day.

The insecurity, the rage; you lie to your editor about how long the story will take, you beg not to have the plug pulled. And then about the fourth week we had a breakthrough moment. We witnessed a violent chase and residents of the project recognized we were journalists instead of cops. The doors opened. What happened is the classic thing where people start bringing you their stories. Even the drug dealer on the street who says I can't talk to you tells us who can. It starts to break open. Suddenly we were in the middle of things. The neighborhood drug bosses were watching us all the time.

The people I found most willing to reveal themselves, most tragic, were the young women prostituting themselves to get money for drugs. It was very complicated working with them. These girls, some as young as twelve, would sell themselves for two bucks. It was devastating to myself and to Ed Barnes to witness this.

Don McCullin talks about a starving kid—in Biafra I think—who wouldn't let him alone. Don took his picture, gave him food, and yet he couldn't do anything more for him. The child followed him. The girls were the same way. They'd offer us sex all the time, simply because we'd spoken kindly to them. We'd go there and tell them we wanted to do a story, and sex was the only way they could show affection. And this made our jobs and our lives more complicated, because you just can't get involved with your subjects, and not being able to help them got to be emotionally difficult. We stayed as long as we could, and then the story closed.

People say why does a story close? Most stories close because they're just too fucking draining after a while. You just wake up in the morning and you say, I don't want to go back to that nursing home. I don't want to go back and see that person. Or I can't go back to the crack houses in Red Hook, and that was it.

Richards also covered the drug scene in North Philadelphia.

That one started very differently, because the person we used as a guide in North Philadelphia was a drug addict named Sarah, who at first had tried to rob us. By the time she tried to rob us, we were so tired and getting nowhere that we didn't care. I wouldn't exaggerate and say we didn't care if she shot us, but we were so tired. We just laughed at her. If someone came up with an Uzi, we would have laughed at them too.

Anyway, it was a phony pistol, but we didn't know it right then. She ran away and we ran after her. Then finally she talked to us, the first person who really reacted to us, and we offered her a job as a kind of researcher. Later we were highly criticized by a Philadelphia newspaper because we paid her fifteen bucks a day to go up to doors of crack houses, gun dealers. Critics said we were encouraging this woman's addiction by paying her this money. Truth is, that newspaper was upset because we told this terrible story before they did, published before they did.

Paradoxically, when we got most known on the street, it became more dangerous for us. We were set up for a robbery. It was a matter of time before some kid would have hurt us, I think, simply because it would be an interesting thing to do. Our work was pretty much completed anyway. The article ran.

My time with Ed ended there. He went back to *Life* and subsequently to *Time* magazine and international assignments, while I wanted to do a book. After failing to get Ed involved in the idea of a book, I went off on my own for a number of months in east New York, another drug-troubled neighborhood—this one in Brooklyn.

Richards has produced nine books. Two were self-published.

You're working for magazines, usually not the writer. Although you respect the writer you work with, it's not your voice. Still I find myself responsible for the article, warts and all. If one of my books really sucks, it's because I did a bad job. If the book upsets people, it's because I intended it to. I'm responsible, not somebody else.

Photographic books reveal you. If you're a wonderful photographer but an egotistical asshole, it'll show in the book and it'll show in the design of the book. If you're confused—and a lot of us are a lot of the time—that'll show in the book. It's a good self-study. When it's all done, you know who you are.

The book with Dorothea—somehow the fact that we got her words down in a book—was the beginning for me of a healing process. Same with the drug book. I know it sounds so naive, but I do feel like each of us has a social obligation, and books are like paying off a social obligation.

Now that I have a child, I do stories on issues that might affect him. Like the majority of parents, I don't want my child going to war, still he should know of world history, of the issues involved in modern wars, in order to make choices. I don't want him using drugs, but I can't, any more than any parent, stop him from using drugs. All I can do is tell him about what is out there. My family is probably the major impetus for my continuing to work. That and the fact that after all these years of being a photojournalist, I'm not sure what else I could do.

When I was talking to photographer Jeff Jacobson recently, he reminded me of something the now-deceased photographer, Ethan Hoffman, had said to him. "Jeff, don't worry. If you do a really bad job, you won't be hired again. But if you do a really good job, they won't hire you again, either." I've struggled to do good editorial work, but lately the assignments are fewer and fewer.

People have been asking forever about the death of photojournalism. I say it's not going to die, but it's definitely a different time. Rather than head out to report on and show a situation, photographers are being asked more and more to illustrate editors' ideas, writers' ideas, even advertisers' ideas of what the world's about.

I have a wonderful wife, Janine, who really doesn't cut me much slack. I mean, she's not the person who's gonna listen to my emoting a lot of the time. She's the person who I call late at night and say, "This story sucks. I hate the business." I vent and then get back to work. Janine hates the business and the egos in photography probably more than I do. She's a very tough person in that respect, but she always encourages me and holds us together.

As for tomorrow, I'm looking at going back to Auburn, a tiny town in Nebraska, and doing not photography, but a film about the old farmers living there. But who's going to want a twenty-, thirty-minute film on old people? I'm doing it because I've got to keep what I love alive.

Susan Meiselas

Central America and Human Rights

Susan Meiselas studied anthropology at Sarah Lawrence College and graduated in 1970. She took her first photography class at Harvard, where she completed a master's degree in visual education and worked as an assistant editor for documentary filmmaker Frederick Wiseman on his 1971 film, *Basic Training*.

She began a documentary project, *Carnival Strippers*, her first summer with a camera. During the year, she taught children to read and write using photography in an experimental program for public schools. *Carnival Strippers* would become a book, a show, and her entree to the Magnum photo agency in 1976.

The following year she traveled to Nicaragua to photograph the civil war between General Anastasio Somoza García's dictatorship and the Sandinista opposition. Her book, *Nicaragua*, resulted from two years there. Meiselas was also in El Salvador during the country's civil war of the 1980s. She photographed the uncovered graves of four murdered American nuns, which helped prompt U.S. congressional investigations into El Salvador's right-wing death squads and the American role in the war. Together with journalists Ray Bonner and Alma Guermoprieta, Meiselas documented the massacre of civilians by the Savadoran army in the village of El Mazote. For her work in Central America, she was awarded the Robert Capa Gold Medal and the Leica Medal for Excellence among others.

Meiselas also helped coordinate the exhibition and publication of *El Salvador: The Work of Thirty Photographers*, a role she reprised with Chilean

Lena outside the girl show,
Essex Junction, Vermont, 1973
(© Susan Meiselas/Magnum)

photographers who witnessed the human rights abuses of the Augusto Pinochet regime in *Chile from Within*. She has also codirected two films, *Living at Risk* and *Pictures from a Revolution*, with Richard P. Rogers and Alfred Guzzetti.

In 1992 Meiselas joined other journalists and activists at Kurdish refugee camps on the border of Iran. Intrigued and appalled by what she witnessed, she launched *Kurdistan: In the Shadow of History* with the aid of a MacArthur Foundation fellowship. A major portion of the project was devoted to collecting and rephotographing pictures from anthropologists, missionaries, photojournalists, and the Kurdish people to help create and archive a visual history of the Kurdistan. The project gave Meiselas the opportunity to explore "the role that Western image-makers have played in shaping the West's and the Kurds' own picture of that history." Her innovative web site, www.akaKurdistan.com, was developed from this material.

After nearly forty years as a photographer, she has actively continued what she describes as her "point of engagement" by using text, sound, film, and other people images trying to see the photograph as a cultural artifact. Her 2001 monograph, *Pandora's Box*, explores a New York S & M club. In 2008, *Susan Meiselas: In History*, a monograph of her work was published and exhibited at the International Center for Photography in New York City. She continues to be an active and leading force in the Magnum photographic cooperative.

For my first project, *Carnival Strippers,* I spent three summers traveling with women who were doing striptease in state and local country fairs. I developed relationships with women who were often transient. Sometimes they would start working on one weekend and end the next because their boyfriends would pull them off the show. My relationships with the managers as well as a few of the girls extended over more than one summer. I wanted to assimilate into their working environment and portray what was happening. It was as important to me to capture their ideas about what they were doing as it was to photograph them in the process of their working lives.

I showed my work in small galleries right from the beginning, putting photographs and text on the walls. The most successful installation included sound. Everyone was represented—the various managers, the clients, the women, their boyfriends—by mixtures of voices that you could hear floating in the background as you were looking at the photographs. The sound wasn't precisely linked, neither were the texts placed alongside the photographs of specific people. I wanted to recreate the feeling of that environment. In the case of the book, which I produced later, I built a parallel narrative so that those voices, when read, would bring you into the process of experiencing that world in a different way than the photographs alone could.

During the five years I was working with carnival strippers, I taught in the public schools as an artist-in-residence. I trained teachers to work with kids using photography, and I worked in the classroom myself to develop a curriculum using photography to teach reading and writing. In 1975–1976, while I was beginning to edit *Carnival Strippers*, I chose not to continue as a public school teacher and tried to figure out how I was going to make a living as a photographer.

It was with two pieces of work, both with a documentary approach, that I went to Magnum. I showed them the *Carnival Strippers* portfolio and another essay on the basic training of women in the army, from one of the few jobs that I had managed to get—the *Daily News,* of all places. I became a Magnum "nominee" and started to work in the world of photojournalism, but I've always kept my documentary approach.

Magnum is about family in a strange way. There's something about being inside a collective of artists who continue to create and invent ways of surviving—sometimes sharing out of self-interest and sometimes not. Echoing exactly the human experience. This could happen within or outside of Magnum. For me, it just happens to be a little harbor. It's kind of a place where I go out from, out into the seas with all the torrential rains and currents and unpredictability that are out there at sea. This is a place that I come back to, one that's always there for me. There may not be a friendship with each member, but many have shaped my thinking.

My life changed radically when, two years later, I headed off to Nicaragua. By chance, my arrival coincided with a crisis inside the country, I decided to stay, not to hit and run. I wanted to go beyond the news event and document what I saw as history. I was fascinated and felt that I had to explore everywhere. It was knowing back roads. It was knowing neighborhoods. It was knowing people in places, so I could get a sense from them as to what was going on. Those relationships are not sources exactly, as writers always have to have, but they help shape your perception of what's important.

You don't always know where you're going or what something is going to lead to. It's discovered, not planned for. I never went to Central America looking for a guerrilla or an army officer or a this and a that to juxtapose. Very often newspaper photographers are forced to work in much tighter time frames and have to illustrate certain kinds of stories. I was capturing the world I was seeing, completely following my own sense of what was important.

Assignments were very erratic. I was living cheaply, for five dollars a night throughout most of the period, until the war got intense, and it was really unsafe to live alone in a small place. It was rare that people would hire me to do a specific thing during the time I covered the war in Nicaragua in 1978 and 1979. Later, in the early eighties, I would be assigned to work with a particular writer to do a certain story elsewhere in Latin America.

The difference between my work in Central America and the earlier documentary work was that I could be on the road with the carnival strippers, come home, process the film, bring it back, show them the contact sheets, and then bring them prints of the images they wanted to give their fathers or their husbands or their lovers. There was a much closer, more intimate relationship with the carnival strippers.

I came up against different sets of problems in Nicaragua, partly because it was a war. I couldn't always get back to the subject. I couldn't find them again. Very often I didn't see the photographs, because I had to send the film out of the country to have it processed. Magnum was distributing to several international publications, and they were editing work that I hadn't always seen before shipping the film. I shot black and white as a sketchbook, to keep a record when the boxes of color slides were dispersed.

It was powerful to suddenly discover an image that I had made on the cover of the *New York Times Magazine,* reporting the insurrection in Nicaragua, before the war actually began. I was excited about that, but I started to feel some caution about what was implied by that power—the responsibility that comes with that power—to get it right. There is an illusion of control that we all have. For me, getting the names, the places, and the details of what is in fact going on is so important. But beyond my own books, the images are out of my control.

Magnum participates as an intermediary in shaping what magazines are given to work with and in helping make sure they get the details right. But once the material goes to the magazines, difficulties can develop. There were definitely examples of images used to accompany text that misrepresented the feeling I had at the time I photographed. Some were just mistakes and some were intentional. Part of the struggle of being a photojournalist is dealing with a medium that moves very fast: then we shipped film out by plane, while now everyone is digital.

When I finally put together the book, *Nicaragua,* it was very hard for me to see what pictures I had in relation to what I had missed. The enormity of the experience was so much greater than whatever I could render in seventy-two images. That is always the biggest challenge in making a book. That process is completely different than shooting stories or watching how what you shoot gets edited into illustrated magazine stories.

Though we might have more control through bookmaking, the distribution of photography books is still pathetic. There are many reasons for small audiences. In some cases it's the tendency to believe that the photograph carries all the meaning and therefore there's no other kind of text that might be helpful to a reader. Sometimes it's because the publishers themselves are isolated and not connected to enough sectors that might value the work. It's still a very primitive business. Sometimes I've felt like, "Why don't I just put the books in the trunk of my car and go door to door selling them?" I remember when we did take a lot of the El Salvador books to a major demonstration in Washington, D.C. We were selling the books to people who already knew about the issues—an obvious audience. But making books should be about creating a new audience.

I don't know if Amazon.com or web sites will help generate another kind of global community that we could never reach before. Is independent-authored production going to be supported or smothered out? Can small archives with limited resources compete against the capital that creates bigger conglomerates and then pressures to further control serial rights? These are critical questions for our survival in the future.

We need to continue to push traditional boundaries. As a documentarian, I have also been concerned about the aesthetics of an image. But if a photograph is in a gallery and it's sold to hang on a wall, does that make it fine art? Or, is it fine art because we're no longer interested in its caption and/or the context from which it came? I believe that the important question is how to seize opportunities to expose our work to a broader audience. If there's a gallery that's interested in the work, can you render the complexity of what you know through the installation? There are moments where the formal is of less concern to me than the narrative function of a photograph, but I'm always looking for that thin line that I'm walking between form and content.

I shot *Carnival Strippers* in color and in black and white until I decided which I preferred. At that time, I was shooting recording film and experiencing many problems with exposure. There was no color negative with high speed at that time, so I worked in black and white. I liked the grainy feel of the pushed film.

In Nicaragua I again shot color and black and white, using two cameras, but I progressively felt that the work should be in color. It was expressive of the way people dressed and painted their houses. It caught the spirit of optimism about what was happening. This was quite different from El Salvador. In El Salvador I shot with two cameras, because at that time magazines expected color, but I really saw the brutality there in black and white.

There were criticisms when the Nicaraguan photographs first appeared. There were people that felt that I was aesthetisizing violence in Central America. There were people who just thought color was inappropriate. But it was not the first time people had used color. In Vietnam there was fabulous color by Larry Burrows. I saw that, but I don't think I was thinking about it in the abstract. I was looking at the world I was in and trying to figure out the appropriate translation to capture what I felt about that place at that moment.

There is an ongoing challenge for us, as documentarians, to continue to be committed and engaged, while at the same time innovative. I fear we have deadened out. You see this in exhibitions, which are often handled in precisely the same manner, or with similar variations. The same is true in magazines. There is a huge amount that still can be done in print, despite the efforts made by Alex Harris and Bob Coles with *DoubleTake,* or Colin Jacobson's *Reportage,* or, going back a few years, Peter Howe's *Outtakes* [a project of trying to print work that was shot, but never published]. Only one of them has survived. Why?

A lot of people buy cameras and film, and a lot of people buy photo books of a certain kind. The obvious example is the "Day in the Life of" series. Now, what's the problem? Why aren't people interested in what we documentarians are passionate about? Why are we in such a small ghetto?

Doing documentary work is not just building the relationships and shooting. It's also finding the spaces, be they magazine pages, books, or exhibition spaces, to transform and present the world we see differently. To get work into a public space is not easy. But we have to figure out how to do that effectively, not to mention the biggest problem, which is finding the sponsorship and the support.

We cannot always assume people are going to be interested in what we are involved in. We have to find ways of taking people someplace they don't expect to go. There was a time when we could surprise people. They would go to an exhibition in a museum and discover that it was so-called "photojournalism." That period was quite exciting. We were creating another environment, transforming the walls into a different experience for people who were going to museums in the traditional way.

When working with the material from El Salvador, I wanted to get the photographs into any kind of environment I could, from public libraries to storefronts, to the Museum of Photographic Arts in San Diego or the International Center for Photography in New York. The greatest success was in a public library in Rochester, New York. In order to go anywhere in the library you had to pass by a photographic display about El Salvador, at a time when U.S. military aid was intensely supporting that war.

I was trying to figure out what happens when this work is on different kinds of walls. What dialogue can it open up? Those are the kinds of explorations that we need to continue to do, and this involves partnerships. It's not just the photographer's problem. We've got to find partners willing to experiment with ways of getting people involved with "other" people and distant places.

The book that I've just done on Kurdistan is about encounter—the encounter of a variety of westerners, be they missionaries or anthropologists or photojournalists—looking at how they saw the Kurds and how they shaped the way the Kurds were seen. I see myself in that tradition of encounter and witness—a "witness" who sees the photograph as evidence. A lot of my work has been based on a concern about human rights violations. That's where that word is the most appropriate. But the other side of "witness" is that we do intervene, and we intervene by the fact of our presence in a particular place. We change how people see themselves sometimes and how others may come to see them. I'm also concerned about how we see ourselves in the process of our role as witnesses.

When some of us began working in the early seventies, already the magazines of the sixties weren't hiring people to do what we dreamed we were going to do. We read the stories about Margaret Bourke-White or Robert Capa going off on long assignments and being guaranteed fifteen-page spreads, no matter what the subject. For my generation, those expectations weren't met. It is still tough for many of us with a lot of experience to get work today. Our production can no longer be sustained by editorial work alone. Does that mean that we give workshops and inspire people to do what we do, creating a geometric relationship of greater difficulty for all?

I don't see a major revival of documentary, although the current generation of students is again interested, after going through a decade where there was a tremendous assault against or controversy about documentary and the validity of documentary. I think there were issues that came out of that period that put some things in question, which was very, very positive, although it paralyzed production for many people.

The interesting question is, will there be a further extension of the vocabulary and the language of documentary? Can we go further than we've gone? That's what I still find myself excited to think about.

Sebastião Salgado

Workers

S ebastião Salgado is an economist who decided that photographs could better express his concerns than his economic reports. He made this discovery after borrowing a camera from his wife, Lélia Warnick Salgado, on a business trip for the International Coffee Organization in 1971.

Salgado left his native Brazil because of the military dictatorship in 1968. Relocated in Paris, he worked as a freelance photographer for several years. He was on assignment for the *New York Times Magazine* covering Ronald Reagan when the assassination attempt on the president occurred and took photographs that were widely reproduced internationally.

In 1977 Salgado began work on a social documentary project on indigenous life in Latin America that culminated in the publication of *Other Americas* in 1986. He also covered the famine in the Sahel, in Africa, working with the medical relief group, Médecins sans Frontières. A collection of these two bodies of work culminated in major exhibitions and a book, *Uncertain Grace*, in 1990.

Salgado has said that, "You photograph with all your ideology," and he is an activist as well as a photographer. On his family's farm in Brazil, for instance, he has established a forest restoration project that models a different type of economic development in the area.

In 1982 Salgado was honored with the W. Eugene Smith Memorial Fund award for humanistic photography for his work in Latin America. For several years, he has pursued boldly conceived multiyear projects concentrated in the Southern Hemisphere. *Workers*, which pays homage to manual labor-

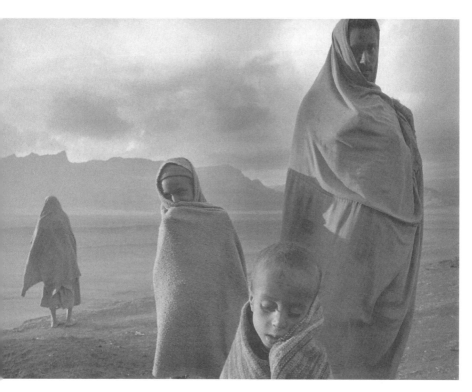

Ethiopia, 1984
(© Sebastião Salgado/Amazonas/Contact)

ers in many parts of the world, was published in 1993. Shortly before
Workers was published, he embarked on a seven-year project *Migrations*
(2000). This project chronicled mass migrations in more than 35 different
countries. Salgado photographed refugees, exiles, orphans, landless
peasants, homeless families, and boat people, all of whom have been
forced from their homes by explosive population growth, environmental
degradation, natural disasters, and economic pressures.

In 2004, he began a new and ambitious photo project called Genesis.
Its aim is to show the unblemished faces of nature and humanity. It
consists of a series of photographs of landscapes and wildlife, as well as
of human communities that continue to live in accordance with their
ancestral traditions and cultures. Salgado has described it as "a body of
work that is conceived as a potential path to humanity's rediscovery of
itself in nature." To coordinate these projects, he and Lélia established
Amazonas, an agency that she directs in Paris.

I don't know if my photography is a passion. Passion is something that
you can have one day and then the next day it disappears, replaced
by another passion, by another wish. It could be that it is a way of life.
I came from a reality that I've lived with from the beginning—that was
my country, that was my family, those were my friends, that was the
school that I went to, those were the political movements I worked
for—before I became a photographer. I continue to do exactly the same
thing, but now I include photography. I believe that it's more than a
passion. It's difficult for me to imagine being any other way.

I began like an amateur and remained an amateur for two or three
years. I tried to understand what my wish was. I tried to do portraits,
I tried to do sports, I tried to do many different things because I had a
passion for photography, for the camera. In the end I discovered that
the stories that gave me the most pleasure were the same stories I did
before, not as a photographer, but as an economist, as a student.

I had found what was important in my life. I believe that ultimately
what you do in life is the thing that you are most capable to do, the
thing that you are most concerned with. I don't believe that you do
many different things in life. You do the same thing in different versions, but it's always the same thing.

I discovered this for myself when I was photographing in the Sahel.
It was practically the first story I did, photographing the problems of

starvation in 1973. And soon I did a second story like this, and that's more or less my life until now.

I've seen many difficult things, many hard things. It is important to have the capacity to adapt and, at the moment that you are photographing, to put these things in the context of your experiences in the other parts of your life—like the side of life you live when you are in your home.

You see the whole thing. You see yourself acting, photographing to show something to the other side, to people who did not have the opportunity to be there. And you have the idea of the link between these things. In the end you see documentary photography more as a vector than anything else. And as a vector it links points of the various concepts of "normal" life. The human situations you see that are very difficult are part of life; the situations that are very easy are also part, and they must be shown. They must be linked.

I have never put myself in a situation where I have a moral question about whether or not to photograph, such as, "Do I have a right to photograph when the death is there in front of me, the suffering is there in front of me?" I never ask myself these questions, because I asked myself the more important questions before I arrived there. Do we have the right to the division of resources that we have in the world? Do I have the right to have the house that I have, to live where I live? Do I have the right to eat when others don't eat? These are the basic questions.

I believe that there is no person in the world that must be protected from pictures. Everything that happens in the world must be shown and people around the world must have an idea of what's happening to the other people around the world. I believe this is the function of the vector that the documentary photographer must have, to show one person's existence to another. Sometimes we meet people in mainly rich countries—sometimes in poor countries, too—that are so shocked to discover that some people have such a hard way of life. These people are very serious, very honest when they say they are shocked because they never really had the opportunity to see. And when you show them, when you discuss the situation with them, they become integrated with the problem, and the problem becomes part of their life.

The most interesting function of this kind of photography is exactly this: to show and to provoke debate and to see how we can go ahead with our lives. The photographer must participate in this debate. I don't believe you do this because you are good, or because you are bad, or because you have a mission. You don't do it because of any of these things. You do it because it's your way of life. And in doing this you are minding yourself, you are minding your children, you are minding your wife, you are minding the things that you love most in your life. How can the documentary photographer help to assure the survival of all these people and to assure the survival of the next generations? Documentary photographers have a slice of the responsibility—they must provoke a discussion. You don't go to a place to create good images, to create beautiful things. That's not what it is about. You have your own way to show them, and the photographer must find his own way.

In my case I prefer to work on very long-term stories. For all the stories I do, I write an outline. I create a framework where I concentrate my energies and my ideas. Of course, in this framework there are plenty of doors and windows. I can come and go by any one. I can put things inside and take things out. Using this method, it is much easier for you to evolve and to work with people. How are you to prepare the reportage? How are you to raise the funds? What about the magazines that will use these pictures or the organization with which you will be working? Does an environment exist that will allow you to give to them and receive from them? I try to work in the most open way. For example, I never produce a picture to show the end of a story. All of my pictures, without exception, were made as the story unfolded.

When I went to begin to photograph the project in Mozambique, Rwanda was not really in a state of civil war. A month later the civil war in Rwanda began. It was impossible for me to anticipate this, so the framework changed. I had a general idea of what was happening there because I read a lot before I arrived, and I also consulted people. But the test of the information comes when you are in the country. Only then will you see how real the things presented are, how difficult or easy they are, how important they are to you, and what part of the story you must touch to make it real, because you have a country, a huge country, in front of you. You have a huge number of refugees preparing to come back in addition to the ones inside. I remember when I first came to Mozambique, I spent about thirty days there, but for at least ten days I was organizing my story. I was looking, going to places, getting different things, to see where the refugees were coming back.

I made my second trip to Mozambique because I thought a lot of different things would be happening, and it would be the right time to photograph. But, by the time I arrived, all things had changed. The programs had changed. Things had happened in surrounding countries. It was necessary to go back a third time, really, to close my story.

You don't go to do one picture. You go to build a story. In the end, I believe that documentary photographers are people that love to tell stories. These stories are made with a big sequence of pictures. When I worked in Zaire with the people who came from Rwanda, I gave about fifty-five pictures to the magazines. In the fifty-five pictures I have a sequence. I have the beginning of the story, I have the middle of the story, and I have the end of the story. I have the captions that can accompany these photos. If you read the captions, you read my story. If you read the pictures, you read the story. That's the point. Sometimes people say, "Oh, you go to make good pictures of poor people." The people don't understand peanuts when they say this, because I never go to do a picture. I never go to do a good picture. What is a good picture? No. I go to stay inside my story, to try to understand what's going on, to be close to the people I photograph, and to create a flow of information that we can use to communicate something.

When *Life* magazine or *Time* magazine or *Stern* magazine has an idea to build a story, to do a story, it's their idea. They create the story, and they ask a photographer to go and shoot it. Or a photographer has an idea for a story for *Life* magazine that would represent one event, that is, one story.

With documentary photography the difference is that the photographer must have a big concern. You must have a big ideological affinity with the subject you will be shooting, because if you don't, you cannot remain sincere and empathetic for long. You must strongly identify with the subject. Then when the photographer first actually encounters the subject all of his preconceptions change.

At this moment, the way you look at the people you come to photograph, the way you relate to the people you come to photograph, the way you relate to your story, and the way you relate to the organization you are linked with are forever changed. Now they are a part of you and a part of your work. The people that you are photographing are a part of the universe in which you are living in the deepest way.

You change the region, you change the language, you change the country, but the story continues to be the same. After six years of shooting, I finished a story about the working class. I worked in forty-two different places of work in many different sectors of the production process, like agriculture, light industry, heavy industry, and miners. Each year I spent at least eight months in the places of work, living with the people, some for months, some for weeks. I have a very good idea about what the world of production is today. I understand how modern the world is today, how the means of production are linked. In practice, you realize that some theories were correct and some were not. You begin to make corrections, and sometimes you go in a direction that is completely different from the one you had in the beginning. All of these discoveries along the way make this flow of information very, very interesting.

I've never made a picture meant to be shown exclusively in one magazine. I don't have a closed agreement with one magazine, and I don't have an agreement with one kind of medium. For example, if I have an agreement with one magazine in one country, I will have an agreement with another magazine in another country. That allows me to have a group of magazines, a group of different countries, a group of different art directors, a group of different editors of magazines with whom I can exchange ideas and publications where I can present the photographs.

In addition to magazines, I work with a group of nongovernmental organizations. Nongovernmental organizations for me are very, very important, because they are so dynamic and positive. That work is as important as the magazines. For example, Médecins sans Frontières saw my work and asked me if they could use my pictures. I accommodated them initially, because I already had the pictures. I never sell pictures to these organizations. I give them the pictures, because the magazines have already paid me. The organizations use them in their newspapers, their shows, their posters, their television campaigns, and that kind of thing.

I'm trying to work with the new electronic media. I'm trying to do a CD-ROM and to use pictures on television. I'm doing a lot of small shows. For example, I'm preparing a television show with one of the United Nations organizations about Mozambican refugees returning to their country, which will be shown in Mozambique, Tanzania, Malawi, Zimbabwe, and in South Africa. The documentary photographer today must adapt to and accommodate the new ways we can use pictures. There are more uses for photography and documentary photography than ever before. When you see, for example, the CD-ROM's capacity to use pictures, you discover that it is probably as important as a book. In fact, it's capable of showing much, much more than you see in a book, and it could make documentary photography more accessible because it is more cheaply and quickly produced. You can change language; you can do different versions, different translations in many languages.

And this is the point: to see how we are capable of adapting ourselves to the technological evolution of the world and to take advantage of this change of tools. It will always be necessary to have a photographer there to get the image. It's only the field that's changing. We must accept that there are more photographers than ever before and that we must live more densely than we have lived until now.

Documentary photography has always been hard. We probably have more opportunity now than before, because, even though many of the big "picture" magazines have disappeared, so many others have appeared in their place. We have all these big newspapers in this country that have Sunday supplements, Sunday magazines. And many nongovernmental organizations publish their own magazines. How many possibilities are there to do CD-ROMs? How many possibilities are there to do films from still pictures—where you film the pictures and you tell the story? That means that possibilities to use photography are as great or greater than before in proportion to the number of photographers and the general population.

We cannot continue to tell the same stories *Life* magazine did in its heyday. We must learn about and integrate what happened in the thirties and the fifties and the way stories were told, but we must see what's happening with this story today. You must live intensely the story you intend to do. The opportunities are there.

There is much, much more to photograph now than you had before, because the population of the world has more than doubled in forty years, and communication is much better. There is another way to see—television. It pushes the stories more quickly than they were pushed before. Urbanization is more than before. The world's problems are probably bigger now than they were, so there are more stories happening now in proportion to what we had before.

Whether the image lives as an historical document is for history to determine. You cannot foretell history. It would be a bit pretentious to say that I'm a historian. I hope people look at my pictures because my pictures tell the story accurately. I try to link my pictures with an historical moment that we are living. I believe that these pictures will stay or they will disappear depending on whether or not they ultimately are linked with the historical moment. It's not because they are good pictures or bad pictures.

People who want to do documentary photography are not artists in the sense that an artist's work can stay. It's not this. It must be your life one hundred percent. If you find you cannot do this, you must find where your passion really is. But if your passion is in photography, documentary photography, that must be your way of life.

Graciela Iturbide

The Indigenous of Mexico

Graciela Iturbide was born in Mexico City to an upper-middle-class family. After her six-year-old daughter, Claudia, tragically died, she gave up a conventional family life to study cinematography. As a student at the Centro Universitario de Estudios Cinematográficos, Iturbide met and became an assistant to Manuel Álvarez Bravo, Mexico's foremost photographer.

In 1979, at the invitation of the painter Francisco Toledo, Iturbide traveled to southern Mexico to study and photograph the Zapotec Indians in Juchitán. Her book, *Juchitán de las Mujeres*, emphasizes the traditions and customs that shape the values of their precolonial, predominantly matriarchal society. Juchitán is "a place the conquistadores never reached," she said. On the basis of this work, Iturbide received the prestigious W. Eugene Smith Memorial Fund award for humanistic photography in 1987.

Although most of Iturbide's work is about Mexico's indigenous peoples—throughout the course of her career she has documented the Mayo, Totonae, Tarasco, Kickapoo, Seri, and Nahua Indians—she has photographed the role Mexican traditions play in immigrant communities, particularly the "cholos" of East Los Angeles. She completed a short essay, *En el Nombre del Padre*, that discusses the tradition of the yearly goat sacrifice in the province of Oaxaca, Mexico. Critics have described her as having

The original interview with Graciela Iturbide was conducted in Spanish and translated by Almundena Ortiz.

Nuestra Señora de las Iguanas,
Juchitán, Mexico, 1979
(© Graciela Iturbide)

"extended the concept of documentary photography, to explore the relationships between man and nature, the individual and the cultural, the real and the psychological." She continues to create imaginative bodies of work and inspire the next generation of photographers in Latin America and beyond.

When I met Manuel Álvarez Bravo, the world of photography came alive to me. I went with him into the field. Bravo never really worked on a theme. He would just photograph what he found.

My education as a photographer was little by little, going to festivals, parties, finding the images. My first real photographic essay or photography with a theme was in the desert in Sonora [California] with the Seris Indians. I was interested in the culture of my own country, and I realized how important it was to work in a thematic way. I made a book of the Indians.

At the same time, Francisco Toledo, the painter, invited me to go to Juchitán and asked me if I wanted to make a book. I would donate the exhibition to the House of Culture in Oaxaca—that was the objective of my introduction to Juchitán. So Juchitán was my first developed theme for photography. I had some freedom when I was doing this project; it wasn't like a job. Juchitán was totally my own creation.

My own country fascinates me, even though I work a lot outside of Mexico, including in Europe and Madagascar. But I feel more of a passion for Mexico, and I feel safer working here. I've also been working with Mexicans in the United States, in East Los Angeles, in the San Joaquin valley. It's part of my country's situation.

I go to the community first, always with my camera so they know I'm a photographer. I speak to the people and normally I stay and live with them. I try to involve myself in the legends, because they're related to the festivities I'm photographing. I also read materials that are related to the topic, for example, in the case of Juchitán I read [Miguel] Covarrubias.

It's little by little I speak to the people. I read a lot about the place itself, I speak to the fieldworkers. We sort of work together, and after a while the fieldworkers and the people in the community invite me to the festivities. They tell me about when a fiesta's going to happen. So we work together, it's not an aggressive confrontation.

For the Seris project I stayed for a month. That's the time that I had to develop the work. But in the case of Juchitán it was around fifteen days at a time, and then I would go back to Mexico City, because it was very intense. There were a lot of festivities, you had to go to the dances and actually dance so it's very intense. They drink a lot, and I also had to drink.

It is one of my principles that whenever I work with a community, I always bring prints back. It's different if I go and photograph festivities somewhere. But if I work with a community, that's always something I do. It's different when it's only a one-day festivity because you really can't go back and give prints to everybody.

The Seris had only been photographed by Americans and with Polaroid color film. So, when I did my project, I went back and did a show for them to see in one of the little houses there. They would say, "No, we don't like it," because it was black and white. But later, each one grabbed their photograph and took it home.

After I did the book on Juchitán, "The Woman of the Iguanas" became a celebrity. She has had about forty different journalists go and photograph her and talk to her. The journalists don't really understand what she's about. They come and ask her, "Why are you a feminist?" and really in the Zapotec culture we call it the matriarch culture, but it's their own culture. We cannot translate our Western ideology to them. So, they don't understand.

It's been easier for me being a woman and working in the field. I go and I stay with the women, and I have never had any problems. It's interesting because if I had been a commercial photographer and I had been working in publicity, it would have been different. There's a lot of competition, and being a woman would be a problem. But in the field people take care of you.

I've been more and more interested in different cultures in my country. For example, the Seris women have no relation to the women in Juchitán as a community itself. The fact that I'm a woman and working in the field has facilitated things for me, because I live with the women, I go with the women to the market, so it's very nonobtrusive. Of course, I focus a lot on the women, because I'm living with them and it's easier, but I also photograph men. And my approach, it's a woman's approach because I am a woman.

The men in the field do take care of you. For example, in the Seris case, initially I was there with an anthropologist, and the Seris were not very happy about my being there. But later they warmed up to me and even came and gave me a little heart that they had knit for me. They don't even speak a lot, but they would hang around and they were comfortable.

In Mexico indigenous cultures are very marginalized. The rest of Mexico doesn't really pay attention. They don't even acknowledge their existence. Except this is changing, for example, the Zapatistas movement. I am interested in Mexico as it is—or as it was—and I'm also interested in the changes now. Many of those communities were abandoned. They had no roads, no anything.

The Seris case is very interesting. The community was a rich community by indigenous standards. They were given permission to fish in the Sea of Cortez, and the Americans would buy a lot of crafts from them, so they had money. I have this photograph of a Seris woman coming down a hill, and she's carrying a big tape deck. That to me is fantastic. Or, sometimes the Indians would dress in a tux and would go to the desert, and that's a part of them. I just stand there and observe, and it fascinates me.

My pictures upset some of the bourgeois, the upper class, the mainstream in Mexico. At least they know there is another part of Mexico that they have not acknowledged. But the people that see my photographs in a show in Mexico, it's not like they're going to have a social conscience after that. They just see it differently. Mexico's very difficult in that sense.

I don't pretend that my photography's going to actually change the world or make it a better place or anything like that. I photograph this way because I want to. The camera is like a pretext to put me in a situation, to go to a community so I get to learn about them and I get to learn about my country.

My photographs deal with the dignified aspect of humanity, even if I'm photographing the worst of situations. And there is a very deep complicity or dialogue between the person who is being photographed and myself. Of course, one of us is holding the camera. But if that dialogue does not exist, it just doesn't work. For example, in the case of Juchitán, there's a photograph I have depicting "El Rapto," a custom in which a virgin bride is deflowered by her husband-to-be before the wedding. If she is not a virgin, the wedding ceremony doesn't take place. This is the first time that this has been photographed. But they were the ones that asked me to come help photograph, because they know the way I photograph.

Mexico has always had a tradition of social documentary photography. We really don't know what term to give it in Mexico, but it's always been there. For example, Tina Modotti, [Edward] Weston, [Henri] Cartier-Bresson, [Paul] Strand. There are young photographers working in the social documentary tradition because of this legacy. There are no magazines where you can work or make things for publication, but young people are still continuing to work in photography. Mexicans don't have as many places to publish as Americans or Europeans. Europeans and Americans have traveled to Mexico and India the most to photograph. These countries have been a mecca for those photographers.

Manuel Álvarez Bravo is a special case. He's a very intelligent, cultured man, but he also had a very close friendship with the muralists when he started. And because of the muralists in Mexico, he met Andre Breton and of course his work was published and known in Europe. Initially when Breton came to Mexico, Manuel Álvarez Bravo was asked to make a photo for the cover of an exhibition catalog, for which he presented "La Buena Fama Durmiendo, 1939" ["Good Reputation Sleeping"], but in the end it was censored. He was fortunate enough to know these people and be well-known. Then again, later on, a lot of the time nobody bought any of his work.

He had the same problems that other people faced, that his work was known in Europe, but he was not recognized in Mexico. He had to do little odd photography jobs, illustrating books and so on, to make a living. He is a personality well-known in Mexico, he has a good reputation, but it's not like he is glamorized like a painter or anything like that.

Now that there are some international awards, more Mexican photographers have been exposed, and their work has been published more. For example, I'm working with Maya Goded, the woman who won the International Fund for Documentary Photography award. She's going to present a book that I'm helping her to edit.

Of course, in Mexico we don't even have schools of photography. We learn in life. You go, you do a little job here, and maybe you publish and someone sees it and calls you, but it's just little by little, there's not really a structure. There used to be a school called the Mexican

Council of Photography. There's a place Centro de la Imagen where photographers are able to show their work, and there is a space for lectures from both Mexican and international photographers.

On the other hand, we are a small community of photographers where we feel there's a responsibility to help younger photographers, help them out, talk to them and that sort of thing, so there is a niche, a tight community of photographers. There's a lot of enthusiasm and a lot of photographers showing their work to each other and pushing each other.

Also, because of the nature of my work, I get to travel, I get to do symposiums or show work. So I do travel, especially in Latin America. I've been to Cuba quite a few times, to Spain where I gave a symposium. When you are there you are a part of that community of photographers, you keep track of each other. So in that respect, I feel a part of the community.

Antonin Kratochvil

The Fall of the Iron Curtain

Born in Czechoslovakia (now the Czech Republic), Antonin Kratochvil was a child when Soviet communists seized power after World War II. His family was sent to a relocation camp for five years and lived in sub-human conditions. He fled to Austria in 1967 but was forced into a refugee camp before escaping to France, where he was drafted into the Foreign Legion and sent to North Africa. After an injury, he again escaped, this time to Holland, where he was able to take a course in photography that changed his life.

The influence of his refugee experience is felt vividly in his numerous photo-essays, such as those on street kids in Guatemala and Mongolia, Tibetan refugees, and war-torn Afghanistan. He spent twenty years, before and after the liberation of Eastern Europe, documenting the problems of refugees, economic dislocation, political chaos, and pollution in the former communist nations. This work was collected in his book, *Broken Dream*, published in 1997.

Kratochivil, who now lives in New York, is a founding member of the VII Photo Agency and has worked for numerous magazines including *Natural History, Rolling Stone, Fortune, Time,* and *Newsweek,* in addition to doing magazine celebrity portraiture. His many awards include the Leica Medal of Excellence, the Ernst Hass Award, and the International Center of Photography's 1991 Infinity Award for Journalist of the Year.

His most recent work, *Vanishing,* represents a collection of natural and human phenomena on the verge of extinction. What makes this

Tar Factory, Romania, 1978
(© Antonin Kratochvil)

book so innovative is the twenty years it took to produce, making it not only historical from the onset, but a labor of love and a commitment to one man's conscience.

I was born in 1947, after the war, a little brief moment of freedom before the communist coup. My parents were singled out as class enemies, and we were all sent to concentration camps for reeducation. I got my "education" there. We lived in a pig stall. That was my introduction to justice.

Before the "Czech Spring" of 1968, I was active with a student underground group, passing out leaflets. The secret police started to arrest a lot of us—there was a fink in the group—and many ended up in jail and many left the country illegally. We didn't know then that there would be an amnesty later. One friend worked for the train company and would smuggle people out in the train's water compartment. I walked and crawled under the barbed wire to Austria. It was dangerous; many people who tried to cross were shot without warning.

I left Czechoslovakia believing that people would be willing to help you because you'd suffered so much. Nobody gave a fuck. They put me in Traiskirthen, the infamous refugee camp, where I lived for a year and a half. It was a horrible place, with lots of killings and rapes. My cousin was killed there, thrown out of a window by some people who didn't like him.

Traiskirthen was a meat market. The Americans and Canadians would come through with their quotas and take only doctors, engineers, educated people—those good for the economy. Young guys without an education, like me, and old people were left to rot there. They're not going to put you through school; that would cost them money. It was before the great sympathy about the Russian occupation of Czechoslovakia, and nobody was giving anything.

Finally, Sweden took me, out of humanitarian consideration. I was designated like a guest worker and got a seasonal job working in a hotel. After the season was over, I was on the street. They just said, "This is it, goodbye." I had to go back to Traiskirthen. After about six months, I snuck out.

I was nineteen or twenty, on the street, homeless, with no money. I started stealing food, got busted, sent to prison, and deported. I wound up in France, where I was arrested for being in the country illegally. They gave me a choice, join the Foreign Legion or stay here and rot. I was sent to the desert in Chad [Africa], where I learned to dig a hole in the sand and lay there while tanks rolled over me. I would have to attach bombs to the tanks as they rolled over.

I was injured and sent to Marseilles, where I escaped over the wall of the fort. By chance I got to Holland, which changed my life. By that time the mood was more sympathetic toward the Czech refugees. With the occupation of Czechoslovakia by the Russian forces, the world took notice, and said, "Hey, you know, let's help these people." The media created the sympathy. I was on my way to being a bona fide loser. Sometimes you get a break.

I enrolled in art school and got a scholarship. I studied two and a half years and I graduated—the biggest achievement of my life. (Laughs) Actually, it was a breeze for me; I discovered I was a photographer. When I was going to school, I never really photographed what the other kids did. They were preparing themselves for careers in commercial photography. I was on the street. My first essay, which I did at school, was an essay on a decrepit old folks' home. I was so poor that I only shot one roll of film. Every frame had to count. Every paper had to count.

One of my teachers saw it and loved it. He got it published in some sort of leftist newspaper, and it created an uproar. The government actually closed the home down and improved the lives of those old people. I said, "Shit man, you can actually do this with your photography?" It's tremendous. I thought, "I want to stick to it." I'm going to go out there and do this because I really have this keen sense of justice in my brain, however twisted it is. That's what I set out to do, and I'm doing it still today. There were little corners I had to turn, but basically I'm drawn to this, because I feel I owe it to these people since I rose above it. I never really analyzed it, like psychotherapy, but that's probably it.

I just follow my gut. Sometimes I run into things, like the Mongolian street kids. I was out on assignment, photographing some idiotic story for *Details* in China. I go to this train station, and I see these homeless kids—but they're not doing drugs. I've shot homeless kids before, in Guatemala, places like that, but these kids were working for their money, making an effort. They were trying to maintain some kind of order, some kind of discipline, to try to sell Coca-Cola, go get the luggage for money. They didn't steal. So I tried to get some money to go back. I approached the *New York Times,* they said, "We did street kids in Afghanistan." Then I found this guy, Bruce Stutz, who was the editor at *Natural History,* and he sent me back. I went to Moscow, so I was near Mongolia, so I spent three weeks there.

I try to stay as long as I can. But I train myself, because I am a magazine photographer and I have been most of my career. I know the limits. Most of these things, if you get two weeks, it's fantastic. So, I work all day long, and I work in black and white so I don't need to wait for sunset. Sometimes I feel I have to go back. With my Eastern European project, *Broken Dream,* it was twenty years of going back.

The important thing is the prep work before. You should read about it, get all the information about it, as much as you can. You have to line up a fixer—somebody in the country who speaks the lingo and can fix things if there is a problem.

For instance, in Afghanistan, a group of mujahadeens climbed up on the truck where I was sleeping and decided to kill me. It was right before the Russian invasion, and they thought I was a Russian adviser. I knew I was in trouble when they tried to read my passport upside down. It was an American passport, but it had my place of birth as Czechoslovakia. They all knew about the 9mm guns manufactured by the Czechs. They held loaded guns to my head for two hours—it seemed like an eternity—while the fixer talked to them, told them I was on their side, whatever he could think of. Of course, I couldn't understand any of it, because I didn't know the language. I was very calm; I just thought, well, I'm going to die. The fixer saved my life.

Another fixer, in Rwanda, drove me into a minefield. He didn't know jack, so I was telling him, "Don't make a u-ey, just back out." Rwanda and Zaire in 1994 was the worst situation I've ever photographed. There were so many people dying; it was like the camps after World War II. There were piles of bodies and bulldozers making mass graves. A lot of people covered the war, but nobody was prepared for such mayhem. You see dead bodies in conflicts, but nothing like that, and it was hard.

Sometimes you photograph something you don't even know is going to be that difficult. Recently, I worked for the Rockefeller Foundation on a report about poor families around the world. I went to photograph a family in the state of Bihar, in India, and discovered that the family was living in bondage to a landlord. They were slaves. They had owed the landlord money for generations, and the debt would be passed down to the sons.

I had brought some money to pay the father of the family for the story, but the landlord told me that he would take the money and apply it to their debt. Instead, I invited the man to the landlord's house and gave the man his money. He just touched it and passed it to the landlord. I didn't know what to do. Later, I gave him more money in private. The Brahman class was basically in a conspiracy to keep those families in debt. The teachers were also Brahmans and would sign papers saying the poor children had attended school, when they were actually forced to work in the fields. Even though it was formally illegal, they protected the caste system, their way of life.

Another difficult story was in 1997, when I did an assignment for *New York* magazine on a missing child. I worked with the parents, who were still looking for him. They thought that if the story came out, maybe someone would see him or he would come back. The kid was about seventeen and had been seen last in a bar on the Upper East Side. There was still hope, but so much anxiety, waiting by the phone. They speculated about everything. Since I'm a father myself, it was a heartbreaking story for me. Eventually, the boy was found floating in the East River, but they still don't know what happened to him.

Oftentimes, when a magazine gives you an assignment and you bring the goods in, they expect something else. They just want to go with what is a popular trend, or they don't want to be too controversial about it. In this way, they suck the real juice out of the story, because the strongest images might be a little bit out there, and they want to tone it down. They have the right to say that. They have their own reasons. They have their own jobs on the line. That's all part of it.

Like this prison story at *New York Times Magazine*. The picture editor wanted to do it really badly. She kept it for three months. She hit them every meeting with it. They said no. They stonewalled her. But sometimes even the chief doesn't have the power—it's the money guys, the advertisers. A lot of photographers bitch and moan, but I feel sympathetic for the picture editors.

All kinds of noise gets in between you and the public, so then you get more perversion, like the sound bite. In a very twisted way, I feel fortunate I could actually be in places like Rwanda—that I don't get it secondhand from the TV screen. It really effects you, the smell of it. You get this antiseptic version of it on the TV screen, but if you're there, you're enriched in life. And you're not really afraid, because you know it's part of life.

Many press photographers never look back. That is not what I do, I turn back and I look behind. That's my role. They go for the shot, because they have to get the shot. I'm freer. When the CNN dish leaves, then it's my time. You can relax and get down and do it right.

I was lucky to do the *Broken Dream* book. In the beginning people here didn't really care about Eastern Europe. Then the Soviet Union disintegrated and people took notice. I was able to come close to the psyche of those people, because I understood it. Often the press reports are bad, because they go for the blood, not the psychology of the place. I know that terror is in the eyes.

I saw it in Peshawar, Pakistan, over a three or four year period when it was the staging ground for the Afghan war. All the journalists covering the war had to hook up with mujahadeen there to get inside Afghanistan. I'll never forget the terror of the refugees living in the camps on the northwest frontier, near Peshawar. The place was filled with agents, like the crew-cut American I met who told me he was selling irrigation equipment. That was the standard line for the CIA men and mercenaries who were running guns through there for the mujahadeen. There was also KGB and KHAD, the Pakistan security service. There were regular car bombings.

In the months I lived there, I made a home away from home on the third floor of the Hotel Green. I even had a bird in a cage. Late one night a car bomber blew up the lobby, killing the receptionist and a guard. I thought that whole place was coming down. I said to myself that at least I wouldn't have to pay the hotel bill. No such luck.

I want to go to places that people don't give a damn about. Once I was in Mexico, on vacation with my family, and I read a little report in the international edition of the *Miami Herald* about the Cueta prison in Caracas, Venzuela, which they called the worst in South America. According to Amnesty International, prisoners are routinely tortured and killed there. With the help of my agency, we got permission from the minister of justice to photograph in the prisons. There's always someone in these governments who tries to make a difference. The ministry wanted to draw European attention to the prisons in order to force the military and police to reform them.

When I went in, they showed me the best parts of the prison. I had to bribe the guards to get into the other parts. Even then, the guards were too afraid to go in with me. Gangs with guns ran those areas. There were bullet marks everywhere, as well as cholera and sodomy. They don't feed the prisoners. When I said I wanted to photograph a lunch line, they told me, "Well, we're not ready yet." I waited for three hours while they worked to scrounge up something to feed them, and of course it was for my benefit. If you want to eat, you have to buy the food.

One of the dungeons hadn't been opened for months. The door was so rusted that the prisoners had to push it from the inside to get it open. Coming in from the light, I couldn't even see the prisoners, and it was dangerous so I had to work fast. I just put up my camera; I was shooting blind. I developed the pictures back in New York and luckily they showed the situation—the knives, the guns, the drugs.

I want to bring the light to these places. I was in prison myself. Sometimes I'm anxious before I go, but once I'm on the ground, I make a decision to be there and I'm not afraid. I'm much more scared of horror movies. I had to cover my eyes during *The Shining*.

You have to be aware of yourself, of course. Prisoners and soldiers are attuned to fear; I believe they can smell it on you. It changes the situation completely by making them suspicious. They suspect you are doing something wrong because you're not sure of yourself. You have to know why you're there.

There are a lot of press guys that are desensitized, but I don't feel like that. I'm not putting myself above the people I photograph. To those critics who have qualms about photographing difficult situations, I say: "People ought to know. I'm just the messenger."

Donna Ferrato

Living with the Enemy: Domestic Violence

Donna Ferrato began working as a freelance photographer in 1976. A former member of the Black Star photo agency, Ferrato has published work in *Life, Stern, People,* the *New York Times,* and other magazines.

After witnessing a man beat his wife while on a magazine assignment in 1985, Ferrato launched a project on domestic abuse for which she won a W. Eugene Smith Memorial Fund award in humanistic photography. Ferrato traveled throughout the country to hospital emergency rooms, shelters, battered women's therapy groups, and self-defense classes to photograph the effects, and often acts, of domestic abuse. The story first appeared in the *Philadelphia Inquirer* in 1987 and became a book, *Living with the Enemy,* which has sold over 40,000 copies worldwide since its publication in 1991. That same year Ferrato founded the Domestic Abuse Awareness Project, a nonprofit organization that utilizes installations of Ferrato's photographs to raise money to combat domestic abuse.

Ferrato has received many awards, including the Robert F. Kennedy award for humanistic photography and the Kodak Crystal Eagle Award.

I was on assignment to document love, not to photograph domestic violence. Accidentally, I discovered a woman could get beaten in her home by the man that she loves. I never considered that.

This was back in the early eighties. I was more naive then, always looking for love. So, there I was, photographing this couple who

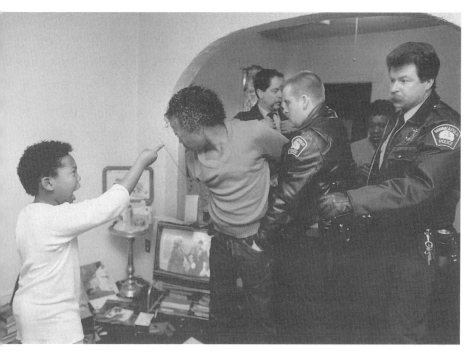

"I hate you for hitting my mother.
Don't you ever come back to this house," 1991
(© Donna Ferrato)

seemed to have a great love. One night this man attacked his wife. He didn't care that I was there. I photographed it because I was shocked to the soles of my feet to see a woman being beaten.

Who could she call? I saw her calling the police. Then he grabbed the phone and said, "She's beating me." He had me confused, and it took a long time to figure out what was really happening.

I remember calling a photographer from these people's house, wailing, "This great love story I've been working on, it's not. What am I going to do?"

My friend said, "Just stick it out, keep looking."

I went into denial. I never even developed the roll of film. I wasn't looking for a Pulitzer or to get it published. After I got a picture of a man beating his wife, I threw that disgusting roll of film into a drawer.

When I told my editors at Japanese *Playboy* what I photographed, they said, "You're fired."

It's been a long process for me. I get sad when photographers—experienced or amateurs—come to me and say, "How can I get my name out there? How can I get people to respect me? How can I get the assignments?"

They ask, "What am I going to get?"

My feeling is it's not what you're going to get. More like what are you going to give? What are you going to learn? There's so much to learn out there with a camera. It gives us power for educating ourselves and for educating others. We have to be patient, try to learn as much as we can until there comes a point where we have something to share with other people. And that doesn't come for a long time.

I rode over six thousand hours with cops around the country to get the pictures. You have to be there.

When I took the picture of the little boy shouting at his father, I'd been riding with the cops in Minneapolis for a month, usually on the four-to-two shifts. Nothing was going on. A lot of the things I had already seen. There were times when I asked, "Can I take a picture?" and people said no. So I watched. I respect people's rights to say no. It's not insulting. I just say, "Hey, I understand. It's up to you."

By watching I'm learning, but I needed to get *the* picture eventually.

I was riding days as well as nights. We were on our first call to go to this house where the boy had called the cops. It was early morning; I didn't have a flash on the camera.

We got inside, the shades were drawn, and it was dark, very dark in the house. The woman at the door was screaming, "My husband's in the back room."

Police rushed ahead. I asked the woman, "Ma'am, I'm from *Life* magazine. Do I have your permission to take pictures of whatever happens from this point on? I don't know what's going to happen here, but I promise you I will not publish anything unless you sign a release."

I said this fast. She said, "Yeah, I don't care." So I followed the cops and started taking pictures. The little boy was crying. "His knife is under the bed mattress." They flipped it. I'm trying to get my flash out because it's dark, and I needed to bounce light off the ceiling.

I was fumbling, feeling like Columbo. The police were handcuffing the guy, and every time he budged, they beat him. The wife was crying, trying to stop the police.

They take him out into the living room, finally. I am in front of them, camera and flash ready. Suddenly the little boy opened his mouth, pointed his finger, and accused his father in a way that I had never seen anyone do. We were stunned at the depth of the angry feelings from the mouth of a child.

They took the father to the cop car. I rode down to the station, because I wanted to hear his side.

As we were leaving, I said, "Ma'am, about that release. . . ."

She said, "What magazine did you say you were from?"

"*Life*."

She said, "I thought you were from *Ebony*. No way."

I said okay. I'm used to it. So, in the police car the father told me how he hadn't been violent with his wife for ten years. He's been in a program. Used to be a drinker. Wasn't a drinker anymore, but his wife was using drugs and had blown the family savings. He snapped. These complex shades of gray, most of the time, are never seen because there's no follow-up.

Back in New York, I developed that roll and knew that the boy shouting was *the* picture. When Peter Howe at *Life* saw it, he wanted it. But I didn't have the release.

A month later, I went back to Minneapolis to their home in the middle of a Saturday. The husband answered the door. I explained why I was there, and he said, "Come back and meet with my wife. She and I are back together."

I couldn't show them the picture; that's magazine policy. But I described the photo. "This is the toughest picture that anybody will ever see about what a child really feels. People must understand what children go through when fathers beat their mothers."

They signed the release.

My releases are ironclad. They're lengthy. Photographers who work in foreign countries don't have to get releases. In this country you have to get releases, and not just so you don't get sued, but also because it's the responsible thing to do. They better know that these pictures are going to come out in a magazine. When the parents saw the picture, they hated it. But it was too late. They signed the release.

Also, I try to make sure nobody puts false stories with my photographs.

An artist who was in a group show at the Whitney Museum [of American Art, New York] took that boy's picture and used it repeatedly in her collage about sexual abuse, insinuating the wrong things. I went after her and the Whitney Museum. The Whitney lost, but this artist won't give me any guarantee that she will never show the artwork again. It jeopardizes the integrity of the people in the pictures, everything.

I wanted [*Living with the Enemy*] to be a mainstream book that would get to the people who needed it. Every mainstream publisher turned me down, year after year after year.

A woman named Melissa Harris worked at Aperture. We met, and she said, "Please, Donna, bring your work in to show Michael Hoffman [executive director of Aperture]." I'd already had an encouraging letter from Aperture a couple of years before, but I didn't take them seriously. Melissa set the meeting up. Michael was interested. I was slow to respond.

I ignored him and kept trying to find bigger publishers. Meanwhile, he was sending me letters saying all the right things. Finally, one morning I woke up and said, "What a dummy I am! Here I have someone who really wants to do it. Why don't I give them a chance?"

When the book was published, I thought that would be the end of it. Then a shelter in New York City approached me with the idea of having a fund-raiser, exhibiting fifty photographs, inviting their wealthiest donors to come, charging them a lot of money to look at these pictures, giving autographed copies of *Living with the Enemy*.

They raised $300,000 in one night. I started thinking, "Ha! These pictures have a power to do good."

When *Life* magazine published information about the show on the editor's page, I got calls from shelters everywhere. That's why we established the Domestic Abuse Awareness Project [DAAP] as a nonprofit. The idea was to send the exhibition around the country to teach groups how to raise money and educate people at the same time. Usually, battered women's groups plan fund-raisers at the ballet, something cultural. Rarely do they have a chance to show their rich patrons the force of domestic violence. One men's group in Washington State raised $86,000 in a week with my photographs.

For the last four years, I've been learning how to use these pictures in campaigns, public service announcements—way beyond the magazines stacked in the newsstands. We work with the criminal justice system, with the sheriff's department, with the prisons and hospitals.

Magazines have to pay standard usage rates. The money supports DAAP, to pay for an executive director, and to pay for the office expenses. I don't take a salary or percentage. We have two shows that travel. This month it starts off in Milan, hosted by Italian feminists. Then it goes to Holland. The Men Against Violence to Women are bringing it to Israel. Another show is traveling to Tennessee to seven different hospital sites, raising money for battered women's shelters.

These photographs are the backbone of many domestic violence campaigns. Michigan's Health Department has a series of PSAs [public service announcements] on TV, pamphlets that educate people across Michigan. There's the Matilda Cuomo campaign, in English and Spanish, on TV and Stacy Kabat's Academy Award–winning film, *Defending Our Lives,* which was about women in prison.

I go out and try to raise money for DAAP. I also have an agent who books speaking engagements for me at universities across the country. I've appeared at forty different colleges over the last two years. I get through to kids, show them my pictures, tell them stories, and learn about what young kids are facing in their own relationships.

We are learning together that there are some really crazy, violent men out there and few who are willing to confront them. We put all the responsibility on women and children to protect themselves. We've been doing a really lousy job protecting women and children.

I want to make the subject of violence against women and children something natural to talk about, to get the facts out, and to make it fun to learn about. I'm not against men. My biggest influences have been from good men in my life, starting with my dad.

[Photographer] Philip Jones-Griffith, was also a good influence. When I got discouraged that nobody wanted to give me assignments, thinking maybe I should sell the old pictures of domestic violence because I needed to get it out there, he'd say, "No, Donna, have faith in yourself. They don't want to give you assignments, because they're stupid. You just keep working, keep quiet, keep your costs of living low, don't let anybody control you." Philip always told me the work was good, and he'd never seen anything like it.

Philip believed in me. The fact that he was president of Magnum and saw everything being done gave me the confidence. Philip's book [*Vietnam, Inc.*, (1972)] was the most incredibly strong, honest, and compassionate book about war I'd ever seen. I respected him. His book showed the truth about war, no bullshit or glorification of death and suffering. He showed what soldiers do. His pictures showed the inhumanity of men to other men, to women and children, to the earth.

The photographer I admire is Robert Frank. I studied the retrospective of his life's work, and I saw his heart, his suffering, his joys, and his pain. His photos are very moving.

I always wonder: "How does a person inspire a movement? To make changes?" If I don't like something, I don't complain about it. I figure out how to change it. That's what I try to do with a camera.

Things are working out without a plan. I keep following my heart— things just come together. Photography is in my blood—I love to photograph the daily life, the people I love. Especially my daughter. She's the pride and joy of my life. Everything I do, I do for Fanny to help her understand what it means to be female, how she must stand up for her rights.

I love darkroom work. I haven't been with an agency since I left Black Star three years ago. I am a lone wolf and do okay representing myself, except I miss Howard Chapnick [the late president of Black Star photo agency]. I am pretty stubborn. I'll turn down an assignment because it's not right for me.

Photographers need to think about how they can make contributions to put their ideas across clearly so they can show there's a reason for their work. Photographers must do their own proposals, research, and budgets, meet with the editors, represent themselves, figure out ways to make their work a vital tool needed by the community, by the society.

We have to face it—the magazines are not there for us, they haven't been for a while. American magazines fund fewer and fewer social documentary projects.

A lot of the photographers are disgruntled, but many are used to having things fall into their laps. It's going to be a particularly difficult struggle for the single-minded photographer who wants to see things change, to make a difference.

I always tell young photographers, "Discover the world. Take pictures. Live cheaply."

Someday, I want to write a book on love and living from the heart. To show things from my early years as a secretary and then as a wanderer. I did everything I could just to be able to take pictures. I worked on a farm; I traveled like a gypsy. I learned so much and had so much fun. Nobody owned me. I didn't have a credit card. I lived off the kindness of strangers generous to me who gave me food to eat and a darkroom to print in.

All these years, and I still don't have my own darkroom. But, it sure is sweet getting older. Those ten years, when I was working on my book, I was very low-key about it. I just had a lot to learn. I still do. Boy, do I ever.

Since the interview was conducted, Ferrato reports that she has gotten her own darkroom. Her book about love is nearly done. Best of all, she said, she is in love.

Joseph Rodriguez

In the Barrio

Joseph Rodriguez's early life in Brooklyn was troubled by drugs and petty crime. After a short term in prison, Rodriguez attended the School of Visual Arts in New York and dabbled in photography for several years. Then Rodriguez met photographer Larry Clark while helping to hang the exhibition "Tulsa," Clark's work about drug addiction. Rodriguez told Clark that the work moved him, and Clark replied, "Listen . . . just go out and take pictures."

Rodriguez took Clark's advice, and he also enrolled in the International Center for Photography (ICP) to study photojournalism. Fred Ritchin, a teacher at ICP, organized a project with nine students on East Harlem that was to revisit the area Bruce Davidson documented in the late 1960s in his acclaimed work *East 100th Street*. Documenting East Harlem turned into a four-year project for Rodriguez. The photographs appeared in *National Geographic* and became his first book, *Spanish Harlem*, in 1995.

With grants from Pacific News Service, the Alicia Patterson Foundation, the International Fund for Documentary Photography, and the National Endowment for the Arts, Rodriguez moved to the West Coast to photograph gang life in Los Angeles in 1995. Three years later his book, *East Side Stories: Gang Life in East LA*, met with critical success. Rodriquez continues to use his own prison experiences to document ex-inmates trying to readjust to life outside prison. He managed to turn his life around and he likes to say that his life changed from one of shooting drugs to shooting pictures. But not everyone finds a way to break free from the cycle of offending. His experiences have pushed him to continue a deep personal

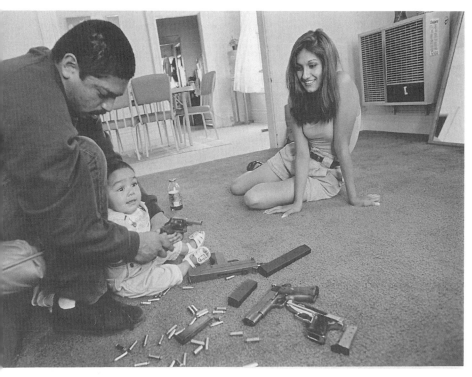

The morning after a rival gang tried
to kill Chivo for the fourth time,
he teaches his daughter how to hold
a pistol, East Los Angeles, California
(© Joseph Rodriquez, from *East Side Stories*,
PowerHouse Books)

interest in photographing people and families on the wrong side of the law. His latest project, called "Re-entry in Los Angeles," brought him back to California to meet ex-inmates and tell their stories with his camera.

Social documentary for me is very personal. And even though I would like very much to change things, over the years I've been a little disillusioned to see that sometimes it doesn't really turn out the way I'd like it to.

My photography is about where I came from and the struggles of my own life. I have a different agenda in that way. It's not a news agenda.

It's also about humanity, but not in the old cliché *Family of Man* way. Now is a very important time for us to see humanity. I wish editors would get that idea in their heads. I think we could probably bridge some gaps, like racism, if we could actually start learning about cultures in a much more human way, as opposed to these flashy, sexy, violent images that come out of Hollywood.

It's funny. You see people, just ordinary people on the street and see how they're dressed—some with tattoos, some with hot, sexy fashion. This is the image of today, the whole "notice me" thing. "Notice me."

I think it's important to have passion—I really do—in your own work. It keeps you going. At the very beginning, I did anything I had to do. I only allotted myself two or three rolls a week. I drove a cab on the weekends and assisted a wedding-studio photographer in Manhattan. Whenever I could get up to Spanish Harlem, I'd go up there. Passion is about being in the spirit of things. I think lots of work is intellectualized too much in this country.

As a kid I was always told to shut up, you know, be quiet and speak when spoken to. I could never get my voice out. Photography is my voice.

One of the difficult issues for photographers is dealing with rejection. I went to the *New York Times Magazine,* and they said, "Well we're not doing stories about poverty." I went to German *Geo.* I went to *Stern.* That is probably the most difficult thing to deal with—besides the times you think your work is not ready.

We live in an era when everything has to be done quickly. Whether it's magazine editors or television producers, they all want results quickly. I think one of the most urgent issues to address is how much time it takes to tell a good story. For myself, I just want to be able to get enough money so I can have the time it takes to do my work in a responsible manner and get it out.

In my twenties I kept thinking about the three D's: desire, discipline, and determination. Those are the qualities that actually changed my way of thinking and my way of being. The desire to be a photographer was always there. I was determined. It was the discipline part that was kind of tough. I was disillusioned, and I was depressed, and I had my lows and my highs.

I'm not strong all the time. I go through periods where I have to pick myself back up, and I have to go out there and come back and go out and come back. People look at me and say, "Wow, you know it's very romantic what you do." Yes, there is a part of it that is romantic, you know, but it's also hard. It's lonely. It's people telling you most of the time they are not interested in your work.

I've been behind bars. I know what drugs are about. I've had these struggles within my own family. We've been poor, so don't come and ask me, "What right do you have to do that?" I've been there. These experiences helped me get close to the gang kids I photographed, because I gained their respect. But there are various ways to work. People don't have to go through these experiences to be good photographers. People think you have to be struggling or starving to be able to document people's lives.

For me it's important to be able to show a little bit of the positive side of life and to try to give that balance, to give respect to people. There's a lot of heavy-handed photography today. In America social documentary has always been like, "Where's the problem? Let's try to document it so we can correct it." But after looking at other influences of documentary photography in Latin American, Africa, Scandinavia, and Russia, I feel it's a little more than that. It's also about people's lives and showing something positive.

I always wanted to photograph gangs. The reason why I wanted to do this was simply because I was paying attention to rap music and what these kids were talking about. I wasn't going to get my research from newspapers, because they already have an agenda that's obvious in their writing.

I guess I had this romantic view of doing a gang essay because of a photographer named Bruce Davidson who I've always admired. I remembered his Brooklyn gang essay that he did for *Esquire* with Norman Mailer. He was documenting this gang in the neighborhood where I grew up, and I knew some of his subjects. Before leaving for Los Angeles I was naive. The nineties were totally different.

I heard about the Community Youth Gang Services in Los Angeles. I walked in there the first day and sat down, and nobody talked to me for about four days because they thought I was just another media person. Finally I got to talk to one guy, and after two weeks I met more people, and then I met a family.

I got close to this family, and through them I began to meet these gang members. This was in Watts. Things were quiet at that point. It was after the riots of 1992, and the Bloods and Crips, the two biggest black gangs in Los Angeles, were having a truce. But in East Los Angeles things were really going crazy. So at that point, I began looking at the newspapers; I watched the news to see where the action was. There was a drive-by, and a two-year-old was killed, and there was going to be a funeral. So I went to the family's house cold. I didn't know them. I knocked on the door, expressed who I was and what I was doing, and they let me in and told me the funeral was going to be the next day. I covered the funeral at the church and the media was there. The television people were in the back. I walked up to the front of the coffin.

You know, there's always this uncomfortable feeling of having the camera and people staring at you. You have to swallow that to make pictures. I guess it's like acting. You have to change yourself and really get into it. So photographing the gangs was very difficult. Then I went to Stockholm, where I was living at the time, to process my film.

I felt this project should be black and white. Black Star made a small foreign story for syndication. It made a little bit of money. One editor said to me, "Well, you know we need a little bit more action. We need some guns. We need some more blood." I went home very despondent.

Later, with the assistance of Sandy Close of Pacific News Service, I edited some prints for grant submissions. I applied to the Alicia Patterson [Foundation] fellowship and later for the International Fund for Documentary Photography fellowship. I received both grants and decided to move to Los Angeles a year later.

To be there every day was the only way to do it. I went back and started all over again. I started going back to this one gang, and I couldn't get in. Then I went to a school where I connected with one gang. I was photographing them until the police arrested some of them and found some of the photos I made of them. The police gang unit confiscated the photos, and this whole problem began. The police told the gang members that I was working with them. The gang thought that I set them up, and because of this my life was in danger. I had to flee that neighborhood and find a new gang to start over with.

Talk about being depressed. You couldn't get any lower than that. I had to start completely over. It took a really long time to get in with another gang before they would even begin to trust me. It took another month and a half before they could even start to trust me. Every day of the year and a half that I worked, I was questioned whether or not I was a cop. Even after I witnessed a drive-by shooting, even after hanging out with their moms and taking their girlfriends to the doctors, they were still paranoid about me. The danger, too, got me down from time to time.

The kids kept asking me, "What are you doing here?" And I said, "I'd like to make a book about you guys." And they said, "Why would anybody be interested in us?"

In the gang work and the East Harlem project, I told people it was going to be a book. It's always difficult five, six, seven years down the road when your work finally comes out. So I try to be as straight up with them as possible about what's going to happen. I tell them it could be a magazine story. With the gang work, I wouldn't go back to them with some of the magazine stories, because I didn't think they were done in good faith. And it would only make the gangs look bad and feel bad, so I'd rather wait until there's a book, something a little more substantial and a little more honest.

I spent a good year and a half photographing them, and it's very important to note that out of the whole project there are less than three hundred rolls of film. There was a lot of driving mothers to court and back, taking them food shopping, picking up kids from school, helping this person, helping that person, trying to talk about jobs, you know, this whole thing. You get involved. You become like a taxi driver. You become like this den mother. They were trying to come up with a name for me. They were calling me "Kodak." They were calling me "Fuji." There was all this crazy stuff. Finally, they just called me "the photographer." That was my name.

You know from your gut when you're onto something. My heartfelt vision of photography is to look at Latinos here in the United States. And I kind of knew what these kids were about. I liked their music, I hung out, we drank beer, we went to fiestas. It wasn't like, let's document these guys with the guns and all that stuff.

There was one situation when they said, "Come on. We're going to go on a drive-by." And I was like, wait a minute here. Will I be implicated in a possible murder? I don't think that's gonna work too well.

I think there are a lot of photographers out there that get kind of stuck. They do commercialized editorial work and they seem to be pretty good at it, but they seem to be very depressed. They don't have anything personal going on with their own work. They don't seem to be making books or putting their work into exhibitions. For me, I think that these are important goals for us photographers. I try to tell them, "Get yourself a small project going on the side so you can be happy with your own work, so you can be happy with yourself and you're just not getting caught up for the money of it." I guess I'm not in it for the money, so I don't know any other way to say it.

In photo agencies the time factor becomes a big problem. It gets to a stage where you have these editors sitting there, and they're typing up the captions. And sometimes, it's like, oops, they made a mistake. Or, I didn't get to check it in time, but darn it, it's out there already.

One time a magazine was going to use the picture with the baby and the guns from the gang series, and the caption information was misleading and unclear, and if I hadn't caught it, oh my God, it would have been a disaster. Their caption was something like, "He did this carjacking and that's the reason for the guns," and that wasn't the truth. The correct caption of the picture is, "Last night they tried to shoot my father." That's the reason why all those guns were there. Mistakes happen. They miss one, and it goes out, and it's just gone. You lose control.

You have to digest your own work. Because once it goes out into the world, there are always going to be people that complain or criticize what you've done or what you haven't done. I went through a lot of guilt with the gang project, documenting things that were very violent. And even though this is their life and they know I'm there, it comes up, "Why are you doing this?"

There's a part of me that lets the editors get something from me if they want. If they want me to photograph it, okay, I'm going to try to do it, simply because we have to make a living. So there's this sense of giving in.

If I can make pictures on a particular assignment for myself, then I'll try to use those pictures somewhere else. So I think it's very important to put a perspective on the work. For instance, when I go out to do a corporate assignment, I just try to close it off and do that corporate assignment and say, "Okay, for a week I'm going to do this." Then I just try to do my personal work later.

Photography has been a beautiful thing for me. I don't mind saying I had a drug problem and photography saved my life. That magical thing. It's being in the darkroom and really having that connection and watching the image come up and saying, "Wow, this is mine. It may not be the greatest thing in the world but it's mine." And it's the richest thing. I'm not monetarily rich, but I feel very rich in another way.

After a couple years in the business, you start to put things in perspective. You learn a little bit. You know the agencies are going to eat you up. When I talk about photography it's a very passionate and a very holy experience. It's hard to deal with editors. They don't understand what it means, that it's part of our life. This is not a job. Seven days a week, 365 days a year, I'm working and thinking about photography. It drives our families crazy.

Dayanita Singh

A Truer India

Born in 1961, in New Delhi, Dayanita Singh is the oldest of four sisters.

Singh studied at the National Institute of Design in Ahmedabad, where she created a book on the tabla player Zakir Hussain, who also became a mentor. The book was published in 1986. The following year she moved to New York, where she studied with photographer Mary Ellen Mark and attended classes at the International Center for Photography.

After returning to India, Singh worked as a photojournalist for *Time, Newsweek*, the *New York Times*, and other international publications on stories ranging from AIDS in Bombay to behind the scenes at the Ms. India beauty pageant. Singh shifted her focus away from the poor of India to create *Family Photos*, a series of "academically composed" portraits of upper middle class Indians.

Her book *Myself Mona Ahmed*, published by Scalo, covers thirteen years of photographing Mona, a eunuch whom she also sees as her friend. "The best part for me was that she [Mona] wrote the text for the book herself, dictated as e-mails to the publisher in Switzerland. So she decided what was told and how."

Dayanita is best known for her portraits of India's urban middle- and upper-class families. In recent years she has shifted her focus to Goa, saying that living in a village there has shaped her art in unexpected ways. "This part of the India is slipping through the cracks, unnoticed, uncelebrated, in the rush to keep up, to modernize, globalize, westernize. These images of people working, partying, or resting at home show

Marie, daughter of a sex worker,
days before she too is put on the job,
Kamathipura, Bombay
(© Dayanita Singh)

Indian life without embellishment." Her work explores another side of India: the place that she belongs to and understands.

Singh credits photography for her ability to stay single and travel widely in India's class-conscious society. "I cannot think of any other profession that would allow me such diverse experiences," she said.

What drew me to photography were my childhood memories. They come from the photographs my mother took of us as children. As the first born I was the most photographed, often to validate an important moment. Once I was placed on a chaise lounge in the Oberoi Hotel in Kashmir, so my mother could show her family that she had lived in a five-star hotel.

While at design school, we had an assignment to photograph the moods of a person. I went off to photograph the tabla player Zakir Hussain. It was then that I realized what an amazing tool a camera is. Suddenly the world was mine. I could enter any situation as a photographer.

Through Zakir I entered the world of the classical musician and bunked classes every winter to travel with him and photograph. My final project in design school became a book on Zakir. He became a "guru" not just in photography but in a life philosophy.

Since the beginning of my photography I could not separate my life from my photography. This continues to create problems in work, but I will not have it any other way. If I got a strong photograph but nothing happened, then it was a waste for me. But if I had some great interaction with you and the film went bad, that's ok, it's just my connecting point.

One of my early assignments was from the *Philadelphia Inquirer* to do an AIDS story in Bombay. I went to do the story and was horrified by what I saw and heard. I couldn't convince anyone in India to let me work further on it. That's when I contacted Jocelyn Benzakin at JB Pictures and said, "Either they are crazy or I am crazy." She was fantastic. She supported all my expenses for about two years.

My work was not published in India, which still makes me angry. This was 1988 and 1989, and they said this is a Western phenomenon that you brought back with you from America. They didn't want to look at my pictures. It's still like that. India is still waiting for its Rock Hudson before actively doing something about the problem.

I was so naive with my AIDS work and so idealistic. The photo of

Marie about to be made a sex worker created a lot of sympathy for her in America. People across the world wanted to adopt her. But no one wanted to help the thousands of other such girls in Bombay.

The AIDS work was a five-day assignment that stretched into two years. Then it was too many assignments in the same vein. I was working for an American audience. I was constantly catering to the "exotic disaster" in India, because those were the stories that people wanted.

One day I said enough. I just want to explore my own world. And everybody said to me, "You're crazy, you'll just ruin what you've built up in all these years." And I said no, I don't really understand what it is to be a prostitute, but I do understand what it is to be born in this transitional period in India, to be part of this upper middle class where you are neither middle class nor upper class. You are trying to be both.

I started photographing Indian families in this situation and showed it to a couple of photo editors in America. One editor in particular said, "This is not India. This is Indians in London or Indians in New York."

I said, "You are accusing me of being dishonest. You have such a huge magazine, it's worldwide, you should know better. How do you think I bathe?" She told me it would never get printed. I realized that in my small way I was presenting an India that didn't go down very well. I decided to make it a personal project.

The biggest influence in Indian photography—ninety percent of Indian photography—is very bad copies of [Henri] Cartier-Bresson. He is the absolute God of photojournalism and documentary photography here.

We don't have this concept of independent photography in India. There are no funds or grants for photography. Ninety-nine percent of the photographers work for magazines or newspapers where the work doesn't belong to them. It's just a job. The only people who can afford to work independently are the ones who are working for the international market, maybe eight to ten photographers working at the most. Then there is this problem that you cater to what the editor in New York says they want to see from India.

I find it harsher in the American media than in the European media. The British are going to have a different view of India, of course. They always want the colonial touch, they always want the Raja stories or the last tea planter in Darjeeling and stories like that.

The Americans like either the exotic or the disaster. But I think it's because we have been catering to that and presenting that again and again. Already there's a small shift from when I met the photo editors at the beginning of my project to now. People are able to look at my work and say, "Great, we must put out this different aspect of India."

I get furious when foreign photographers reduce India to blobs of color and exotica. But photographers who work longer and are more specific in what they are seeking have amazing bodies of work. I admire them for being able to enter this alien culture, which often baffles me as well, not knowing the language or the nuances and coming away with such in-depth work. It's the fly-by-night photographers who succumb to that superficial vision of India all in color and chaos. I do not mean this for foreign photographers alone; we in India do this ourselves.

If I keep doing street children in India, then of course documentary photography is dead. If I kept doing stories on child laborers or a story on child sacrifice, which I saw in the *Sunday Times* magazine two or three days ago, then sure photojournalism would be the pits. How much of dowry debts can you see, photographed in the same style?

With the families project, I have given myself another lease on my photography. I want to work with the teenagers because they're changing overnight, with MTV and the current economic liberalization in India. It's going to lead to other things. I am going to feel like I wish that there were five or ten of me.

With the changing nature of publishing it would seem documentary is dying. But the more I work, the more possibilities I find to sustain that work. It's such a great time in India. Even if for the next two years or five years the market is bad, it will work out.

I used to think, Oh my god if I was a photographer during independence, what a time, from British colonization to independence, but it's like that now. It's even a stronger time to be a photographer.

Fazal Sheikh

Portrait of a Refugee

Fazal Sheikh, born in 1965 in New York City, has a Kenyan father and an American mother. He graduated from Princeton University, where he studied with photographer Emmet Gowin in visual arts. He has received numerous grants, including a National Endowment for the Arts fellowship, the Leica Medal of Excellence, a Fulbright scholarship, a MacArthur Fellowship, and is a recipient of the International Henri Cartier-Bresson Prize.

He is a documentary photographer who uses the personalizing power of portraiture to bring the faces of the world's displaced people into focus. In 1992 Sheikh's concern over the refugee problem in Africa led him to the northwestern border of Kenya, where thousands of Sudanese refugees had gathered. Sheikh stayed for several weeks photographing the refugees, using a large-format camera, a tool most often associated with landscape photography. His aim was to provide a more in-depth study of the camp refugees than ordinary photojournalism could afford. His photographs were collected and published in the book *A Sense of Common Ground*.

In the mid-1990s he found Afghan refugees, who had fled after the Soviet invasion of their country, living in camps. He returned to the camps in Kenya where Somali refugees had been living for a decade. He found children he had photographed ten years before, now grown into adolescents, who knew nothing but life in the camps. Since then he has worked in Mexico, Cuba, Brazil, and most recently India, where his latest book, *Moksha*, examines the lives of India's dispossessed widows.

Ajoh Achot and Achol Manyen,
Sudanese refugee camp, Kakuma, Kenya, 1993
(© Fazal Sheikh)

In contrast to the often sensational, mass-media depictions of humanitarian crises, Sheikh takes formal portraits of his subjects—living among them and earning their collaboration. With names printed prominently next to their images, mothers, children, wounded soldiers, and tribal elders assume stately poses, hold pictures of loved ones, and gaze directly at Sheikh's camera, producing what have been described as understated studies of human dignity under devastating circumstances.

He established the International Human Rights Series, which collaborates with institutions, international galleries and human rights organizations, so that his publications and exhibitions can reach a much wider audience.

In 1992 I was given a Fulbright fellowship to document the Swahili communities of the Kenyan coast. I traveled to Kenya and began preparations for the trip to the coast. However, in the year since my last visit, nearly five hundred thousand refugees from Sudan, Ethiopia, and Somalia had flooded into northern Kenya in search of a safe haven from the civil wars in their home countries.

Before heading to the coast I decided to make one trip to the refugee community on the border with Sudan. I was given permission by the United Nations High Commission for Refugees to visit the Sudanese refugee camp at Kakuma, a small village in the northern desert. This camp provided sanctuary to more than twenty-five thousand Sudanese refugees. Of that number, twelve thousand were "Unaccompanied Minors"—children between the ages of eight and eighteen who were either orphaned or separated from their parents in the flight from their homes.

On the appointed morning I arrived at the airport for a preflight briefing by the United Nations spokesman. In the course of his description of what we would encounter, he told us about the "Unaccompanied Minors" who had been abducted by the Sudanese People's Liberation Army, forcibly conscripted, and sent to military training in southern Ethiopia. Many had walked more than one thousand kilometers through the desert in search of sanctuary in Kenya.

Later, as the plane moved away from Nairobi over the desert, the words of the spokesman resounded in my ears. I remember feeling reticent about my place among the journalists. In an hour we were circling over the camp in our descent toward the border.

On landing the others with whom I traveled immediately began their work. They seemed to know exactly what they wanted. I experienced a kind of paralysis and had no idea how to begin working in the midst of such turmoil. The spokesman's description of how I should meet this place and the throng of people in the camp seemed to banish thought. Now, as I look back upon that time of unknowing, I see what a turning point it was for me.

I decided to stay on in the village, giving myself time to sift though the initial impressions. During the first few days, I wandered throughout the camp without photographing. Eventually, I approached Deng Dau, the elder of the community. He greeted me generously, and we sat together in his home. During the course of our conversation, I asked his permission to begin working in his village. He turned to me and said, "Why do you ask me? I am only a refugee."

The meaning of the words was clear—"If I am a refugee, you may do as you like, and it is not my place to give, or withhold, consent." But the tone of his voice held another, latent meaning. Its tenor laid bare the irony of those words. It had been a trespass for people to storm through the camp without consulting those whom they were photographing. In the following moments, he agreed to the collaboration, and we began a work of documentation, which continued for two years.

With this approach, I discovered a way of working that I have retained on other projects. Now, I recognize the initial sense of unknowing when first visiting a community and embrace it as part of the process. I see it as a sign of receptivity to what the place and the people have to offer. I begin by asking the members of the community for their willingness to collaborate in the documentation. In my recent work among the Afghan villages of exile, the elder's agreement to work with me, to provide insight, as well as protection, has been crucial.

Many of the images that I make are formal portraits. I use a simple Polaroid camera that yields both a positive and a negative. The slow process dictates the pace of the work. The act of photographing becomes an event in the village. We construct the image together. Many of the people have never been photographed before, and the Polaroid provides a point of reference for the discussions that follow in which the residents of the community offer their opinions on how the documentation may unfold.

For so long I have thought about "African" and "refugee"—such loaded terms. The media seems preoccupied with encapsulating communities and paring them down to myopic tag lines. There *is* a horrifying element to the refugee stories from Somalia and Rwanda, but the lives of those people are more complex than the way that they have been represented. Being an African or a refugee is only one facet of who they are as human beings. I would like to balance out the equation, to broaden and challenge our preconceptions as structured by the media.

When I began working on the Somali border, I had a conversation one evening with a Kenyan doctor who was working in the camp's hospital. He told me about Somali parents smothering their malnourished children. These occurrences he described as evidence of the "essentially callous and aggressive nature of Somalis."

Later that night, as I lay alone in my tent thinking about the doctor's story, I decided to spend some time in one of the camp's feeding centers. I was interested in testing the doctor's explanation of the reasons for such incidents. During the weeks spent in the feeding center, mothers or siblings brought the malnourished children—fifty in all—to the center twice daily to receive their treatment. They would sit for photographs, the gesture and gaze revealing the familial bond.

In my last days there a nurse told me of a mother and child who had recently arrived from the desert. The woman was registered in the camp and—as the child was severely malnourished—they were immediately brought to the feeding center.

When the woman saw how the treatment was reviving the children, she broke down. She related the story of how, during the flight through the desert from Somalia into Kenya, she had smothered the first of her two children. Now, in the feeding center she was forced to confront the possibility that what she had thought to be an act of sacrifice in sparing the infant's suffering, might, in some sense, have been a killing.

The body of images, names, and stories from that time, later exhibited in a large grid and a mainstay of *A Sense of Common Ground*, provide a visual response to the doctor's declaration. There is the question, in this case the doctor's assertion, and then there is the documentation that explores the issue. In this way the working process becomes fluid and revelatory.

As I worked in Africa and Afghanistan, I realized that many of the connections and decisions about where to work are based upon intuition.

After working in the tribal area of northern Pakistan for several months, I realized that my time there was not only about documenting the situation of the Afghan refugees and the history of the war, but also searching for the legacy of my grandfather and his relationship to Islam. Although it is inevitable that the photographs are also a product of who I am, I hope that my perceptions defer to or mingle with those of the people that I photograph, allowing the personal chord to resonate with the documentary.

The people in the photographs often look directly into the camera and, by extension, to the viewer. There are no visual gymnastics, and the image is pared down to what I believe to be its essential nature. The sitters present themselves. My role is not to confer upon, but rather to encourage that which is already inherently part of the person to come forward. The strength of a sitter's gaze and an entire life lived in their bodies speaks for itself.

I am unable to predict what will be a strong photograph. The most compelling images have come from remaining receptive to what the place has to offer. A photograph with its roots in my imagination pales in comparison to that which is given in the moment of collaboration. In the time following my engagement with the people, the experience lingering in my mind overwhelms my perceptions of the photographs. It takes quite a while before I am able to recognize the strength of any given image. Time and distance provide a frame and a context.

I traveled with a Somali woman who was working for the United Nations High Commission for Refugees. She was recording the testimonials of women who had been assaulted and raped in the border region. The Kenyan government denied the allegations of such happenings for fear of a negative impact on tourism.

I have always been troubled by the notion that a person becomes the subject of a photograph simply because they have been raped. It is not the sum total of who they are. For their part, the women understood that the images and their stories would be shown in public, and they still insisted upon speaking out. However, I felt protective of the trust that they had placed in us, and I struggled with the responsibility of bringing those testimonials to light.

For nearly three years after photographing those women and recording their stories, I refrained from using them. When piecing together

A Sense of Common Ground, the book from those years, I skirted the issue of their inclusion. I now realize that by omitting them I had perhaps failed in my charge. The women who we met had gone through such trauma that they ultimately wore it as a badge of honor, a declaration that they had persevered in a society that ostracizes and shuns the victims of sexual abuse. Now, when showing that body of work, I include the images and the testimonials in their own voices, unfiltered.

At a pivotal point in my development as a documentary photographer, I read *Let Us Now Praise Famous Men.* I found the marriage of text and image in which both ways of working, both mediums, retained their dignity. They function in separate realms, yet they inform one another. Neither element serves as illustration or embellishment.

In my recent work, that is what keeps me busy. In confronting the complexity of Afghan society, the people's relationship to Islam, and the depths of both hospitality and loss within that culture, I have become aware of the need for text to elaborate upon the message of the photographs.

I hope that my work reaches toward a greater good. However, I am not willing to achieve that goal at the expense of the individual. I believe that it is the individual and his testimony that allows us to access broader themes—through the specific to gain entry to the universal. I want to be able to go to a community and ask that it teach me about its truth. I try to encourage the medium to pierce the alienation in a return to the basics of humanity.

Editors and Curators

Gifford Hampshire

The Environmental Protection Agency's Project DOCUMERICA

Gifford Hampshire received a Purple Heart for wounds sustained in aerial combat in the Pacific during World War II. He was educated at the University of Missouri and enrolled in their photojournalism program. Inspired by the Depression-era documentary project at the Farm Security Administration, Hampshire convinced the Environmental Protection Agency to organize a national documentary project on the environment in 1970 called Project DOCUMERICA, for which he received a Special Citation from the National Press Photographers Association. Retired now in Virginia, Hampshire said, "I am an eighth-generation American, and that is the greatest honor of all."

My father was a schoolteacher and an amateur photographer, and he set up a darkroom in the bathroom. As a boy, I used to go in there and watch him. He put that paper in the tray, and the next thing you knew, there was a picture.

The Depression was on. I was living right in the middle of the Dust Bowl out there in Kansas, and I was witnessing many of the things that the FSA [Farm Security Administration] photographers were photographing.

When I was drafted in 1943, I showed up in Leavenworth, Kansas, and they said, "What would you like to do?" I said, "What about photography?" I thought that maybe I could get into the Signal Corps.

Instead of the Signal Corps, they drafted me into the Army Air

Industrial pollution
(Marc St. Gil/Project
DOCUMERICA/EPA)

Corps, and I wound up as a radio operator and gunner on a B-24 crew. The only photography I did there was to try and get the Fairchild camera going on our bomber missions. My interest in photography lay dormant until I went to the University of Missouri School of Journalism after the war, and got involved in Cliff Edom's classes. They had just started a major in photojournalism at the University of Missouri, and I was one of the first products of that. I was interested in writing and reporting as well as photography, and I always thought about my work as a photojournalist—that was Cliff Edom's term.

Photojournalism, in my mind, was words and pictures. So much of what I'm going to talk about in documentary has to do with that concept. Photojournalism came out of the idea of documentary photography, because documentary photography has always been, in my opinion, an art—because it's the product of an individual's creative effort, rather than an institutional creative effort, rather than a team effort. That's the essence of documentary photography.

At the University of Missouri, Cliff Edom started the photo workshops in 1947; I assisted him. He brought out some of the FSA photographers like Esther Bubbley and Russell Lee. They were on the campus there for a day or so, and we met in the evenings and had bull sessions. I thought then, and ever since, that the FSA was a benchmark in photographic history.

Early on, I had realized that the subject matter of a documentary photographer has nothing to do with sensationalism, nothing to do with the unusual—it has everything to do with the very commonplace events of lives. All the good documentary work you can think of is perceptive photographs of people doing what they normally do.

When I graduated from university, I went to New York, and was practicing public relations work with the Fairchild Corporation. They had a change of management, and *National Geographic* was looking for picture editors. I came down to Washington and I went to work for *Geographic* in 1954.

Geographic was a very successful magazine then, and it is now. They had worked out a formula, and part of the formula was that they looked at noncontroversial subjects. The photographic clichés they were working with—people in red shirts and red dresses in the foreground and all the rest of it—were all very artfully staged, and very undocumentary. But they were open to change at that point, and that's one of the reasons they hired me.

They had a picture editor who was of the old school, Walter Edwards. When they brought in a bunch of pictures that were produced for a particular story, he would throw them on the light table and pick out the prettiest ones he could, without any regard for the story or the truth. If you look back on those old issues, you'll see that quite often the pictures have nothing to do with the story, and vice versa.

I tried to start thinking about the story, about the subject, and select pictures based upon their journalistic value as well as their artistic value—and therein lay the conflict. I and some of the other guys from Missouri, Bill Garrett and Tom Smith, who were there by that time started doing the layouts the way we thought they should be done—by the story.

In one of my first stories, Frank and Jean Shore, a husband and wife team, were in Morocco, and I was assigned to be their editor. I reviewed their pictures and sent them back comments—that was our routine—about what I thought they had and what they might photograph. I got a letter back from Frank Shore saying, "Who the hell is Giff Hampshire, and what does he think he's doing?"

I got straightened out right away. I wasn't supposed to think too much about the story. I shouldn't go to the library and study about Morocco, and I shouldn't read the papers about the problems they were having with the colonial revolution.

I had to back away. When the assignment was finished, we'd begin working on a selection and a layout. I would present that layout in a projection session with the editor, Melville Grosvenor. He would take a personal interest at that point and make changes and suggestions, and those would be done. It got to the point where I went into Melville's office one day with a layout, and he said, "Oh Giff, it's you." And I said, "It is I." Here we go. We knew that we were in for it. I would try to sell my layout and my story. I'd try to present it to him based upon what I thought was a well thought out and logical way, and often that didn't go over very well. He wanted more formula, the tried and true pretty pictures.

I got a reputation. Frank Shore was an assistant editor by that time. He called me in one day and said, "You've probably got a lifetime job here if you'll just shut up, and not think so much."

I'd been talking with Ruth Adams at the United States Information Agency [USIA], and she had started a new, slick magazine for the Arabic-speaking world called *Al Hayat*. She asked me if I'd be interested in joining her agency. It was a mistake, in retrospect.

When I was talking with her in 1959, I was just as naive as I could be about government and politics. All the people I talked to at USIA were Eisenhower appointees. When I went to work there, they were all Kennedy people. I had to do something else. At that point, I'd become a father of twins.

A year earlier, my attention had been caught by an event. The Food and Drug Administration [FDA] prohibited the sale of cranberries that year—a big event around Thanksgiving time—because they had been contaminated with an herbicide. This was the first time I could remember that the federal government had done anything as important as that to protect the food supply of America.

Since World War II, our nation had, all of a sudden, been caught up in things like pesticides and chemicals and plastics. It used to be wood and leather and water and earth, and now it's all plastics and chemicals. There's a lot of harm done there. I was looking for something to do with my life, and I thought, "Perhaps that's the place to try."

I went to the FDA and got a job working in the Public Information office. Over the next ten years there, I worked for four different commissioners. Then the Senate hearings for Bill Ruckelshaus' appointment as administrator of the EPA [Environmental Protection Agency] came along in 1970, and I went. Bill Ruckelshaus sounded like a guy who was really going to get something done.

I applied and was transferred to his staff in 1970. His immediate aides were a bunch of young, interesting, intelligent, go-get-em people from Indiana and elsewhere. We had these bull sessions, and I threw out the idea of a documentary project. It caught on immediately. They could see right off the bat the parallel between the FSA and the EPA.

I became deputy to the director of the office, responsible for day-to-day operations. Meanwhile we were gestating this idea about "DOCUMERICA." When it came time, I said to Bill Ruckelshaus, "There's only one way to do this. If you like the idea, and you think I'm capable of carrying it out, what needs to be done is say it's Giff Hampshire's thing, and I want him to have the support he needs." That's the reason it happened at all.

We even got presidential approval. I had everything going for me when we started, except I didn't have any help. It was just me and my secretary. I wrote the press release announcing Project DOCUMERICA.

I had it pretty well worked out in my head, and it didn't require much of a staff, because we were going to hire the photographers to do the work. All I needed was a setup to handle the film when it came in, and get it processed, and get it into a file.

I said, "There's gotta be a way to manage this file with the new technology." One of the first things I did was get a contract with a firm in Alexandria [Virginia]. I said, "I want to develop a file, where we can look at the pictures by asking for certain kinds of information. For example, every picture has to be identified in terms of its geographic location, date, and its photographer. In addition, we've got to have certain descriptors of the picture: water, vegetation, traffic, solid waste, etc." We actually created the first computerized photo file.

As each picture was selected for the file, one of the contractor's people would write the caption, basic information, and key in these descriptor words. We hooked this all up through the computer to microfiche.

We started the assignments in the spring of 1972, in the South. The idea was that each photographer would be given an assignment of a particular period of time. They were paid $150 a day, plus expenses. They were to be given, let's say, twenty days at that rate. I don't think there were many over thirty days. The idea was that the photographer was to select a subject relevant to EPA interests.

There were about 120 photographers. I gave each photographer an assignment number, and it was sequential. We started with 01 and finally got about 164 assignments. This was a kind of a project that somebody worked for twenty days or so, and then went back to activities that supported his or her living. *Life* magazine had folded, and *Look* had folded, and there were a lot of good photographers looking for work, which was fortuitous, in a way. Also, in a way, it was not, because some of these photographers thought that maybe this was a thing they could live off of. I discouraged them from thinking that.

The first meeting was held in Atlanta, and the photographers who were selected to participate were invited to come to that meeting, and they heard the people at the Atlanta office of the EPA talk about the air pollution problems, the water pollution problems, and so forth.

On the second day, at night, [former FSA phographer] Arthur Roth-stein and I met with them individually. He was helping me select pho-tographers. We'd invite them to come into my room, individually, and the basic question was, "Well, what did you hear that set you off, as a subject?"

Some of them would come up with stuff that was almost directly re-lated to what they heard, and others came up with things that were tan-gential. Often air pollution and water pollution were not very inter-esting to the photographers, but the conditions under which people lived in those environments was of interest. It was of more interest to me, too. I said to them, "Look, I can only sell this program at EPA if it's based upon the EPA programs, but that doesn't mean that we're not connected to everything else."

During the FSA, Roy Stryker, head of the Historical Section, was more direct. He would say, "Let's do a story on cotton," and he'd call photographer Carl Mydans in and say, "What do you know about cotton?"

"Nothing. I know nothing."

"Well, before you leave, you must know a lot more about cotton." And Stryker would get specific about shooting scripts. We didn't get into that. My philosophy was we're dealing with intelligent people here, people who are concerned about things. They have the resources, the intellectual resources, to develop it. All I wanted to know was whether they were interested enough in a subject. If they were, I would make a few notes in a little black book that I kept, and that was it.

They were on their own at that point. We had a contract with East-man Kodak, and they could go to the local Kodak outlet and, using their social security number, get all the film they needed. A lot of the photographers, I found out later on, felt they were too much on their own. They didn't have any feedback, they said. They didn't have any encouragement. They'd call me up on the phone and I'd talk to them, but I wasn't about to get into telling them how to do their assignment, what to shoot. As a consequence, we had a lot of stuff, all over the yard—some very good, some not so good.

I insisted that before the photographer was paid, he or she turn in the documentation—the caption information as well as the images. We would make a selection. We would send it back to the photographer and say, "Do you agree with this, as a selection to go into the file?" We were pretty liberal about it. Whenever the photographer asked for something else to be included, we did.

What we selected for the file was the first and seconds, and the rest of it went back to the photographer. This was government property, but the photographer had full control over those rejects, so to speak.

I told the EPA people right off, this was not to be a propaganda effort. One of the problems they had in the FSA project was that Roy Stryker and others were really propagandizing the FSA programs. "The legitimacy of DOCUMERICA and the value of the images will be from our determination to be truthful, our effort to be objective as best we can," I said.

Today, if someone wants to understand the environment in the early 1970s, they can find the answer partially in that file—to the extent that we did our job properly. That makes it a baseline of what was happening in America environmentally when the agency started.

That's the value of documentary. It has no commercial value at the time, has no real journalistic value at the time, but if you could persevere in doing it, then one of these days, if it's preserved and kept in a public file in the public domain, then maybe it does. If it's in some photographer's file, tied up in his estate, it probably doesn't have any value.

The project started, as I said, in '72, and during '72 and '73 we did most of the photography. In 1974 there was an economic recession, and the EPA had to take its hit along with some other federal agencies. DOCUMERICA really had to take a hit. More important, Bill Ruckelshaus had been pulled out of the EPA to temporarily head the FBI as assistant attorney general, and the whole Watergate scandal happened. He was part of the October Massacre.

Gradually, the guys that resented my doing it in the first place came out of the woodwork, as it always happens in government, and they found their opportunities to snipe at me. One of them wound up being my boss. In the final analysis, he had the budget. So we had to cut out the computer program. I cut out various things, but one thing I didn't want to cut out was the photography. There are about another 6,000 images that were selected for the file but never got into the file, because I couldn't afford to have the microfiche made or the rest of it. They're sitting with the other 16,000 that are in the file.

Those are the edited images. Those are at the National Archives [and Records Administration] right now. While the Archives has digitalized the images and they are available on the Internet, they have not made it easy. [Search for DOCUMERICA in the NAIL database at www.nara.gov.]

When I left the EPA in 1980, the project had pretty much stopped. As far as photographers were concerned, it ended in 1976. Up until the day I left, anyone who wanted an image could get it.

As soon as I was out the door, the National Archives people who had wanted to add DOCUMERICA to their still picture collection came to the EPA and asked for it, as the law entitled them to take any inactive government file. EPA agreed that it was not an active file, and it went to the Archives.

I am fairly well satisfied that the federal government, unless something changes drastically, will never be able to sponsor a documentary project again. The only reason it happened is because I basically wanted it to happen. I paid the price, physically and mentally, but it was worth it. It was a lot of fun at the time.

The greatest compliment I ever heard about a project I did was when I once took a publication that I put together to the government printing office and they screwed up the transparencies. They had taken them out of the slide covers and scratched them. So I had this big meeting with them, to tell them what the problem was. And this guy, sitting in this great big office, with paraphernalia around him, looks at these pictures and says, "Well, I could've taken these damn pictures."

And I said, "Thank you, sir. That's the best thing you could have told us because that means we have accomplished our objective." I remember he was looking at this picture of this kid fishing on a creek. Looked like a snapshot to him.

That's the subject matter of documentary photography, and those images have meaning only because of their relationship to the time, the place, and the circumstances at a later date.

I think that documentary happens because a photographer wants it to happen. A photographer decides something should be documented, and he or she puts in the intellectual, as well as artistic, effort. The payoff has to be in terms of that photographer's satisfaction with the work itself, because there's no economic reward, there's no fame and fortune in it.

Peter Howe

Life Magazine and *Outtakes*

Peter Howe worked as a photojournalist for fourteen years before becoming a leading picture editor. Howe covered breaking news stories for the French press agency SIPA, wrote features and photography reviews for London publications, and created the book *Peter Howe's Picture Book of the Salvation Army* (1975).

He joined the *New York Times Magazine* in 1984 and *Life* in 1987 as director of photography. Howe helped to revitalize *Life* by shifting its focus from celebrities and lifestyles to harder-edge journalism. He helped fund and publish works like Eugene Richards's *Cocaine True, Cocaine Blue,* which focuses on the problems caused by drug addiction in the United States. During this period, *Life* was a finalist in the National Magazine Awards three times and received two first-place awards from the New York Newspaper Guild's Front Page Awards.

In 1992 he founded the magazine *Outtakes* for underpublished documentary work. During the same period, Howe was appointed the director of photography for *A Day in the Life,* one of the more successful photo-book series ever published. The National Press Photographers Association and the University of Missouri School of Journalism honored him for Best Magazine Picture Editing in 1993. *Outtakes* ended in 1995. Howe worked for a short time as vice president for Photography and Creative Services at Corbis, the digitally based photo archive. He has been a regular contributor to the *Digital Journalist, American Photo, Columbia Journalism Review,* and USA Today and advises independent photo agencies and photographers on digital organization, storage, and licensing of their work.

Outtakes magazine, issue three,
spring 1993
(cover photo © Nubar Alexanian)

We have gone far away from using photography as journalism and much more toward using photography as illustration. Documentary photography is not being published as much as we think it should. This does not devalue documentary photography. It's still as valuable as it ever was for the right reasons. The right reasons probably don't earn a lot of money, but it doesn't make them the wrong reasons.

The job of the photojournalist is to witness those things that people don't want to think about. When they're doing their job right, they are taking photographs that people don't want to publish by their very nature.

When photography was invented, painting didn't die, but it changed its character and its social position. When television was invented, photography didn't die, but it changed its position and its character. I think that we're still struggling through and redefining the role of what this kind of photography is in the world. If our society ever rediscovers what really is important—socially, intellectually, emotionally—then they'll rediscover how important documentary photography is. One of the things we found with *Outtakes* is the extraordinary high quality of work that came over the transom almost every week. A lot of this work is from people I've never, ever heard of, and I have no idea who they are or how they make a living.

When you come down to it, the problem is that photography is no longer, and hasn't been for some time, a primary news source. The demand for photojournalism, strict documentary photography in the way that it had been used in *Life, Look,* all the British magazines, *Picture Post,* and other places like that, the commercial need for it has literally shriveled up.

We have to look at a new environment, an environment that is not magazine dependent, not even newspaper dependent. We have to look for other areas and other venues to be able to both fund and place photojournalism.

To me, "documentary photographer" and "photojournalist" are almost interchangeable words. I think a documentary photographer has to be a journalist, but a committed one. If you look at it in terms of text, you can get a reporter and you can get a writer. A reporter is someone who goes out and reports. A writer is somebody who gives his or her own personal style, his or her own personal viewpoint and twist and spin to that story. A documentary photographer is a writer rather than a reporter. Great documentary photographers come to their craft with their own preconceptions, their own interests and ideas. They are not neutral observers.

I don't employ Gene Richards to give me photographs like Sebastião Salgado. I don't expect that Gilles Peress is going to give me Mary Ellen Mark. You employ each of those photographers for their vision. I'm not denigrating reporting—it is a complex and difficult skill—but the reality is that most of the time I'm not using photo reporters. And, to me, that is what a documentary photographer is.

A picture editor's only ever as good as the editor of the magazine allows that picture editor to be. You are not the ultimate voice in the magazine. One of the things that always amazed me, and particularly with *Life,* was that it was a picture magazine that was always edited by a text editor. A picture editor is often very low down on the food chain. If you look at the masthead of most magazines, you will see that.

When I was fired from *Life,* I felt I was a victim of some sort of corporate drive-by shooting. For picture editors there's no such thing as job security. You just have to do what you want to do as best as you can and try and push for it as best you can.

One of the things that I think distinguishes photo editors is their ability to articulate to text editors why a particular photograph or photographic project is important. It's a skill that all photo editors need and not a huge number of them have. You can't just say, "It's a really great picture." You've got to actually be able to give substantial editorial and journalistic reasons as to why that particular picture or that series of pictures is important for the magazine.

It's very hard to explain to an editor of a magazine that has to be commercially successful why it is we should depress the shit out of the readers. And, of course, we shouldn't. But this makes it hard to get the really tough stories in, particularly in this country. The perception is that the average American reader does not want to read about the more thorny, gritty side of life. And that is sort of the bread and butter of the documentary photographer.

For instance, there's the wonderful set of pictures that Lauren Greenfield did about growing up in Los Angeles on the other end of the social spectrum. It's mostly incredibly overindulged, overprivileged children in Los Angeles and the values they're brought up with. It's just as serious as doing a hospice for AIDS patients but it's different—and an easier thing to get into a magazine.

I look at *Life* magazine nowadays and you hear people complaining, "They're doing cats and dogs on the cover" or "They're doing the parties of the year on the cover." That's no different than the way *Life* magazine always was. *Life* was the magazine that brought you such groundbreaking photojournalism as "How to Undress in Front of Your Husband," when it was at its most commercially successful and its most powerful. If you go back through all the covers of old *Life* magazines, you'll find eighty percent of them were film stars. You didn't have the country doctor [Eugene Smith's pioneering photo-essay] on the cover.

When [editor and publisher] Clay Felker was at *Life*, he said that the editor would put up the fifty-two covers at the end of the year in order of their sales. The top left-hand corner of the wall would be the highest selling cover. The top left-hand corner was always pretty girls, and the bottom right-hand corner was always sports personalities. He said that it never ever varied.

Publishing magazines is a commercial venture. The difference is that in the forties and fifties *Life* magazine was a primary source of visual news. That's absolutely changed, and the magazine has changed with it.

I am optimistic that despite everything that's against the documentary photographer, there's still an enormous amount of documentary photography being done of very high quality. People are getting it done by whatever means they can.

I don't know what the avenues are going to be. I am very excited about the possibilities of the Internet, but I am worried it may be another area where still documentary photography is left out. The appeal of using photography in an electronic environment now is that still photography takes a lot less memory than moving images, but that's just a technical problem. Once that's solved, you'll be seeing much more video than still photography on your computer screen.

I look at Kathy Ryan's career. I employed her as a deputy picture editor at the *New York Times Magazine*. When I left the magazine, they made her the picture editor, which was one of the smartest things that they ever did. But it has worried me that she's veering much more toward what seems to me to be art photography rather than what I, in my stubborn old-fashioned way, consider to be documentary photography. Although she does use a lot of documentary photography, there's a high proportion of what appears to be conceptual photography. I would expect to see that on the walls of a gallery rather than in the pages of a magazine. I was wondering, whether, in fact, that she's right, that photography as it stands at the moment is becoming much more of an art form than an information medium.

There are times when I feel like the last of a generation, the last of a profession even. I often wonder if I was nineteen or twenty whether I would go into documentary photography. One of the things that I have learned in the time that I've been in this business is that if there is a secret to being involved in photojournalism, then the only secret is persistence. The people who survive and prosper are those people who persist.

I very strongly believe that what documentary photographers do, and what journalists in general do, is of almost unparalleled importance to human society. The act of witness is very important. Without journalism, there's no democracy. Without journalism, there's no freedom.

Colin Jacobson

Independent Magazine and *Reportage*

Colin Jacobson studied politics, philosophy, and economics and, in 1971, entered journalism as a picture editor, a position he has occupied for several British publications, including the *Observer* and the *Economist*.

In 1988 Jacobson joined the original staff of the London *Independent*, where he succeeded in publishing many photo stories. A story about land mines in Cambodia spanned ten uninterrupted pages and helped raise over £90,000 (about $89,280) in aid for mine victims. In the early nineties, when the *Independent* followed many other magazines in scaling down on photojournalism, Jacobson left to found *Reportage*. That quarterly photo-journal was grounded in the same spirit as Peter Howe's *Outtakes*, maintaining a simple format and giving photographers more control over visual presentation.

Jacobson left full-time journalism to teach in 1995. He writes articles on contemporary photojournalism and more recently has become interested in the effect of digital technology on photojournalism.

In 2002 he edited *Underexposed: Censored Pictures and Hidden History*. *Underexposed* tells the stories behind the photographs which have determined our view of history, providing a reality check on events in the last hundred years and documenting the struggle of the powerful, from the cruelty of Stalin's Russia and the chaos in Iran to the horrors of the Gulf War and perspectives on September 11th. Jacobson continues to work as a freelance photo editor in London.

reportage

Special issue The international magazine of photojournalism / Winter 1997

An anonymous young prisoner
photographed by the Khmer Rouge,
S-21 camp, Cambodia,
Reportage magazine, winter 1997

Certainly in Great Britain, and I suspect in other parts of the Western world, the whole thrust of magazine publishing is cerebral. The people who edit magazines, the people who are in the driving seat of publishing and journalism, are word oriented. There is little acceptance that there can be another way of understanding the world, which is more visual, more aesthetic.

It's a very strange thing. With almost every magazine I've ever been on, when they get around to doing a readership survey they find that the thing that people most like and remember about the magazine is the images. But it never seems to make any difference to the way the magazine is put together.

With *Reportage,* I wanted to be in a position where I didn't have to justify the stories all the time. The basic, very simple philosophy of the magazine, which is behind all these discussions about "Photojournalism, is it dead or is it alive?" and "Why are magazines so bad?" came down to one thing in the end. Until you have magazines where the visual decision making is in the hands of people who have a visual orientation, they'll never get better.

A lot of the younger photojournalists in Europe are very intelligent, aware people. Certainly on the *Independent Magazine* some of the best stories we did—even stories which weren't particularly visual, which ended up as text stories with backup pictures—were ideas that came from photographers or picture editors. Photographers know what the stories are about and can push the frontiers of the story, more satisfactorily than the writer in many cases.

The *Independent Magazine* started from scratch in 1988, and I joined just before the launch. I was able to influence the way the magazine was going to look because, strangely enough, it was launched without any very clear idea of what it was going to be. The editor respected people who could fight their corner and justify what they were doing. I was able to use picture stories from the very beginning that I liked. If I said we should publish the story, generally speaking, at least in the first two or three years of the magazine's existence, the editor would accept it.

It was a slightly schizophrenic magazine in the way that the front and the back of the magazine were not very visual; they were quite text driven. But in the middle of the magazine, the heart of the magazine, there was always a picture story—usually eight pages, sometimes as many as ten pages of a self-contained picture essay. Advertising was placed in the front or the back of the magazine.

For two to three years we had that wonderful space for a wide-ranging photojournalism, without any sort of very specific agenda. The text was always limited and there to support the pictures. We took trouble to find the right writer, or writers, who knew what they were talking about. That is rather unusual in contemporary magazines.

The two disciplines, words and pictures, need each other and should complement each other. I wish there were ways to break down those barriers. Photographers and picture editors have some responsibility for the situation, because they tend to be very overprotective or over-sensitive and refuse to acknowledge that words or text can contribute to what they are doing. It should be absolutely clear to everybody that brilliant images are not enough. You need the text, you need great headlines, great captions, great introductions, good text to amplify and expand the sense of what the pictures are doing and give them context and meaning.

One of the great areas of conflict within the picture fraternity is between photographers and picture editors or art directors. There's this awful crisis when the harsh reality of editing for a magazine or newspaper comes into play. You can have twenty wonderful photographs from a story, but you only have room for eight or ten. Space in a magazine is like time in a film or video; both demand a heavy degree of editing. You get into an editorial way of thinking and working, which is to my mind vulturistic—you descend on a body of work. If it's a day's work or six month's work, you're still landing with your claws on these images. It's like losing blood for the photographer, and sometimes for the picture editor as well. But the truth is that editorially you have to do this. Magazines are not in the business of being repetitive or boring, or they shouldn't be. So then you have to pat the photographer on the back and say, "Never mind, old chap, there'll be an exhibition in the future where you can have all your pictures up."

The stories that I remember are strangely not about universal topics, not about the great sweeping aspects of life or society. I really like focused photojournalism, often about daily life and not about the huge, harrowing problems of the world.

Unfortunately, in many people's minds, photojournalism is seen to be about life on the edge of the precipice. So we get drowned in stories about war, homelessness, street kids, unemployment, AIDS, drugs—all of which are photogenic subjects. Of course, we can acknowledge their importance, journalistically and as human beings, but we don't have to keep on doing the same things all the time. I do think that photojournalists are shooting themselves in the foot by constantly returning to these themes.

Photojournalism is being a journalist with a camera. Documentary is more culturally driven, designed for learning to understand one another, to document life at a particular time. It is not for the here and now but for posterity.

The whole Robert Capa era holds up because we as magazine people go back to it. We publish retrospectives on anniversaries and exhibitions. We are all aware that there is a great reservoir of amazing photography. People get forgotten and taken up again because of excellent work they have done in the past.

I'm not so sure about the future. I don't know whether work being done now will have the same resonance in twenty or thirty years time, because attitudes to photojournalism are changing so much within the digital revolution. Speed and simplicity of image delivery seems to preoccupy the press nowadays, and not much attention is paid to composition and story interpretation. I worry about the quality and range of photojournalism—tomorrow's history—now going into the archives.

Anne Wilkes Tucker

The Museum Context

A nne Wilkes Tucker is the Gus and Lyndall Wortham Curator of Photography at the Museum of Fine Arts, Houston. She decided to major in art history after seeing an inspirational exhibition of Vincent Van Gogh paintings during her freshman year at Randolph Macon Woman's College. After obtaining a second undergraduate degree from Rochester Institute of Technology, where she studied as a photographer, she "decided [she] wasn't one." When Nathan Lyons formed the Visual Studies Workshop in Rochester, Tucker joined him for her graduate training. "The idea was to take a broader look at pictures and communication," she said.

Her thesis on photographs of women was completed while she was an intern under John Szarkowski, the former director of photography at the Museum of Modern Art (MoMA) in New York. It was the height of feminism's "second wave." Her thesis led to an exhibition from the MoMA collection, a special issue of *Camera*, and another project of photographs by women that was published as a book, *Woman's Eye*.

In the early seventies she taught and, for photography historian Beaumont Newhall, researched exhibitions of photography in New York between the closing of Alfred Stieglitz's famed 291 Gallery in 1917 and the opening of the MoMA in 1939. During this time, she became particularly interested in the Photo League, which she has continued to research and write about.

In 1976 Tucker was asked to join the staff at the Museum of Fine Arts,

Mastectomy (© Joan Myers)

Houston, which had just received a large grant to begin a photography collection. She became the main force in shaping the museum's collection, and has since curated over twenty-five exhibitions, including retrospectives for Robert Frank, George Krause, Richard Misrach, Brassaï, and Louis Faurer. She has also organized major shows such as a survey of the history of Japanese photography and contemporary Korean photography.

Tucker is deeply serious about how and why photography speaks to the viewer and its place on the world stage. The museum under her leadership has been collecting photographs that move beyond serviceable records to images that "continue to engage, inform, disturb, and challenge viewers long after the immediacy of the moments recede into history." She is currently researching and writing about the relationship of war and photography for a major exhibition, seeking what has been described as broader and unbiased look at war photography. In 2001, *Time* magazine honored Tucker as "America's Best Curator."

We began the twentieth century by believing what we saw in a photograph was true and ended the twentieth century by distrusting every document.

There is an inherent problem in discussing the whole concept of the document at the end of the twentieth century, when you can so seamlessly create in a computer any reality that you want, visual or otherwise. In some ways it is liberating for photography because, as in a written essay, our faith is based on the integrity of the maker. Photographers are liberated from trust being inherent in their medium. Our acceptance or rejection of the information they present will have to do with the reputation of the photographer, the declared intentions of the maker, and what else we know about that subject. In some ways it's probably the best thing that's happened in documentary, especially social documentary photography.

There is a friend of mine who, whenever I talk to him about documentary photography of any kind, tells me I am looking forward out of a rearview mirror—that nothing new in terms of aesthetic form can be added to the genre. This same person believes that a play with a good plot and solid characters is no longer relevant.

A photographer who had done a really beautiful series on a particular family in North Carolina took his work up to a New York museum and was told that his work was passé. This attitude adopts another parallel to writing, which is the hierarchy that fiction is more important than nonfiction and essays are the bottom of the heap. It places too much of the responsibility for whether or not something is art on its formal properties. It emphasizes the hierarchy of form over subject that was formed early in the twentieth century.

The prejudice against documentary work, especially work about controversial issues, also comes out of the practice in the museum world that one didn't buy an artist's work until that artist was dead. The National Gallery [of Art, Washington, D.C.] still has a rule that they can't show a living artist unless they own the work. In essence we apply the same standard to issues. We don't collect during the heat of the issue.

There's a wonderful quote by Therese Heyman, in one of her early Dorothea Lange catalogs of about ten years ago, in which she said that the photographs are art today because the issues that motivated Lange's photography are no longer within our power to correct. To respond to work coolly is supposed to be more scholarly than buying work at the moment of a crisis. For one thing, you don't alienate either side of your public by jumping into a controversial current issue.

As long as I see so much strong work being done in both documentary and social documentary, I find it a peculiar position to devalue, or worse, to ignore these genre. If you want to understand what were the current controversial issues of a particular decade, go back and look at the photography from that period. If we have no reflections on the heart of the social debate for any particular decade, I find that an arid interpretation of culture.

What museums collect can affect history. John Szarkowski once stated at a conference that he had played no role in the making of art, that he merely responded to what was out there. Well that's not quite true. When you're as articulate as John and you publish all these books, you are creating the veins of ideas and information about a specific group of people that are going to be mined by future historians and future artists.

What we collect can affect the pictures that are made. Future artists and historians will follow the shaft already created to mine a decade as opposed to digging a new one down through the mountain, if you will. They will more likely go to the most available sources and the monographs where the work has been gathered, rather than do the nitty-gritty digging out of information in magazine articles or track down the works of photographers that are not in repositories such as museums.

Once work has been done—for example, the civil rights work or even the Photo League work—the museum *should* become the repository for future generations. However, there are also practical realities that govern. For a museum to have collected the work of Photo League photography after the blacklisting was inconceivable. It was inconceivable for the health of the institution. People can rally all they want about how that shouldn't and oughtn't to be, but that's just not the real world. Showing photography—showing any art—that might get your institution into the kind of trouble that the Corcoran [Gallery of Art, Washington, D.C.] and Cincinnati [Art Museum] got themselves into with [Robert] Mapplethorpe's images is not something that any museum professional should do lightly.

We were given a very large collection, a wonderful collection, an extraordinary collection of a thousand photographs a few years ago. There were pictures in it that I don't think I would ever have gotten the trustees to accept as gifts except as part of a collection. The collector had a category that he called "cock penis" with photographs by Peter Hujar and Robert Mapplethorpe and a couple of European photographers. It's an important series to have in a museum, but I could never have raised the money to buy it.

There are two pictures going in our collection that are about having mastectomies. Because a friend died of metastasized breast cancer, I will be the first to admit I am not in any way distanced and impartial from this subject. One is a picture Joan Myers made because a woman approached her. Before the woman had a mastectomy she couldn't find any pictures of other women who had it and this upset her. She wanted Joan to photograph her so that picture would be there for other women who had to make those decisions.

I was on a public panel, and I reported that I have to fund-raise for every picture I buy. I felt that I would never find a donor for Joan's picture as much as I would love to have it in the collection. A woman in the audience then bought the picture for the museum and donated it in memory of a friend of hers who had died of breast cancer. What I love about this picture being bought is the chain of people who shared a certain concern, a certain sensitivity to a phenomenon that has previously been silenced by shame.

Fred Ritchin

The Fish are Last to Know about the Water:
The Emerging Digital Revolution

F red Ritchin is one of the early visionaries in the field of digital
photography and probably one of our most influential and
thoughtful commentators on the future of visual media. His perspective
comes from years in the trenches as magazine picture editor, independent
curator, web developer, political activist, and university professor.

In 1978 he became picture editor of the *New York Times Sunday
Magazine*. It was Ritchin who hired the young and largely unrecognized
Brazilian photographer Sebastião Salgado to photograph the first one
hundred days of Ronald Reagan's presidency. Ritchin describes how
"they were doing one of those stories magazines seem to do too much on
the first hundred days of a presidency." He needed to assign a photographer, and wanted one who did not know "anything about the plaid-
shirted, horse-riding, log-chopping Republican candidate in a cowboy
hat who seemed to first want to be the Marlboro Man and only then the
president." He wanted to work with a photographer who could see what
was behind it all, and he chose a foreign photographer who spoke no
English. Many claim that it was Salgado's assassination images that
helped the photographer gain financial security, prominence, and thus
the freedom to work more in-depth.

Ritchin left the *New York Times Magazine* frustrated with the difficulties, familiar to all picture editors, convincing other editors and designers
as to which were the strongest pictures. In 1983 he founded the photo-

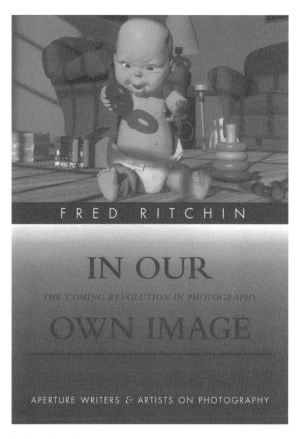

In Our Own Image, 1990
© Aperture Foundation

journalism and documentary photography program at the International Center for Photography, where he served as its director for three years.

Ritchin's keen editing skills and continued interest in the image pushed him to independently curate photography shows on Latin American and Magnum, the photo agency. He also worked closely with Salgado in 1990, on his book *An Uncertain Grace* and curated his first one-person exhibition in the United States at the San Francisco Museum of Modern Art.

Always an acute observer, Ritchin was one of the earliest writers and theorists on the digital revolution, and much of what he discussed and predicted in his pioneering book *In Our Own Image* (1990) has come to pass.

His new book *After Photography*, offers a supple, politically astute, and fascinating account of the dizzying impact of the digital revolution. He is currently professor of photography and communications at New York University's Tisch School of the Arts.

Ritchin has a passionate interest in the social role of photography and he continues to ask the hard questions that photographers often don't want to hear: How did we lose so many jobs, How did journalism become so irrelevant, and "How do you have a Democracy where everybody has a little media empire and there is no front page anymore that everybody starts to share?"

For the most part, the digital revolution affecting photography has not yet happened. People are continuing with what they used to do before, just putting photos on a digital platform. If you did a photo essay on paper that is eight or sixteen pages, now you do a slide show. If you have a single image on paper, now you have a single image on the website. The digital promise is something very different.

I think this revolution promises, first of all, nonlinearity, the web as hypertext, and the ability to link in a variety of ways. It's not an A-B-C-D story, but something where you can skip around. You can image-map, meaning if a photographer has an image you might be able to click on a piece of it and go one direction in the essay as opposed to another. You might be able to click on a piece of it and get sound on the right side, but if you click on the left side you might get a text box. You can play with it and interweave all kinds of media with it in ways you cannot do in print. I think the great majority of digital photos one sees out there do not avail themselves of these new possibilities.

There is also an issue of interactivity, which to me means collaboration. It's a collaboration that happens at the very least among the reader, photographer, subject, and the publication, as well as among all of the various technologies used. The reader may have something to add—certain perspectives and ideas. These can be added to the piece, which can inform the way other readers choose to navigate it. If a photographer does a story on something going on in Uganda, then the reader who knows a lot about Uganda can add a link to a website that's helpful or correct a misperception in a photograph, perhaps re-captioning it. There are also a variety of potential links with the subject.

For example, with digital cameras it's very easy to show the back of the camera to the subject and ask: "Is this an accurate portrayal of you or your environment?" Then the photographer could record the subject saying he or she got it exactly right, or saying, "You photographed me looking unkempt. It's not fair. You got here too early in the morning—it's demeaning to me."

Now you have the voice of the photographer expressed by the picture, and then you have the voice of the subject giving another perspective, perhaps resisting the outsider's voice. You also have the voice of the reader who may in fact be an expert in the field saying, "You know, you should look at it another way as well." You have multiple voices. That does not mean that the person coming to that story has to read or listen to every voice. They could choose to just go with the photographer, proceeding through the story in a straight line like they usually do. Maybe they only have a few minutes to read. But maybe they will want to go back to the story, to its complexities, and it will not only be there waiting for them, but it might have grown more complex in the interim. Of course, all stories don't have to be done this way—there are so many ways to provide different kinds of context.

In my recent book *After Photography*, I suggest using the four corners of the image to provide different kinds of information hidden within the photograph. This would be a new standard in the industry, whereby each of the corners could be exposed by rolling a cursor over it, revealing the hidden contextualizing information. The photographer becomes more of an author of the image by doing this, and as the image is published in various locations on the web, on mobile phones, on iTablets, and other such devices, the photographer's contextualization is not lost. The reader would get used to looking for it—

perhaps the frame of the image would signal that such information is available.

For example, Eddie Adams, who took the famous picture in 1968 of the execution of the alleged Viet Cong terrorist, had very mixed feelings about that picture's use as an antiwar icon, and might have wanted to add his own point of view explaining how he felt the Vietnamese general's action could have been justified. So you could get that on the bottom left corner, either in spoken voice or text. The upper left corner might reveal other pictures taken that day by Adams. There may be two or three other images, which give some sort of a context for the interested reader. So instead of seeing the one iconic image, you see the images before and after to better understand the sequence of events. In the upper right corner would be links to ideas and information on other websites, and the bottom right would contain the photographer's name, copyright, and a link to his or her own site.

This is a draft of ways in which photographers could more effectively take possession of their own work. If a picture is published on a website and then it is republished on multiple other websites, which often happens, all this information embedded in the four corners travels with the picture. If a photographer is published in a right-wing publication or left-wing publication, the author's voice, the photographer's voice, is still included in the image as it travels.

These are ideas that you cannot accomplish in print. These are just some beginning ideas for what indeed will be a revolution when we start to figure it out. At the moment I think we are in a transition point, at the very beginning of a paradigm shift.

Media philosopher Marshall McLuhan had the idea that the fish are the last to know about the water. They don't know it's wet because they don't know what dry is—they have no experience of dry. Certainly a great number of people working in the media don't know what dry is, and as a result they don't know enough about the environment that they are in. I often find it's people in the media who are the most resistant to new ideas. They have often been the most conservative, because this is their background, this is what they know, and they don't see the reason why they should change (the same could be said of other industries, such as automobiles). I will often talk to people who are not in the media and they will say, "Oh, this is great. Why don't we do more stuff like that?" They feel less restrained.

Any revolution brings with it substantive change. In this case it is not simply new hardware and software. But underneath it all, one of the significant factors of the digital revolution, not just in photography but in media generally, is a move toward understanding the world via code. And in photography this shift will be from a focus on appearance, or phenotype, the province of analog photography, to an interest in genotype, a recognition that all living things are code based via their DNA, like digital media itself. Media emerging from code will have a predilection to view the world via its codes.

And, just as significantly, the shift will be from viewing the world via a Newtonian perspective—continuous, emphasizing cause and effect—to a more quantum view of the universe. After all, analog media are based upon a sense of continuity, such as the continuous tones of photography, while digital media are composed of discrete segments (pixels, for example) and quantum physics functions through discrete energy packets. This will encourage a massive reconception of the universe, allowing the exciting craziness of quantum physics, its fertile ambiguities, to become a much more significant part of our consciousness via our media. I believe that we are creating digital media because, in part, we want, at various levels, to reconceive our existence in profound ways.

I think analog photography itself will begin to look like oil paintings, and it will be valued. No question that reference points about where we have been in history and culture will continue to be an important stream in what we call photography. But in a much larger sense we are going to have to be inventing new forms because we have this emerging environment that encourages it. At unconscious levels there is an incredible anxiety about what this all means because we are not able to really bring it to the surface and ask ourselves, "What is this revolution about?" We would rather point to our computer and say that is the revolution. The computer is not the revolution. It is a symptom of it as well as its facilitator, but concentrating upon it avoids the enormous change in consciousness that is in fact already happening.

McLuhan said we all go 90 miles per hour looking through the rearview mirror. I think it is unrealistic to ask that people sufficiently acknowledge these changes as they are happening because people have a tendency to think according to older paradigms in order to preserve, as much as possible, their own worldviews. That's why so much of technology is labeled according to older vocabularies—laptops, Apples, Windows, Photoshop, iPhone—to give the sense that little has changed.

Talking about the future really means living deeply in the present, deeply enough to see and feel what has changed—another insight from McLuhan. What people call the future has, in many respects, already happened, but people tend to think of it is as somewhere down the road. For the most part people have not acknowledged the depth of the changes we are going through, pretending that digital photography is the same as analog photography, only more efficient. People talk about publishing on the web as a massive step, but publishing on the web and making it look like print is simply a shifting of platforms without acknowledging their differences.

Let's say that a photographer is covering a press conference or photo opportunity, a staged event. The photographer feels that the people in power are manipulating the situation. The president of the United States shows up at a factory and they pull out this burly factory guy to stand next to him. The president then puts his arm around him; an American flag is in the background. His media handlers tell the photographers where to stand. All of the photographers make that same staged image, which is meant for publication so that millions of readers will see that the president is a nice and caring guy, a friend of the workers.

But let's say that the photographer manages to walk around and photograph from behind or from the side to show how everybody is forced to stand in certain areas, and the event is staged. Then the photographer decides to say, "Here is that image they wanted me to show you, the readers, but if you roll over that image with the cursor you will see underneath it the second image that reveals the staging." This exercise doesn't cost anything except another frame of the digital camera. There is in fact no cost at all. What the photographer is doing with these two images is exposing some of the constant manipulation that politicians, celebrities, businesspeople, and others use to control their own image. If the photographers do that often enough then those in power will realize that there is no point in staging events because they are going to be exposed every time—so why stage an event? Then the practice of government may change to the point where instead of spending the money on media managers and manipulation, the candidate or the government official may have to actually speak about issues of importance.

It is very possible to at least partially redress the imbalance of power using all of these new technologies. It's not really a cost issue. The greater issue is a conceptual issue, a political issue, a psychological issue, a willingness to experiment.

Why are we so often looking back to the 1930s imagery, particularly that of the Great Depression or even the Spanish Civil War? In the movie industry you don't look back to the 1930s and say we have to do what they did. Quentin Tarantino is not going to go back to make a film just the way they did in the 1930s. But documentary photography has not sufficiently progressed beyond what Dorothea Lange, Walker Evans, and Robert Capa did three-quarters of a century ago. In fact when we entered this economic meltdown of the last two years, there were many asking to re-create the strategies of the Farm Security Administration, instead of thinking of new ways of exploring what has been going on.

It was the director of photography at New York's Museum of Modern Art, John Szarkowski, who pointed out that it's extraordinary how much of American history in the 1930s is based on these pictures by Walker Evans. Because it is photographic, we think it is credible, we think it is authentic, we think that's the way it was, so we accept it. But Evans himself didn't even think the work was documentary—he said it was "documentary style," it only looked like documentary. Evans's work was highly self-referential, a New Englander looking through the prism of his own obsessions. Were his dignified poor really emblematic of the 1930s (were they even all that dignified?), or was that an FSA-style approach to win sympathy for Franklin Roosevelt's New Deal politics? Were his pictures really about the specific Alabama tenant farmers whom he photographed, or were they made into symbols in the interests of Evans's art and Roy Stryker's politics?

The depiction of the tenant farmers by Evans was extraordinary work in 1936. In 2009, I would hope a contemporary Evans wouldn't be doing exactly the same kind of work. She would be doing something different. She might go and photograph the tenant farmers, but might also give a camera to the kids to include their points of view. She might be contextualizing the images by using the statistics of the economy for the last five or ten years. How much does a landowner make versus what a tenant farmer makes? How does that compare to someone in a northern city? What do these farmers think of her photographs, perhaps projected for them right there from her digital camera? Our stereotypes of race and class need to be broken in such ways that we see complexity—this new media encourages such complexity.

When James Joyce wrote *Ulysses* he was trying to understand and articulate what he saw and felt. He was also breaking the boundaries of what we thought the novel was. I don't see how we can have a revolution without trying to break some of the boundaries of what we think photography is. It's insufficient. For all these years I have heard photographers complain about not being published enough, or being published incorrectly by magazines or newspapers. Now there is this wide-open expanse to experiment and to publish. So many have personal websites, but you go to them and all you see is a portfolio. There are a few notable exceptions, but with all this technology, all the computers that dwarf any media technology that we previously have had, why do we see almost only portfolios? I think that this is really an underutilization of resources. Of course, people need to be paid—but that is not the only question.

In 1996 I did a website with photographer Gilles Peress on Bosnia for the *New York Times* ("Bosnia: Uncertain Paths to Peace"). It was a one-off, because the *New York Times* never wanted to do anything like that again, nor did pretty much anybody else. The idea was to see whether it was possible to implicate the reader in the journey the photographer took as a way of exploring what was going on in Bosnia. We were trying to ask people, readers, to join us in a conversation. All of us together will go further than any single person could do. Peress had been there before and knew a lot about it. But he doesn't live there. He is an outsider, but he could provoke a conversation. On the other hand the people who live there may miss some of what is going on because they don't see the outsider's perspective. Everybody could join in these discussions that we have online and make the journey.

We opened it up so that it worked in a non-linear way. People could click and go this way or that way or at any time they could just go to a menu of image choices. They just clicked on one of a bunch of images, almost like a contact sheet. They could pick one and go that direction and we were not telling them where to go. We were leaving it open. We were saying to the reader, "You are mature, we trust you, you are responsible, you know you don't have to follow us step by step. You select where you want to go." We encouraged the reader to be an active reader. People can synthesize these different ideas and experiences and come to some sort of ideas in their own minds on what they think is going on, knowing that there is not one single answer.

The project was shown for three months on the *New York Times'* website. In 1997 they nominated it for a Pulitzer Prize in public service. It was immediately rejected for not being on paper. It took until the end of the year 2008 for the Pulitzer Committee to say that websites independent of the print publication would be eligible for a Pulitzer Prize, at which point the journalism business was failing rapidly. It took them twelve years to acknowledge that what we had done was important. I think that such encouragement, given in 1997, would have had a major impact on the desire to experiment with new forms.

The Bosnia project was expensive. Not everybody has to do that kind of a thing. You could do it in twelve pictures, in six pictures, or in one picture. You can start to play with an image and see what other possibilities there are for illumination. The fact that hundreds of millions of people in affluent societies have access to a computer allows an enormous number of people to create examples which others could learn from and even copy. (They do it now with apps for the iPhone.) When you are in your mid-twenties and you don't have a big family to support yet, it is possible that you could spend some time experimenting to show the way. Just like poets sit around in the middle of the night and write experimental verse. They don't expect payoffs for experimental verse, but they do it. I think that this community should do more to take advantage of these new potentials.

What I like to think about is Henri Cartier-Bresson referring to photojournalism as keeping a journal with a camera. In fact it's a kind of a daily journal. You bring into it the personal and subjective, and the explicit sense that it's not just a mechanical, so-called objective camera that is making the image. It's a person with all their history and feelings and desires and perceptions who is interpreting what is going on. The photographer says, "Here I am in Alabama. These people are poor." The photographer shows what they had for breakfast or what they had for dinner, and all that fills their day. The photographer is saying this is *their* life and this is also *my* life, and the two are entwined. There is a relationship, and it gets to be a richer and more complex story. That is extremely important, because the web, which allows nearly an infinite amount of imagery, text, and sound at this point, is not like a paper-based journal. I think a lot of us still think of column inches, but the web itself is highly expandable. You have a lot more space. I am not saying the reader has to spend twelve hours on this story. The reader may want to spend twelve minutes, but you know some of the readers might want to spend twenty minutes.

I think that we all agree that the so-called objectivity of journalism is a myth that is used to sell journalism to people. The more honest journalism is that we try to be fair-minded. We certainly have biases. We don't know everything, but we try to go into this as open as we can. We try to show some ideas that come out of this—we are both an authority and a non-authority simultaneously.

It used to be that if you retouched somebody's image it was a bad thing because you were manipulating it. But now if you don't retouch somebody then you are not placing them at the summit of the world of image, which is more important than what they actually look like and who they actually are. (The *Newsweek* cover of Sarah Palin, which was not retouched, was criticized as being anti-Palin for that reason.) The world of image itself is a world that begins to supplant the actual world in terms of societal value.

Photography has contributed to us thinking that way. What I am suggesting is that by contextualizing the images and not putting so much of an emphasis on the iconic, we will allow the map to be more important than the territory. The territory has to stay more important.

In France, England, and Israel they are trying to pass laws at the governmental level so that manipulations of photographs of models have to be acknowledged to the reader, because they don't want to encourage bad body images for young people, particularly in the context of anorexia. Finally after over a quarter century of nearly unconstrained digital image manipulation, people for the first time are actually taking interest. That's a small step for humanity. But generally we really have not dealt with the ramifications of this expanding image culture in the photographic community. There are novelists who have commented trenchantly about the out-of-control proliferation of image (Don DeLillo, for example), as well as a variety of social critics, filmmakers, post-modern artists, etc. But the documentary photography community, and particularly the photojournalistic segment, often proceeds with little recognition of the changing media environment. One day, of course, we will wake up and say, "Oh, my God, how did this happen to us? How did we lose so many jobs? How did journalism become so irrelevant? How come we have increasingly autocratic governments?"

When the car or the automobile was invented over a century ago, they called it the horseless carriage, and we still speak of our cars in terms of their horsepower. But imagine if at that time smart people sat around and said, "This new automobile is amazing. We will be able to travel at night, we will be able to travel long distances, we will be able to stay warm in the winter in the automobile and not be exposed. It really is not a horseless carriage. It has very little to do with a horse and carriage. It's a new way. We are going to have suburbia. We are going to have malls—and we are going to have global warming." Then people might have said, "We don't want all the bad stuff coming with it. As much as we can we want to minimize the destructive aspects of the automobile. Let's make a pact between all nations starting to manufacture automobiles that none of them will be more than four cylinders." Of course that didn't happen and now we have global warming and the planet is in danger. This is a hundred years later. Why couldn't we have thought about that earlier and sat down and done it?

Similarly with new media, and photography in particular, why can't we try to maximize the benefits of this revolution and minimize the ways in which we might be hurt? Let's now come up with certain ideas and protocols and build models that other people would follow. You could build a model on a single person's website; you don't need to have *Time* magazine endorse your model. It's not like that anymore. Why don't we come up with new models that would revitalize us in this moment of despair and reconceive photography in broader and more expansive ways that are simultaneously more complex, more nuanced, and more profound, while trying to engage society in some different ways than we did in the days of print and paper?

It is very normal that we don't want a revolution, or at least the pain of revolution. A revolution is a difficult thing. People lose their jobs. People at some very deep levels start to think of relationships differently because of this revolution. You can text people instead of talking to them. You don't have to be in the same room with people. You can multi-task instead of being present. People expect instant gratification. These are extraordinary changes in people's psyches and expectations, and the impact on society will be vast.

Why don't we see this as a Golden Era set of possibilities as opposed to walking around in the doom and gloom? An expanded documentary photography could still bring us to greater understandings and to a greater sense of who we are. That's the challenge. I think that is what we should be teaching in universities now. It is not just the history of photojournalism/documentary, but it's the challenge of photojournalism/documentary. That is where you need creativity, innovation, intuition, and ideas. We're too mired in our past and our past glories. If we could create something instead of all of us trying to be like the photographic heroes of the twentieth century, we could really move forward.

In the Field

Rondal Partridge

Dorothea Lange in the Field

In 1960, Dorothea Lange gave this account of her field experience photographing what would become known as the "Migrant Mother" to *Popular Photography* magazine, "I saw and approached the hungry and desperate mother, as if drawn by a magnet. I do not remember how I explained my presence or my camera to her, but I do remember she asked me no questions. I made five exposures, working closer and closer from the same direction. I did not ask her name or her history. She told me her age, that she was thirty-two. She said that they had been living on frozen vegetables from the surrounding fields, and birds that the children killed. She had just sold the tires from her car to buy food. There she sat in that lean-to tent with her children huddled around her, and seemed to know that my pictures might help her, and so she helped me. There was a sort of equality about it."

Dorothea Lange, one of the greatest documentary photographers in the history of the medium, was pivotal to the development of documentary photography and its fieldwork traditions. Rondal Partridge (known as Ron), the son of the legendary twentieth-century photographer Imogen Cunningham and a master photographer himself, started accompanying Dorothea Lange into the field before he had a driver's license, which he got at age 15 in 1933. His memory of his years in Dory's circle (as those close to Dorothea Lange called her) has been a large part of our understanding of her life and work. His recollections are razor sharp and the stories are memorable and sometimes surprising. One story Ron tells is

Dorothea Lange Photographing, 1930's
Library of Congress, Farm Security Adminsitration

how we almost lost Lange's iconic 1933 photo "White Angel Breadline." Ron explains in an animated conversation (and he is always animated) that the film was developed by photographer Roger Sturtevant, who had a studio in the same building as Dorothea's on Montgomery Street in San Francisco. Roger developed her Graflex cut film magazine holder, which according to Ron held a dozen sheets of cut 4 × 5 film. As Ron tells the story, "Roger said 'Dorothea, there are only 11 sheets in the box' and Dorothea said 'What? I loaded 12,' and they went back in the darkroom and felt inside the magazine and there was one sheet that got up under the leather film holder and never got out. Roger developed it and it was *the* 'White Angel Breadline.' It's a true story, it could have been gone forever. Open the back, oh, there's the film, just open the back and too bad."

Ron not only accompanied Lange but also made many memorable photos of her in the field, as well as his own images. He describes how in California's Central Valley he photographed Dory as she was suiting up with a field worker who was picking potatoes. "Dorothea's going off to pick potatoes to experience what her subject's world is about." Ron repeated over and over, "Dorothea was very, very conscious of how you approach people to make their image." Her sensitivity and ability to connect with her subject made her a master at documentary fieldwork.

We'd drive around and I had a driver's license and she didn't like to drive to photograph and she would say "Slow, slow, Ron, slow." I was a teenager, you know, and I wanna go barreling down and she would say "Slooow" and she'd drive me nutty, but I did go slow.

Dorothea always had a station wagon. Always. She was the first person to really glom onto Woodies, and she had the 1934 Ford square Woody station wagon. It had four doors. We put in a tripod and camera cases. She had a Graflex and the Zeis Jewel, it was a 9 × 12 cm and it had a 3¼ × 4¼ back with a single Eastman film pack. You could pack an awful lot of film into the field with little weight and that's important. We very rarely carried extra raw film. In those days, people used film sparsely. It was a Depression mentality. Twenty-four films could last you three or four days, now it's three or four minutes. We also put in a sleeping bag and coffee-making equipment.

We would take off from Berkeley in the Woody and we wouldn't get very far. We'd get to Walnut Creek, California, and something would appear. We would get to Pittsburgh, California, usually and that was it, and then we'd go up the river road. Now it's all people, but it was wild open country then, and Dorothea had with Maynard Dixon (her first husband and a renowned Western landscape painter) this great love of open space. She didn't photograph it much, she didn't spend too much time on photographing landscape, but when she did, she did it perfectly. Then we would get to Sacramento and it's "Hey, let's go up this road," you know. You'd see it and go out river road. See a tent and we'd stop and we'd wander around, and "How are the walnuts?" "The walnuts fine this year" "Are you going to be picking walnuts?" "Well, yeah, I'm waiting for the walnuts" "And, do you have any other source of income before the walnuts come, because they're not going to be for a couple months?" "No, the county's been here and they've offered me a block of cheese which I took. My wife doesn't want me to take it," etc., and things like that. And then she would photograph them. Dorothea never took a picture unaware. She never went in and took pictures. She never started out taking pictures, and she didn't come out with a camera. If she did come out with a camera, she put it on a tripod and wandered around without it, so people knew what she was about to do. She wouldn't take that many pictures. She would take ten or fifteen photos a day. One or two on a shot. We made East-man Kodak rich.

We photographed simple things: trees, crops, contract laborers from India, and gangs of Pakistanis. We didn't get into the Depression stuff until you hit the main valley near Sacramento, the "Hoovervilles" (shanty towns of unemployed). In Tulare County they had turkey farms. The soil is not very good, and the poor people always end up on the poor soil, isn't that funny? The rich people buy them out and they move over, the rich get richer, and they're still gettin' richer. And the poor are still poor.

Dorothea was very, very conscious of how you approach people and she always said that she put on her mask and walked about being nonjudgmental, said it was the "cloak of invisibility." She did this with everybody. The kids would come to be photographed at a camp. They saw the camera around her neck, and she would set up another camera on a tripod. The camera on the tripod was a come-on. The kids would gather round and ask for their picture to be taken. She was photographing views and they would come up closer and she snapped shots. Then they would run to tell their parents, and she would follow.

That's how she met the adults: the kids go home, she goes walking around, and then they say, "Oh there's that lady," and she goes over and she's "in." That's the way Dorothea handled it.

We went out for two weeks usually, and we would live very frugally. Before motels they were called motor courts. They cost between a dollar and four dollars a day and the dollar ones were pretty much at the end of the row. The linoleum on the floor was cracked and people had pissed in the corners and there was usually a shelf with a little sink and you put a gas stove or something on the shelf and made your own coffee. Usually they had a double bed with wire springs. Dory got the bed and I slept on the floor. The food, we made our own. Usually we made breakfast in the cabin or opened something up. But we would sometimes buy a hot turkey plate, which consisted of turkey, potatoes and gravy, and a side dish of gray overcooked vegetables. But we ate a lot of just hand stuff through the day. We didn't stop to eat lunch, didn't stop.

We sometime did ten miles in a day max. We also got tired of poverty. Poverty is debilitating. We'd get back to a motel and face the next day with more sadness, heat, dirt, flies in babies' eyes and stuff, and we'd say "What the hell," and we'd go up in the foothills to hide out. We'd go up in the Sierra to a hotel where it was cooler and Dorothea would find something to photograph. It could be a lumberman chopping down a tree or something, she'd photograph him. Unrelated to her job with the government, but we did trips to reservoirs and Big Bear Lake and into Hollywood. Once we went into Los Angeles and to the orange groves. I don't think she photographed much, but we did one or two photographs, and then when we got a little rested, the next day we'd go back over to Tehachapi and back into that maelstrom, which was terrible.

I think the main thing was that Dorothea knew more about her subjects than Roy Stryker, her boss and head of the Information Division of the Farm Security Administration. She knew more about what to photograph than Stryker. She knew more about the value of these photographs. You look at the series of Madonna pictures, the "Migrant Mother," (Paul Taylor was with her, not I), and they approached from a distance, and they were talking and the children were at it and Dorothea knew all the time what she was doing. Then Stryker objected to the thumb in the image. Well, somebody said it was Paul's thumb, nobody knows. Stryker made so much noise about that thumb that

Dorothea gave it to photographer Roger Sturtevant, and Roger had these abrasive elements that Eastman used to sell for dodging, and he ground the emulsion and the finger out.

Dory made notes in the field. Every time we went back to the car, Dorothea had a spiral notebook. She would write impressions, background, future, what's going on, what these people did, where they came from, where they were going, and what their finances were.

We would photograph, talk, and find out where people came from. Her notes were as important as her photographs. When we would come back to the car after a very short time she would say "Quiet," and she'd take her notes down and she'd remember the whole conversation, "And if I could get my hands on an acre of land, I'd dig it with my fingers," and she got the essence out of the whole conversation. She wrote these down and sometimes they were long and pointed and sometimes they were short, like "It's a fight between the belly button and the backbone for a bean." There is brilliance in those notes.

She felt exhilarated and alive in the field because her mind was always working, always, always. She was very calm with the superintendents and the people along the road. The people whom she hated were DiGiorgio Farms. DiGiorgio had barbed wire fences, observation towers, and big squares of almonds, peaches, and fruit. The workers were bonded to the land by debt. That's a nice way to say it. They were enslaved, and there was nothing else for them to do. They had to have milk for the children. They had to have it. They went in and knew they were getting screwed. Everybody knew it. And they went in and they couldn't get out, and we couldn't get in, and that was a sad thing. When she was out in the field she'd ask, "Oh, have you worked with DiGiorgio? Do you know about them? Have you heard about that? Have you any relatives in there? Have they been able to get out?" just little questions, you know, she just asked little questions.

Yes sir. "I'm from the gov'mnt and I'm here to make photographs to show the gov'mnt what's going on in California." She wouldn't say gov-ern-ment, and she wouldn't say, "I represent." But, "I'm from the gov'mnt, and I'm here to make photographs, as you can see" and she did, to show people what it was like in California, or Arizona, or wherever she went. "Let's see what's going on." or "The gov'mnt wants to know." And she always did her little speech and she was very modest and very quiet, not distinguished looking really. She was just a little lady, a lady photographer for God's sake, you know. But we never distributed candy and we never sucked up to the people in any way at all.

Once we paid a guy off. We were going up to Sacramento shooting in the Hooverville. There was a road up a levy, somewhere north of Sacramento, not far, ten miles or so, and we went up the road in order to back down and make a U-turn. I was driving in the Woodie. And I drove up by the river and there were the hobo camps. We were not interested. Dorothea rarely photographed hobo camps, lone single men camps. As we backed down, a hobo was standing in the path, and he rushed and threw himself under the back of the car and attempted to get run over. I heard a noise, looked in the rearview mirror, and saw him flip. I put on my brake on the gravel, and *eek!*, there's a guy under my car. The tires did not hit him. Well, he got up and he was burned by gravel, scratched by gravel, and he was screaming, "You tried to kill me! Give me money and I'll go away." I said "Dory, uh-uh, uh-uh." Dory said "Well, you know, Ron, sometimes, sometimes you have to," and my memory is that she peeled off two dollar bills. It was a lot of money. But we paid the guy.

We never developed film in the field. But we took a lot of test shot. Most of the film that she had in the later trips was sent back to Washington. Stryker insisted on processing the stock. The first one she sent back was processed so badly that after that I did the processing. Dorothea and I would do it together in the darkroom, mixing pyro, and developing. I would hang 'em up and dry 'em, and then Dorothea and I would print them. She hated darkrooms. She said "Ron, when I was working in San Francisco, I couldn't stand being in the darkroom more than three hours in a day." She would say this to me at eleven thirty at night when we'd gotten to the darkroom at eight in the morning and we were still in there processing and printing. We'd sometimes be side by side, she using one enlarger and I another one. There are two printers in this world that impress me; Ansel Adams and Dorothea Lange. Dorothea's pictures always have warmth and a sense of roundness and a relation between the highlight, not just brilliant highlights and shadows. The prints had a beautiful sense of roundness.

Reflecting on all of the experiences of my life, I see clearly that photography is a tool like a book is a tool. Among all of the photographers I have known, the one who did it best and had the most influence and whose work benefited society hands down was Dorothea Lange.

Don McCullin

Vietnam: The Battle of Hue, 1968

D on McCullin is one of the great war and conflict photographers of our time, often mentioned in the same breath with Robert Capa. His powerful photographs record human suffering and war-torn countries from images of shell-shocked and dying soldiers in Vietnam, to starving skeletal children in Biafran refugee camps, from the monsoons on the Indian continent to the conflict in Northern Ireland. He has skirted death (in 1968, his Nikon camera stopped a bullet intended for him) and recorded these tragedies with emotion and clarity. His images are beyond the traditional press conflict photo that we are so use to seeing. Their shocking lucidity continues to haunt long after the moment. His work proved so painful and memorable that in 1982 he was forbidden by the British government to cover the Falklands War.

McCullin, working with the brilliant picture editor Michael Rand at the *Sunday Times Magazine,* created amazingly powerful photo essays through the '60s and '70s, that humanely portrayed the world's crisis with depth and authority. His photos have become an iconic record of these troubled times, and generations of photographers have been influenced by his work and exploits, which have been published in numerous books and magazine essays.

He has lived with what he describes as his crimes, his pains, and guilt. He has said that he "used to chase wars like a drunk chasing a can of lager." The title of his monograph and masterwork *Sleeping with Ghosts* came from his realization that he was haunted by his work. "The photos

Don McCullin
Shell shocked U.S. Marine, Tet Offensive
Hue, Vietnam, 1968
© Don McCullin/Contact Press Images

were actually right down at the other end of my house, because my house is like a railway train. It's a great three cottages joined together. Right down at the extreme end from where I sleep are all of my negatives, three or four thousand prints of war and landscape, but mostly war, pain, and suffering. When I go to bed at night, these things must come out and have a merry dance. Even to this day, there's a contamination. I feel the house is contaminated, almost haunted, by the energy of all these horrible pictures."

McCullin's bravery, or insanity as he sometimes describes it, includes a remarkable and brilliant use of light, most often haunting, a frugal use of film, and waiting for that moment when the essence of the human condition explodes before his eyes, recording for us man's inhumanity to man.

Vietnam was in the early '60s and was getting more and more attention. The first picture I remember was, 1963, a picture of a burning monk. It was a quite shocking image; it was done by an Associated Press writer Malcolm Brown. He happened to have a camera and he took this picture and it was such a powerful picture that it started raising hairs on the back of everyone's neck.

Then we got more pictures from Vietnam, and of course being a young photographer, I wanted to get in on this Vietnam story, whatever was going on in this weird country several thousand miles from where I lived. I went into the *Sunday Times*, where I worked, and said, "Listen, I want to go to Vietnam." They said "Well, we're not interested in that, really." I said "Look, we've got to make a commitment." There was a big anti-Vietnam feeling building in our office and lots of left-wing minds. I wasn't politically motivated. I was too rough around the edges. I said to Michael Rand, my art director, that I'd like to get a (case on?). He said "I don't know, I don't know if that's what the readers want to see." I said, "Well, we should be doing it." He didn't say, "No, get lost, forget it." So, I kept coming in. It took me about ten days to get him to say yes or no. And he finally said "Alright, go do it, get lost, get out of my face." They gave me 400 pounds and the air ticket from the business side of things, and off I went.

I drew film from the *Sunday Times*. I always used to take thirty rolls of film, black and white, and I took a few rolls of color on this occasion. It was Ektachrome, which I detested. English Ektachrome wasn't like American Ektachrome. It was crap. It never gave any presence to color. [If it was a color magazine, Michael Rand would say, "Oh by the way, give this some color." He was begging, because he knew what a rebel I was about black and white.]

So I gathered my few things together. I had three Nikon F cameras, two exposure meters, which were very difficult for combat. You had to take the back off the Nikons to load. I use to lie on the floor under heavy fire, on my back, place everything on my chest like a table—this is under fire—and almost like Braille loading and unloading. It was all done by the fingertips and the feeling. There were times like Catherine Leroy (Vietnam War photographer) said, you couldn't pop your head up. It was a very stupid camera for one thing, since you had to slide it off, and doing things like that under fire was dangerous. But it was the workhorse of photojournalism. All it needed was to have a hinge in the back. I had a 135mm small telephoto lens and a 28mm lens. They were the only two lenses I had. I had a military bag for the camera. I've always been fond of military things, like military shirts, kind of safari-like attitude. You needed more than a safari shirt for Vietnam. You needed a flak jacket. The first time I went to Vietnam I'd never had a flak jacket.

Suddenly I found myself on this Air France flight which was the very last plane trying to get into Saigon as the Tet offensive exploded. It did not touch down in Saigon. Can you imagine my apprehension? The plane overflew, because the airport was under attack and I landed in Hong Kong. I went into a deep depression imagining what I was missing! I was in Hong Kong, walking the streets of Hong Kong listening to the radio broadcast. I was in a hotel. I wasn't sleeping with all my anxiety. I'd sold myself on this big trip only to be locked out. If Michael Rand, the art director, had only given me a "Yes" three or four days earlier, I would have been in the battle for Saigon when the Viet Cong first struck. I saw Eddie Adams's picture in Hong Kong. Can you imagine! I was thinking to myself if I'd had a gun I'd have put it to my own head. You can imagine the terrible frustration walking the streets of Hong Kong. It was raining and it was cold. I looked at the light. I knew the light would be the same in Vietnam. My light. Gray, raining, no sun, perfect for great dramatic pictures. I kept going to the British Airways office, saying "Any chance, any chance?" and they said, "Airport closed." Of course it would be closed. You know, it could be closed for two weeks, if you think about it. I was in Hong Kong for five days—I was in such a distraught situation. Finally I went to the British Airways office, and they said "Flight tomorrow." So I managed to get on the flight to Saigon, which was only about an hour away, and I arrived in Saigon.

I got to my hotel, and the plan originally was to go to the north of Vietnam. I immediately got accredited and the next morning jumped on the flight to Danang and to the press center. I handed over a letter of accreditation from my newspaper, and accredited cards and press cards and things. You got accredited, it took a couple of hours, and then you wound up with your Mac V card, which gave you the assimilated rank of major. It was a high priority, which meant you could go to the airport, demand a seat on the plane, and if there were no seat, you could have someone thrown off. I don't think to this day any journalist ever did that. When I got to the Danang press center, I thought I was going to Khe Sanh.

In Khe Sanh the enemy pinned the American army down for weeks as a diversionary tactic to allow a North Vietnamese regiment to slip in and go for the real prize: the city of Hue. When I was at the press center, I looked up as I was arranging my travel, and the man I was eating with said "Oh look, look, look, there's *Life* photographer David Douglas Duncan!" And I looked up and I said, "My God, I can't win!" You know, I've been shut out and there's Duncan just coming out of Khe Sanh and you knew he was dripping with rolls of brilliant film. Do you know what Duncan did? He flew all the way to New York in his fatigues and went into the *Life* office. I thought, wow, what a silly thing to do.

I knew right away when I saw the haggard-looking face of David Douglas Duncan, I was out of business. I was so depressed—what was I going to tell the *Sunday Times?* Then this fellow said, "Well if you don't mind me saying so, the Fifth Marine Battalion is going to assault the Hue Citadel. Why don't you go with them? Would you like to go?" I said, "Please, please!" Of course, you know, I could see this as the only way out, but it had its dangers. As a photographer, when you get on a story and it's late—you're late—you have to take the added extra risk. That's where you have to really get smart. You know everyone is scoring left, right, and center. Eddie Adams got the great picture, Duncan got the second great pictures, and where are you going to fit into all this? This is the danger: to catch up to these people, you take the most appalling and foolish risks. I had to go back to England and justify being late, but it wasn't my fault I was late. I could have been early! I could have had it all! But oh no, because the office took their time, I had to then find myself in this position of the risk-taking business, which war is anyway, whether you're late or you're early.

I was under the Marine press corps, and they were going to truck in. I jumped into one of these trucks and then we went but very slowly. I remember it was dark and it was rainy, and I thought, fantastic. I knew I could shoot at 125 at f/8 in that kind of light with Tri-X. I knew it, I knew my exposures. I was going into a deep kind of psychotic preparation and I was so excited! Because I thought I was being saved.

We reached the south bank of the city of Hue, separated north and south by the Perfume River. The city was waiting for us. They were waiting for us. It was so overcast. I spent the night on the southern part of the city. I knew the Marines were going to go by amphibian landing craft the next morning. We just bedded down in a headquarters, which was huge and looked like an old granary. You find a space, that's your space. There was never a pillow. I used to take my boots off and cross them, and sleep on the soft bits. I used to sleep almost in a fetal position with my cameras so that nobody could steal them. I mean, who was going to steal my cameras when I'm amongst American soldiers? Nobody! I had a kind of a fretful night. I wasn't really sleeping, I was drifting. I was anxious because I was behind on the story, because I was aware this might happen, this might not happen. I was actually playing games with my mind. I didn't need that, I needed a good night's sleep. I scrounged some nourishment which came in the shape of what they call C rations, food in a tin. People usually gave me the things in the C rations that they didn't want, and it was always ham and lima beans. I loved them!

Photographers like Eddie Adams and Larry Boroughs came from very powerful organizations. Associated Press (AP) and Time-Life. If you said, "I'm with Time-Life" to the American authorities in Saigon, "I want to do this, I want to do that," they'd get you there quicker than you can flick your fingers or flash your eyelids. Time-Life was, for them the ultimate goal. The cover of *Time* or *Life* magazine was the jewel in the crown. The rest of us, who were foreigners and outsiders, never had the same impact. Nevertheless, we were never normally refused. The Army guys looked at me with some kind of curiosity—not suspicion, curiosity—why is he here? Soldiers would come up and say, "Excuse me, sir,". . . nobody ever addresses you as "sir" in my country, in England. It's part of this cultural thing. "Excuse me, sir, you don't have a weapon. Would you like a weapon?" I said, "No, I don't want a weapon, I'm not here for any purpose other than as a photographer, and secondly, it's against the rules of the Geneva Conventions." I said this in a sarcastic way, for journalists and press people do carry weapons. The soldiers did look upon us in a curious way.

When you wake up in the morning, you're stiff, you're hungry, and you're anxious. First thing in the morning, you do the human functions and get something to eat. You smell coffee, and then you go scrounging. That's the part of my life that I don't like, you know, becoming a beggar. I had these accreditations, which entitled me to eat in officers' messes. There are no officers' messes under those circumstances. You're in the combat field, it's every man for himself, and so you scrounge. I found coffee, but it's not what I drink. I drink tea.

So after all these things, you have to just get on with the photography. But you know, you have to move mountains before you can even take your camera out of the bag. That's the funny thing about being a photographer. It's all going on, it's all happening, but you have to get permission, you have to get there. I said to the colonel of this battalion, "What's going to happen now?" He said, "Well, first of all, we've got to secure the southern part of the city. So we've got to send patrols out. Why don't you go with the patrollers?" So I followed the patrollers, and it was a bit boring and a bit dull. I was with these great big beefy men with all their stuff, and they're swaggering around because there was no gunfire at that point. The whole city was dead and quiet. The storm was waiting to come and hit us.

We went through the suburbs in the southern part of Hue. They went into this house and I waited outside. This black soldier came out and I said, "What's going on?" He said "Dead gook." Then he came out and walked past me. I thought, I'll go and have a look inside. It must be a dead man in there, a dead North Vietnamese. I went inside, there weren't any dead North Vietnamese. There was a mosquito net, which was silently shrouding something. There was a candle at the head of this mosquito net, which I thought was curiously dangerous. When I looked gently inside the mosquito net I found it hard to find anything. It was strange. Like what's going on here? There was a child lying there, dead. A little boy with a shirt on. I remember all these details to this day. We're talking about decades ago. These details never leave my mind, they're forever imprinted. I was angry with this soldier because I thought, how dare he call a little boy a dead gook, who had been killed at war and abandoned by his own parents in their haste for their own safety in their own home. Why should this tragedy have visited this little boy's life and that family's life? I thought, excuse me for saying this, fuck you! I don't want to be with you people who talk about children who are dead, as gooks.

They went on ravaging and kicking doors in of people's homes, and I went back to the command post. The colonel was there, and he said "How'd you get on?" I said, "Oh, fine, fine." I didn't make a fuss about it. Then I asked, "When are we going to cross?" He said, "We're going to cross today."

The Fifth Marine Battalion was assembling down by a kind of jetty. I saw a very tall military-looking officer smoking a cigar with lots of gold on his epaulets. I assumed that he was in charge. I went down and said "Good morning, sir," and he said, "What can I do for you?" I said, "I'd just like to know where the loading is going to take place." He said, "What has it got to do with you?" I said, "Well, I'm going across." He said, "You're not going across on any of my boats." I pulled out my card which gave me the assimilated rank of major. I said to him, "Well, I am accredited. I am allowed to do this." He said, "Not on my boats, you're not. You can go away."

I'm not very good at arguing with people, and I could see right away I was wasting my time with this fool of a man. But I did look out of the corner of my eye and saw that the Vietnamese troops were also loading. I went away from this officer. He had this fixed stare that he wasn't even looking at me when he spoke to me. It was arrogant. The mere fact that he had this kind of stare that was going somewhere else, I used to my advantage. I slipped behind him and went the direction I came. I swung back around to where the Vietnamese soldiers were loading, and I said to the Vietnamese captain who was there, "Can I hitch a lift?" He said, "Oh, come on, come on!" So I got onto the boat, and then they pulled the ramp up. We were fully loaded, then the boat started making its way down the Perfume River. As we went down the river, I passed this arrogant naval officer standing there. I stood up, and gave him the finger, and that was the most satisfying thing. I got to the other side, and I wanted to be with the Americans. I felt more secure with the Americans because I didn't speak the language of the Vietnamese, so I split from them.

I immediately started hearing gunfire. I went toward the gunfire, gingerly, because it's no good running into it and getting yourself killed right away. I could see groups of Marines taking cover. I saw a group of Marines leaning over somebody. It was one of their first casualties. This man had been hit in the face with a bullet. He had his face bandaged and he was oozing saliva mixed with blood from this tremendous wound. I thought, well, here we go. Here we go, let's start shooting pictures. Let's do the job. And I looked at him, and I put my camera up to my eye, and he immediately spoke to me with his eyes, because he couldn't with his mouth. It must have caused him an enormous amount of pain, because he looked at me with his eyes, almost saying no to me. No. So I put my camera down, put it away, and I went away. I've always tried to seek consent when I take pictures, because you don't have the right to take pictures. You don't have the right to trespass on people who are already suffering. I went away and thought, don't get too upset about this. This looks like a situation where you're going to have lots of opportunity.

The soldiers I was with were making their way slowly down the road, doing things I wouldn't particularly approve of. They were dragging tables out of houses and setting up M-16 machine guns on the tables, totally exposing themselves, foolish! I thought, these are trained soldiers! What in the hell are they doing, exposing themselves straight down the middle of the road with a table, and all standing there as if they were at some game fair and turkey shoot? They were just begging for trouble. I was amazed that their senior ranks didn't say, "What in the hell are you doing? You've got to stop this. You're going to draw fire."

They moved on down the road, and by that time, nightfall was coming. At nightfall we looked for shelter, because we started receiving mortar shells from the other side. Then we entered this eerie night of American star shells. They were fired by mortars, and then they would be parachuted down very slowly, making a very strange noise, going *vu-vu-vu-vuvuvu* and petering out. They would be up lighting the area in a kind of bronze, kind of a yellowish light. They were sinister. They would shadow things and you'd see, kind of—weirdness.

We started being shelled by the North Vietnamese, mostly by RPG rockets, which means an awful explosion. At the same time, phantom jets were dropping napalm, and they have to drop it behind us, to get it in front of us. I used to see these canisters making yet another sinister tumbling noise, and I used to say to myself "Keep going, keep going," because you didn't want an accident. Many accidents in wars, you know. Shells are always falling short on their own lines and killing their own people, and then the idea of a huge napalm canister tumbling over your head. You say, "Keep going, please keep going." Then we were getting offshore shelling from massive naval vessels, dropping these huge shells just in front of the gridlines. Again, you know, any mess-up like that would wipe you out.

You were worried about the enemy, you were worried about the good guys. Quite frankly, the enemy was not my enemy. I was totally impartial to their cause and the American Army's cause. I knew what the Army wanted and I knew what the North Vietnamese people wanted. They wanted some kind of success, victory, and survival.

The next day, we had some shelling, and it progressively got heavier each day. I was with a Marine and we ran and got into a dugout, this hole in the ground. But the funny thing about the hole in the ground, it was obviously the place of an entrenchment that someone had dug horridly, but it wasn't. Something was weird about it. There was a terrible smell coming from it, and also, it was soft. We quickly realized that we were sitting and crouching on the stomach of a dead North Vietnamese soldier. We were compressing his stomach and it was probably the excretion of his body's fluids and matters. There was this terrible appalling smell, plus the beginnings of his decomposition. We quickly vacated that dugout under fire and shelling and found somewhere else separately. Then it started becoming grotesquely like *All Quiet on the Western Front*. You were embracing bodies. You were quietly praying for survival, and this is only the second day.

I didn't have a motor winder. I was shooting single frames, which is the best form of discipline in my opinion. The actual motor winder is a fantastic thing, but you can still do the job without the motor winder. In a way, I think it's almost better, because you have time to compose your pictures. All my life I've never used the light meter in any given camera, and I've never used any cameras that became automatic. I've always been a manual photographer. My biggest problem then, of course, was I had to get up and use the exposure meter. I've always had this saying that I didn't want to be killed only for people to find that my exposures were wrong on the film they found on me. So, it makes sense, doesn't it? I wasn't a very intelligent educated man, but I had a streetwise sense of trying to survive. Common sense is the best piece of education you can ever operate under.

I was slowly moving with the soldiers, bodies littered everywhere. Bodies started to appear more and more. I started seeing soldiers do funny things. Within two or three days, the soldiers started aging. You sleep rough, you don't wash, you don't bathe, you're not particularly having a great cuisine experience. It's the beginning of the breakdown of you, physically and mentally. You're sleeping next to dead bodies, within range of dead bodies—the whole thing is not normal. Then on top of that, you're having these life experiences of dying, not just dying, that might be a quick way out, you know. I saw terrible injuries. When I look back after forty years of warfare, I think, my God, aren't I lucky, I've got a jawbone left? Aren't I lucky, I haven't got an eye or half my face missing? But then, I was so involved in the photography that my main problem was, get the exposure right, get the composition right, and get the picture right. because I had to try and do all of those things in the space of a split second.

I slept under a table every night. Someone said to me, "You should get yourself a helmet. You should get yourself a flak jacket." And I said, "How am I going to do that?" He said, "Well, go down to the first aid tent, down to the end of town." So I doubled back down to the end of town. I found a mountain of discarded equipment—helmets, flak jackets, with different people's names on them. I became like Joseph, the man who wore so many colors in the Bible. I had somebody's helmet with somebody's name on it, somebody's flak jacket. They'd been injured and taken away. I was what you might call recycling stuff to keep myself alive. I had something on my helmet: Kalamazoo. I didn't even know where that was, must be in America somewhere. Then there was the sign of the ace of spades from the cards, and then on the back of my flak jacket there was something else. But I didn't care. It was like life support for me. There's nothing worse in war than to have a naked head when there's thousands of rounds of ammunition flying around. Then I got back into the battle.

One time this soldier and I suddenly looked down together, and we both said "GRENADE!" We ran in different directions. He was a bit big and lanky. He wasn't like me, I was fast and I was down on the floor in a depression, and then this huge explosion. I got hit with all the rocks and stones, and my leg was the only part I couldn't cover up. I literally thought my leg had been blown off. I started shouting, "Corpsman, corpsman!" I looked at my leg and thought, that's funny, there's no blood. Then I realized it was the stones, which can hurt you. Then I looked over and saw him and I saw all this blood coming out of his head. It could have been me. It's very strange, because when you think of war, there's only so many ways a human body can respond. People don't think about that, you know.

I tell you something, when you're running with a helmet on, it's not easy to keep it on. It wobbles. Then you're running with one hand, it's all very disturbing. The flak jacket was a welcome relief for me. It doesn't stop a bullet, but it kept me warm at night. I put my head in the helmet as a pillow, and I took my flak jacket off and laid it over me as a blanket.

When I look at the photos from my time there now, I can still remember what was happening as I took most shots. For instance, there's a picture of a soldier I took throwing a grenade. I had to anticipate that man throwing it. One shot at 250 at f/8. Everybody who sees the picture immediately thinks the man has been struck like the Robert Capa picture. I'm pleased to say he wasn't. He was struck, but several seconds after this. You could see the grenade going. You could see the kind of terrain we were working in. I had to stand up for that picture. I just had to anticipate his movement. I look upon this picture as a great javelin-throwing athlete, and within moments, he's been brought down, destroyed, in tears and pain.

My photograph of the Marine sniper with the binoculars is called "The Eye of War." The eyes are so intense, but also exposure-wise, difficult, because you had to get under the helmet, no flash. I would never use flash, and I hardly did in my whole life as a photographer.

There is a photograph that I took of an injured soldier that really embodies the pain of war. His back is against a brick wall, his helmet is off, his arms are draped over the shoulders of two fellow Marines who are supporting his slumped body. The soldier's listless face is looking up to the heavens. I align this to the crucifixion of Christ. I was just photographing and I think I only got one frame. I said to them, "Bring him over, bring him over." Then they brought him over, and I took my cameras off and I put them down on the side of the wall and I put him on my shoulder. I got his arms around my neck and I carried him away from the battle. I stumbled at one point and I thought both of us were going to fall down and increase his pain. I put him on my back. I was 31, and I was strong. I arched myself over to ease the burden of the weight, and of course, every movement was killing his legs. He had a bullet through both legs. I got him back to the compound and there was a Marine colonel there. He was a man from the southern states of America. His name was Byron. He looked at me and he said, "Outstanding." I was embarrassed, really. But from that moment on, I was one of them. The soldiers would come up and say, "Have you eaten, sir?" And I'd say "No," and I was lying. My backpack was full of ham and lima beans. I was always afraid of being hungry. I was always afraid of waking up and not having anything to eat, because food, when you're young, is your energy. I found men opening tins of C rations and giving me the best ones, like the fruit cocktail.

One day I found I'd been sleeping a few meters away from a dead North Vietnamese soldier. There's a photo of it. After two Marines came along and tried to find some souvenirs from his body, they discarded all his personal effects. Then when they went away, I took the liberty of trespassing on this man's personal effects and trying to make a history of his life by showing what he was. I actually moved objects, which is one of the only times I've done that. I had to, and I did it because I felt it was significant to make some connection with this man's sacrifice and become this man's voice. Because he was dead, he was not going to be able to tell me anything. Those pictures tell you something. They say he's a human being

One of the biggest mistakes I ever made in my life as a young photographer was running away thinking I had the story. You must never think you've got the last drop of juice out of a lemon. If you can drop a ton weight on that lemon, you're absolutely sure you've got the last drop. I wanted the pith, the juice, and the skin of this story. This was the one story it was tempting to run away from. By the time I got ten or twelve rolls of film, I wanted to run away. I kept saying, "No, no, no, there's more to come, there's more, there's more." By the time the twelve days were up, I knew I'd got the best of it, because things started slowing down. The North Vietnamese by then were vanishing very quickly, just leaving behind, sadly, their dead comrades.

Twelve days, it's over? I'm finished with my film, I need to get back and tell the story. By then I'm anxious about my film, by then the casualties were up to seventy killed, and a couple hundred wounded in this battalion. I said to myself, "This is it." I wanted to get back, and I wanted to see my film. Can you imagine not having processed your film after twelve days? I wanted to see the first day's film.

I went back to the evacuation areas where they were taking the wounded and the bodies. There was a padre. He had offered me the Last Rites several days before and I declined them. I had been in a room full of wounded and tired men, about four or five days into it, and the padre came and said, "Excuse me, gentlemen, but can I offer you the Last Rites? Because tomorrow, you know, could be very heavy." He frightened me and I was afraid. I thought, don't encourage death, you know. He was trying to respect it. I said "No thank you, Father." On the last day when I decided that was it, I've done my thing, Catherine Leroy, the other photographer, and I were both walking back toward this evacuation area, and when we got there and the padre said, "Do you people want a lift?" I said, "We'll just wait, Father." He said, "Take my place." I said, "I couldn't possibly do that." One of the chaplains had been killed in the battle. He was shot by a sniper in the back of the head, and this padre had survived, I said "No, I can't take your place." He said, "Please take my place. You'll give me enormous pleasure." I said "Okay." I was mad, I was totally insane. I was unwashed for two weeks. I was wearing the same underwear and the same clothes. The C rations that you eat for two weeks don't do your intestines a great deal of good. Piled on top of the experience of fear and shock, your stomach is in a bad way, your mind is gone. I said to the padre, "Can I offer you my apologies for the way I treated you the other night?" He said, "Don't even say a word about it. You didn't offend me at all."

I flew all the way to Danang, and I arrived at the press center. I was a man who was lost, a man who had lost his soul, who lost his direction. I think I actually looked like the man in that picture, the shell-shocked man. I had to come down from this strange place I had been. I took off all my vile, filthy underwear and my combat things. Someone supplied me with some fresh combat things and clothes as a gift. After all this, I lay in bed. I didn't know whether I was sleeping or not. The bed was spinning around, my head was spinning around. I was in chaos. Then I got the C130 flight down to Danang, still not talking to anybody, still looking weird. I was looking at fresh-faced soldiers coming up to take over. I was not a human being. I arrived in Danang and I went to Air France. I booked my ticket. I got on the plane, and it lifted off, and I was still clinging to my film.

The Air France plane flew to Paris. I then contacted the *Sunday Times*. For two weeks I had not spoken to my editors. I use to leave London and think, okay, there's nothing I can say to them, all they want is film. Don't bother with any trashy prickle prattle of conversations. I informed them I was coming by telex. They knew I was coming, They said, "Go to Paris, you'll be met." I went to the lab where Henri Cartier-Bresson gets his film developed. They took my film, and they processed it in an Ilford developer which was an unforgiving developer, it was tough. In a way, I think they may have chosen the right developer. I wouldn't have done that. I always used to process in D76.

To my astonishment, most of my exposures were right, throughout the whole lot. Very few misfires. All the very best pictures were exposed properly. Then I grabbed the film and the contacts and went to London. I went to the *Sunday Times* office the next day after I'd been to see my wife and children. They ordered the prints and I made the prints. I'd already marked them off. I had this amazing privilege. I use to edit all my own film. I use to mark my best edits and give them to the editor and say, "This is my story." Rand would say, "Okay, looks good to me, give us the prints." I went home, made the prints in my little darkroom. They were done on 10 × 12s. The original prints are that big, many of which have now been stolen.

In the office I stood there and watched them do the layout. Rand said, "Right, okay, we'll open on this, we'll do that, here's the cover. Blah blah blah." You couldn't have done that ten or fifteen years ago with an editor. I had this amazing privilege. "You know," he said to me, "this is really good, this is really strong, now piss off." He was pleased.

It was a story of survival. I survived that tremendous battle. But at the same time, I managed to survive my professionalism. I persuaded them to send me. I could have come back empty-handed. That would have been the end of me. When you say to editors "I want to do this,

I can do this," and you can't come up with the goods, you're in serious trouble. They're not going to trust you anymore. My photography came from my experience, my spirit, my emotions, and my eyes, of course, which are all part of the same family. What I used to take pictures were my eyes and my emotions and my feelings. That's what it was all about.

Bill Owens

Suburbia and a Passion for Seeing His World

I n the mid-1960s when Bill Owens was working in Jamaica and the West Indies as a Peace Corps volunteer, a photographer came to photograph the area. He saw what a photographer does and thought, "That's me. I can do that." In 1966, once he finished his commitment with the Peace Corps, he knew that he wanted to be a photographer. He enrolled at San Francisco State University and took a visual anthropology class from John Collier Jr., who had written a book on the subject and had worked as a photographer during the Farm Security Administration (FSA).

In 1968 Owens landed a job as a news photographer for the *Livermore Independent* in Livermore, California. At the end of the '60s, "everyone was moving to the suburbs. You could buy a house for $2,000, with only $99 down—a two-car garage, a swimming pool, and a Kenmore washer and dryer, all of the things that come with the good life." Owens saw that this new generation of suburbanites was far ahead of him in material consumption and that it was going to be a while before he caught up. But he slowly became disenchanted at what he saw and wanted to document the materialism of the new suburban culture instead of take part in it.

He cobbled together some free time in his schedule and secured a grant for expenses. His photographs, taken between his daily newspaper assignments and through the contacts he made on the job, were published in the book *Suburbia* in 1972 and gained him much notoriety. But the book and his efforts to build on its success weren't paying the bills.

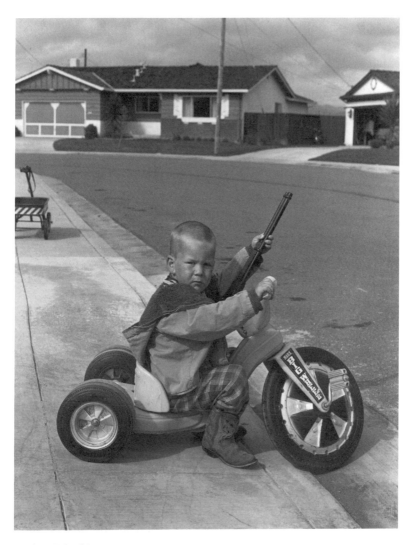

Ritchie, Suburbia, 1972
© Bill Owens

Deciding to branch out, he tried his hand at self-publishing, even writing a book *Publish Your Photo Book: A Guide to Self-Publishing* in 1979.

In 1982 Owens sold most of his camera equipment and tucked the photographs from *Suburbia* under his bed. He still needed to make a living and it was time to try something new. Since his college years he had dabbled in home beer brewing, so he parlayed his hobby as a brewer into one of California's first brew pubs (Buffalo Bill's in Hayward, California) and happily made beer for many years.

Almost 30 years later, his early work was rediscovered by collectors and museum, and Owens returned to photography. *Suburbia* was reprinted to much acclaim. He had numerous exhibitions and reemerged, this time with a digital camera around his neck. Many of his early books have also been republished in new expanded editions. No subject is too ordinary for his camera, a close up of Jell-O or porta potties against the western landscape. As his website says, "Every now and then Bill Owens takes a picture."

As a young adult, I knew I wanted to change the world. I was upset when I came back to America from my stay in Jamaica and the West Indies with the Peace Corps and saw all of the affluence and no concern about what was really the problem. The problem really isn't the poor people, it's not the Eskimos, it's not the Indians. The problem is middle-class people and their consumption.

I had gotten married in 1963 and we had a baby. When we moved to suburbia, people my age already had two cars, a swimming pool, and washer and dryer. It was going to take us a while to catch up. I was just appalled that we lived in such a material society and decided I wanted to document that. I wanted people to become aware of the materialism of the world we live in. In the '60s, early '70s, our conception of the greening of America and being more attuned was to put a brick in the back of the toilet to conserve water.

I started my project off by writing a statement of work. You have to have a mission statement to know where you're coming from and where you want to go. When you do visual anthropology you gotta know where you start and where you end. For all of my books, I always have a shooting script. After you do the mission statement, you can put it away, but off of the mission statement comes the shooting script. The shooting script gave me a road map and kept me focused.

I would write down, for example, "The project will record by means of a photographic survey the new suburban culture. Particular emphasis will not be on the traditional suburbs surrounding urban centers but on the new suburbia—instantly developed tract communities." These tracts were dramatically transforming the small-world towns into affluent urban governments, i.e., Livermore 46 miles from San Francisco grew from 16,000 to 35,000 people.

When I worked on this project, the closest mall was thirty miles away. Basically, malls and mini malls hadn't happened yet. To be a good photographer I still had to develop skills. I had read some place that to do anything well you have to do it 10,000 times. I knew I had to learn how to shoot the camera and shoot it over and over and over again, 10,000 times. The best place to get that discipline was working for a newspaper. Every day you shoot six to ten assignments. When I came out of school, the first and only job offer I got was at the *Livermore Independent* newspaper.

I went to work for this small-town newspaper in California shooting everything. I shot Friday night football games. Saturday mornings would be slow. Mondays I photographed the new people running for City Council, the junior women's club. I did everything but traffic accidents, because my little paper didn't believe in photographing them. In the deep suburbia of Livermore, Pleasanton, and Dublin, California, it was all right in front of me: a crossroads of two major highways, mountain ranges, and a complete community. On Saturday morning you could drive to all three towns and see kids playing soccer games, kids training and diving at the local high school pools, people shopping for their groceries. It was all right there happening, and I wanted to document how people lived. I knew I didn't have to travel. You just had to see it, and most people don't see their own culture.

But something else also happened. I knew documentary photography could not be done with a 35mm camera shooting rapidly frame after frame. I wanted to slow the process down, and along came a new camera into the marketplace, a Pentax 6 × 7, which had interchangeable lenses. I bought one immediately because it had a 55mm lens. The other thing that helped me make good shots was using a strobe. Soon I started shooting with a bare tube, which means I had one camera handheld, one strobe handheld, and the other strobe on a slave. Almost every shot in *Suburbia* was done with two strobes going off. I had taken a workshop from photographer W. Eugene Smith and he talked about how he used strobe in "The Country Doctor" essay. Eugene Smith knew how to use strobe, which shocked me.

I raised a small amount of money and with a small grant I could leave the newspaper one day a week—work four days a week at the paper and one day on my project. I shot it in fifty-two days. I got to a point where I knew I had to stop so I stopped.

At the beginning of the project, I ran an ad in the newspaper and just started working. The ad said something like "I am doing a documentary on Livermore. Let me photograph your kids, your pets, your house, whatever. Call me, Bill Owens. I work at the newspaper." Because I worked for the paper, I had credibility. The ad ran in the Livermore paper for about a year, all the time, three times a week.

Occasionally people would call me up and say, "Come on over for coffee." I would go over and sometimes there would be nothing to photograph, just nice people. I met a lot of people that way. I would go see them again in two weeks, and maybe that time the garage door would be open and I would see something, or the neighborhood girl might be sick and playing with her Barbie dolls. Sometimes I would walk in the house, and boom, the bookcase would be just perfect to photograph, or I would just do a simple portrait of the family.

The picture of Richie happened because the Larsons lived next door to me. Art Larson became a friend of mine. He sat on the City Council in Dublin. So when I was out making my rounds on a Saturday morning or Saturday afternoon, I would drop in and have a cup of coffee with him. I would talk about my photographs and discuss what to photograph in the community. One afternoon I was leaving their house and there is Richie, the next-door kid out in the driveway. I had been in and out of that house twenty or thirty times before Richie appeared there. You couldn't drive around looking for him. You couldn't dress him up. He was just there. So serendipity plays a very important role in your photographs, to pull all of those cosmic things together—the cowboy boots, the gun, the Big Wheels, and the flat-top haircut. It's all there in one simple image.

I used Chong Lee, a printer in San Francisco, to print for me, because I couldn't keep up with what I was shooting. Every Saturday I would come in with ten to thirteen rolls of film, process them, and make my own contact sheets. So if I had thirteen rolls, that's twenty-six contact sheets. I would go to Chong and have him print. He was always two to three months behind me on printing. I wanted to stop printing, to be able to step back and take a look at what I had done. I wanted to see where the gaps were, what was missing.

In any book you have to have two to three pivotal images that sew the book together. Richie and the Tupperware party image are seminal to *Suburbia* and say this is who we are at this point in time. I just tried to keep my focus. I had a child and a wife, and you have to be home at night or you are divorced. I couldn't just move to New York City and make it. I kept going on my project, and in the end I had 500 prints in a box before I went looking for a publisher. It is pretty hard for them to say no when you've have 500 prints.

Once I had my box of prints, I wanted photographer Wayne Miller to look at the work to give me advice. I went up to Wayne's house and he looked at the project and he looked at me and he said, "You don't have any sex." I said, "What?" He said, "No sex." Well, you've got to remember the year was 1971. For me to cross that line, to dare to show genitalia, I couldn't do that. You would be destroyed. Your credibility would be destroyed, because you would have to pay to have it set up. I was really kind of stuck. I thought about it, and finally I decided to take the chance and put out the word through some people to say I was looking for a couple who would pose for me in the nude. One of them finally said, "I know this guy who works at Ozzie Davis the automobile dealership. He and his wife posed for a little trashy magazine." So, supposedly, they were use to posing in the nude. I got in touch with them and went over to their house. Their front room was straight out of Levitz, with the chrome table, the big overstuffed couch, etc.—I wanted to photograph it. I talked to them for a while about posing in the nude. You can't ask people whom you've just known for 10 minutes to take off their clothes. I was thirty-two or thirty-three years old and they were the same age. Eventually, I said "Let's see the bedroom and why don't you pose on the end of the bed." The only thing the wife did was take off her bra. I let her hair hang down. The husband was in his underwear and she was in her underwear. That shot became a key shot of sexuality, because the bedroom had flocked wallpaper and parquet floor. There are no curtains on the window—it was weird.

More than anything else, I would drive around looking for overviews trying to find the right long shot to make a photo that symbolized suburbia. I would go out on a Saturday morning, drive up a hill, look down, and see a guy pushing a lawn mower. I could get the scale of the houses and the hills in the background.

Certain scenes I shot over and over again, like the junior women's club meeting, Lions Club meeting, Rotary Club meetings, those kinds of things you do on a weekly basis. One of my best shots is the girls at the beauty contestants. You go over and over it and finally you say to yourself, "I am not getting this right. What am I doing wrong?" You look at other photography and realize you need to do this. You need to be in this position, standing right here at this particular moment to make that shot. When I did my beauty contestants, I just waited until the girls in the bathing suits turned their backs and then I had all the backsides of the bathing-beauty contestants with the judges on the left-hand corner of the frame. Shooting over and over is really important because you get familiar with the subjects.

When I photographed the Lions Club three or four times, I got to know the people. You sit next to your friends, and when the superintendent of schools is up on the stage, it's really easy to reach down in your bag, drag out your camera, turn on your strobe, walk up in front of 200 men in a room with your back to them, and take a picture of the superintendent of schools. They just say, "It's just Bill from the newspaper taking a picture." So I was able to have the credibility of the newspaper, even though I was often out shooting it for myself.

I knew everybody! I could go back a year later and knock on their door and show them a print. Most of the time I couldn't give the prints away because people's image of photography is a picture in a little frame up on the mantel of them and their wife in a studio. To offer them a picture of them and their kids eating hot dogs on a Saturday afternoon at their house, they don't want that shot necessarily.

I kept going back into the community. I was not a stranger in a strange land. This was my community. Time was on my side and I had plenty of it. I could go back and reshoot anything I had missed, like the photo of the kids climbing the tree and picking all of the leaves off at one time. You know, that was easy. I was out looking for interesting moments. I didn't even get out of the car to make that shot. I just shot it through the window with a telephoto lens. I would then just knock on the door, and a kid would answer. I would say, "Here is a picture. I am going to need to have you guys sign it so I can publish it in a book." They would say, "No problem." I would ask, "What do you want to say for a caption?" "Well, my dad has me pick all of the leaves off at one time. We think he is crazy." The moment just ends up being a really delightful shot.

When I finished the project and *Rolling Stone* was ready to publish it, they said, "You've got to get releases." I said, "I am a journalist, I don't have to do releases." They said, "You've photographed in people's homes. Go back and get the releases." I was always telling stories and they asked, "Why don't you get captions from all of the people, too?" So I just wrote up a little something on a 3 × 5 card for a release. I went to see the couple who posed in their bedroom. I flipped the card over and showed the release. When I went to have them sign the release card, I said, "What do you want to say about yourself?" They said, "Oh, we let sex take care of itself." It was just perfect to let them speak for themselves. I was in and out of there in not even an hour.

I am one of these photographers who really gets upset when people repeat their images. I never show the same face twice, never show the same home twice. I want every image to stand on its own. So you just see one shot that is a barbecue, even though I photographed two or three other barbecues. None of those other shots worked. I would look at other people's work and say "Oh my God, this person doesn't know how to edit." You need to go to work for a newspaper. Because if they don't like it, if you put too much white space in the image, they just cut off the edge of the photograph. Newspaper work gave me that discipline. I am a news photographer. I look at so much photography today that doesn't have basic composition. Come on. If this photograph doesn't have any composition, it goes in the trash. You haven't worked for a newspaper.

As a documentary photographer, you are going out there to satisfy yourself to make an image and communicate a message that will stand on its own two legs. It is very hard to make an image that is going to stand on its own legs. Today, it is a different world. You've got to have permission to do things, whereas in my day you could pull it off easier. I think there is a difference in attitude. I like to call myself a documentary photographer, not a photojournalist, but my discipline is photojournalism. There are not that many people doing documentary photography, because there is nowhere to go with it. Nobody will publish your book. It is occasionally taught in school, but it is something you do out of your own personal desire and your own personal demons to prove that you have the right stuff.

Larry Fink

Social Graces

Larry Fink was born in Brooklyn in 1941 and took up photography when he was a kid, starting with a Rolleiflex and a 120 foldout camera. His family was left wing and so he says "I was very well aware at a certain age of class consciousness and all of the various struggles for justice that we human beings are pushed to try to solve."

Music also drew him in, but photography held center stage. In his twenties, he started to photograph the Black Panthers and Malcolm X. One of his early acts was to curate "The People Protesting" in 1967 at Columbia University. People of every type of photographic expertise were asked, "to do a kind of a document however they wanted" of the first large, nationwide peace march in Washington, D.C. He incorporated Diane Arbus, Bruce Davidson, and many other photographers into the show.

Fink studied photography with Alexey Brodovitch and Lisette Model at the New School for Social Research in New York City and has had solo exhibitions at the Museum of Modern Art and the Whitney Museum of American Art in New York, as well as in major retrospectives at Les Rencontres de Photographie, Arles, France, and the Musée de L'Elysée, Lausanne, Switzerland. His photographs have appeared in the *New York Times, Art in America, Vanity Fair, Vogue,* Time-Life Books, *New Yorker,* and *Village Voice.* He is a professor at Bard College.

Over the course of his career, Fink has been a powerful social critic and has authored numerous books. His scathing comment on the 2000

Pat Sabatine's Eight Birthday, April 1977
© Larry Fink

Bush presidential election, "The Forbidden Pictures," was set to run in the *New York Times Magazine* in the fall of 2001. After the events of September 11th and the ensuing reluctance for criticism in the media and general public, the images were pulled and were not seen until exhibited at Lehigh University, Pennsylvania. This body of work has continued to come under extreme attack. Fink's tableaux set Bush administration look-alikes in the opulent world of Weimar-era painting, referencing the decadent depictions of painters Max Beckmann, George Grosz, and Otto Dix. It's pure Larry Fink: ironic, political, laden with intellectual art historical references, and visually arresting.

His seminal book, *Social Graces*, was first published by Aperture in 1984, and has gone on to become a classic, reprinted by powerHouse Books (2001). By using a flash and a medium format camera, the images chronicling the social graces of the rich and the poor are thrown into high relief, demanding that the viewer observes critically. The project spans five years in which Fink traveled between two worlds to document parties, exhibition openings, and the rural farm community of Martins Creek, Pennsylvania, where Fink lives on a farm. When asked how this project began, Fink says, "It started when I was born," and he laughs outrageously.

I was born with my umbilical cord around my neck and I came out like a screaming, bloody maniac. My father was asked a question whether he wanted my mother or me to live, and he said that he didn't give a damn about me but he loved my mother, so I came out as a welcomed guest, but perhaps unwelcomed if the situation were more dire than it actually was. Which is to say I was born a duality. *Social Graces* by its nature is a duality between rich and poor, two distinct classes with very similar rituals. The rituals are, in this case, about parties. At parties, you are privy to very exhibitionistic, sometimes uninhibited, sometimes very hidden ambitions or predilections.

This analysis of that ritual is about the people in each specific image but also about the difference between the class that has to uphold statutory values and the class that has none—and who has a better time.

I have this political background of concerns and also a background of elitist left-wing thinking. In the '60s many of us thought that because there was an intellectual hunger for social change in the air it would spread incrementally throughout the whole American population, which it did not. The struggle for all of those values became ba-thetic, drifting to social illusion and then disillusion. However, out of all of those various ideological constructs, I thought that the revolution was about to come, and I wouldn't buy property nor would my father. My mother thought the system was about ready to fall even though she was wearing minks. She liked the system a lot and Dad had a Stutz Bearcat roadster. They went to Florida and she had to quit the Communist Party because the party was puritanical like everything in America. They were decent people and they were full of justice. My mother organized all through her life. My dad was an insurance man, golfer, and a bourgeois guy and was also really smart.

With all of those various kinds of influences, I'm this leftist photographer. I was working for the peace movement in the '60s, trying to make a living as a photojournalist, working for *Pageant Magazine* and the *Saturday Evening Post*. I went to the Dominican Republic during the revolution and got scared out of my brains. I photographed the Harlem riots and at the same time I was teaching in Harlem. I was asked to join Magnum and I didn't because I was a teacher and I couldn't go off on big assignments.

Social Graces started out as a project to photograph the bourgeoisie as if it were a dying sociological class, just like I was Eugene Atget with a Marxist bent trying to preserve all that was good or bad about the Paris of my interior mind. It was going to be the last pictures of the bourgeoisie. I really believed it was about ready to fall. My work started at Parsons School of Design, which was a pretty bourgeois school. I was teaching there and all the kids were having fancy, decadent costume parties. Nothing is more decadent than the imitation of decadence. They really personified it, and there the pictures started. I also started to use flash in a very serious but very clumsy way for the first time in my life. That is not to say I hadn't used it before, but I always thought it was invasive and I didn't want to be an invasive photographer. I was interested, like Cartier-Bresson or W. Eugene Smith, in the dignity of man and I wanted to be a mobilizing bystander rather than an aggressor.

You have to understand that *Life* magazine and photographers like Wayne Miller used flash bulbs. Then Harold Edgerton came along and developed strobe for the War Department during the Second World War. So strobe light was out there, but nobody was using it the way I started to use it, which was with a certain level of invasive brutality mixed with the curiosity that comes with being human. I was trying to find out what it is about my fellow man that is powerful. It was really like "Wow." I was getting the fleshiness of these decadent kids and stuff in a way that I never had seen before, in my work or in others. I wasn't that self-conscious. I just had a mission, not a goal, but a mission in mind to go over and photograph this bourgeoisie life that was going to be dying. One thing leads to another.

From the Parsons School of Design parties and episodes, I started going to debutant balls and balls at the Russian Nationalist Club and the English-speaking Union—at that time very upscale digs. I was let in there by some of my students at Parsons who took a liking to me. I told them about my project. I got dressed up in my tuxedo and went to the ball with my camera in hand.

At first I was using a Rolleiflex camera and my day would start at dawn. I would get dressed up in my tuxedo and then jump into a 1957 Willies Jeep and drive to New York. It doesn't go faster than 45 miles an hour. I would park it in a garage near the ball, and go to the ball with the camera. For four or five hours I would drink, photograph, socialize, and then drive the goddamn truck back to my farm in Pennsylvania, develop the film, and go to sleep at dawn. It was a long day. I had the darkroom in the bottom of the barn. I made 11 × 14s. I'd stick 'em up, smoke a joint and get completely unclear, and then try to get clear about what I had. I had a big hunger to keep on going to these parties. I myself was an imbiber of many, many different substances of abuse, so I had a good taste for the rapture that people were getting into at the party. I wasn't much of a party guy but I certainly knew what pleasure was and so I went with it.

Some of the earlier talk about my work was that it was about attraction and revulsion, and I think that probably is true. I went to debutant balls in the most seditious way, but treated this issue impishly. I was really nervous about shooting, so when I would get to the party in my tuxedo, I would immediately head to the bar and swag down three or four gin and tonics, so I could equalize myself, get social, and then move into the crowd and start to be attracted to the people I was attracted to. No particular rhyme or reason about that attraction except it was very, very intuitive. I was drawn to the physicality of certain groups of people who were doing energized kinds of things. I didn't go to the ugliest and the most obsequious, those laden with pearls or whatnot. I didn't have a precise agenda politically. I just went to where I was attracted. I meant to document the class and to do a little bit of harm, though I'm not a harmful person per se. I actually had a pretty good time photographing and talking about whatever bullshit I was talking about.

This work was private for years and years. I knew what career was but I didn't have a career in mind for these photos. I never thought it was going be a book some day. I was reasonably independent of any motivation that signified ambition save for the ambition of doing the work. I didn't go to museums to show my work. I had virtually no colleagues. I've always been a guy who's been oddly very friendly but oddly isolated, not in my soul, but by choice.

I was contact sheeting it and cataloging it as I worked. I was an organized person even though I was smoking a lot of grass then. All the while I was playing piano and whatever else I do. It kept going that way, and at a certain point it was getting really interesting to me. I was starting to use the flash with more and more angularity, starting to develop a style, if you will. I never put the flash on camera, it was always off and, at some point, it started to illuminate itself in ways where I really started to become seduced by its mystery, and also by chance. Chance is always the greatest educator.

I'm onto that for about four or five years and then *bang!* One day I'm looking for a cheap lawn mower 'cuz I have no money to speak of. I drive down Little Creek Road and there's John Sabitine with a lawn mower shop. John, this big burly guy, says "Hey, what are you doin'? I never seen you before," blah blah blah, and a relationship is formed on a thirteen-dollar mower which breaks every week, so an even bigger relationship is formed. By the second trip or so, I'm in the household with Gene Sabitine drinking the grease off the top of the spaghetti sauce with a great deal of relish, and hangin' around there. They're having parties and family gatherings and things like that. I'm photographing and not once do I ever think "Ho ho, I'm on to a big Marxist project here. Here's the poor and here's the rich." I'm not thinking about that. Just "Wow, these are really funky people. These guys are so open. They're happy, they're horrible, they're angry at each other. They just hang out like nobody I've ever seen." Years later, when the work started to be shown, New Yorkers would look at them and go "Oh my God, who are those people?" They would go into a kind of vomitatious apoplexy toward the baseness of them all and they became exotic. I never thought of them as exotic, I thought of them as people. I just see people for people period, regardless of class or any other type of attribute.

I'm printing the work and I'm thinking I'm a fine artist or a documentary photographer or whatever I am. It was exciting. I am making pictures that I have never seen before. I win a Guggenheim, and I win another one, and I get an NEA (National Endowment for the Arts grant). Holy shit. These grants give me a terrible conflict because all of a sudden here I am Mr. Marxist underground doofushead but I am the Guggenheim fellow who can waltz around Park Avenue. My leftism is being taken from me. It is a funny kind of process of growing up. Needless to say, getting two Guggenheims leads to somebody asking me to do a show, a Guggenheim show. Then people from the Museum of Modern Art get acquainted with my oeuvre. I go see Susan Kismaric (MOMA photography curator) and she asks me to come up and see John Szarkowski (chief photo curator). He has very smart words to say about things and he immediately gives me a show, and I am fucked up. I mean I'm so completely plagued by duality it's unbelievable. I call up my wife, Joanie, and I say, "They want to give me a show at the Museum of Modern Art," and she says "Oh my God." I'm all choked up, completely happy, and horrified at the same time.

The pictures came forth with so much energy that everyone was gossiping about them. I thought "Wow, this is great." It was fabulous and I learned that the institutions I was so poopooing from this leftist stupidity were the places from which you can educate everybody. All of a sudden my life became much more complex, and rightly so. Then I was reviewed and I was exceedingly happy and absolutely horrified all at the same time. It was a lot of pressure, and yeah, I liked it. That project ended with me on fire.

I got stopped in my tracks by all that success. So what happened to me? I didn't have any more grants to win and in the mid-eighties or so Joanie, my wife, and I broke up. I didn't have any money; print sales weren't that significant and I had an overhead. By this time I even had assistants. As luck would have it, with the emergence of fine art photography and documentary photography, kids were going into photography and college programs were booming. Kids were going to school and studying my work, of all things. They came out of school and they had to make a living and they became picture editors at various magazines, which were still vital at that time. They called me up, wondering trepidatiously "Will it work? He's an artist, you know." Will I work? Are you fucking crazy? You know, I gotta work! So I got hoisted into projects of one kind or another, party or business stuff with all the contradictions of working in the field. Now when I work in the field, I still work with the same amount of force. I see every assignment as a grant. People recently asked me to come photograph the Masters Golf Tournament with all those funny people. Great, they're gonna pay me x dollars and I'm gonna work for several days. I haven't thought about photographing golf before but I'm there and that's good.

I'm not a street photographer. I used to be. I couldn't be anymore unless somebody really paid me for it. Why would you wanna stick your big camera in somebody's nose while they're having a kiss on the sidewalk? In this day and age, it's immoral. But if you're in a scenario where people are accommodating and accepting, then it's ok.

Social Graces was how many years of work, six or or seven, for Christ's sake. I moved around a lot artistically and so I was always in between. Is it documentary work? Sure it is, but is that really an important ethos? Not necessarily! I wanted it to be akin to expressionism. To document is my social concern, but my real concern is to create art, not with any particular big "A" elitism, but art in the sense that it pushes past the mere look of things and brings the already conventionally informed mind into a relationship with transformation, emotional and spiritual. It must approach the edge and simply and vibrantly hover. Also, accessibility was always the most important thing. I wanted to create work which was first accessible so it could not be denied to anybody. It needed to be expressed for the proletariat, if you will pardon my old archaic words. Regular folks and intellectuals, all could come to it and gain something from it, which was absolutely imperative and still is today. And then it can take into concern every other level of interpretation in the aesthetic world.

David Goldblatt

Once an Enemy:
Apartheid and the New South Africa

D avid Goldblatt was born in 1930 in Randfontein, a gold-mining
town near Johannesburg in South Africa. His grandparents were
Lithuanian immigrants who fled the persecution of Jews in the 1890s. As
a child, Goldblatt was raised in a family who emphasized racial tolerance,
but he grew up in the racial segregation of South Africa that, beginning
in the early 1950s, was institutionalized into apartheid. He became
interested in photography in high school and pursued a career in magazine photography with little success. Discouraged, he joined the family's
menswear business and began working part-time on a university degree.
Following his father's death in 1962, he sold the clothing concern and
began working full-time as a photographer.

In his early foray into photography, he tried to photograph some of
the activities that were taking place in opposition to state apartheid. As
he describes, "I did them badly, very badly. I had no technique. I didn't
have a clue about how to approach these things. I was quite hopeless."
Despite his early experiences, he had a deep and heartfelt commitment to
his homeland. He felt that he had to tell the world what was happening
in South Africa, "because nobody seemed to be taking any notice. I had
visions of becoming a sort of a missionary with a camera."

But unlike the small number of like-minded photographers, trying
desperately to put a face on the terrors and crimes of apartheid, Goldblatt turned his camera away from the clashes and focused on the state

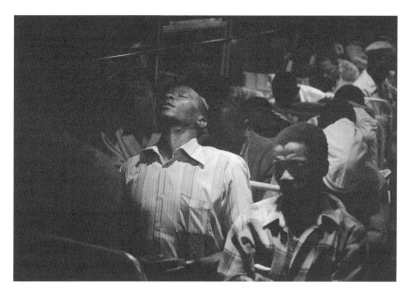

The Transported of KwaNdebele, 1989
© David Goldblatt

of being and the condition of this society. His work appeared in numerous books including *In Boksburg* and in the Carnegie Inquiry of 1984, which published its associated book *The Cordoned Heart.*

After more than five decades, Goldblatt now works in color and continues to document the changing political landscape of his country. His photographs continue to be what have been described as astute and subtle observations of his homeland, a society trying to find its way after apartheid. Even in this post-apartheid era, apartheid continues to inform his work.

Over the years I have become interested in some particular aspect of South African society. If you look at my whole body of work created over the last 55 years you'd find that there would be very distinct pieces of work. Each of them is very different from the others because I needed to design my approach to the subject matter. The subject to me is always primary. Without the subject I'm lost. I see things that really excite me because they exist, they make me itch, and I've got to scratch the itch. I scratch it with a camera.

When I started taking photographs seriously, the National Party had just come into power, 1948. These were the people who enforced the policy of apartheid. We'd had segregation for over 300 years, but this was a new kind of thing. It was much more systematic, it was ideological, extremely complex, and detailed in its application. I began at first to think that I had to be a missionary. I had to tell the world what was happening in South Africa because nobody seemed to be taking any notice. I had visions of becoming a sort of a missionary with a camera. I did some photographs of one of the first incidents of clear-cut apartheid on the Johannesburg railway station. I sent these pictures off to *Picture Post,* which was one of the great photographic magazines of the time. It was not photographic in the modern sense; it was an illustrated photographic magazine like *Life* and *Look.* My photographs were politely rejected but when things really started popping in South Africa in the 1950s, the editor sent me a cable "Please send photographs—anything."

I then started trying to photograph some of the activities that were taking place in opposition to apartheid. I did them badly, very badly. I had no technique. I didn't have a clue about how to approach these things. I was quite hopeless. The climax occurred in a big political meeting in the Trades Hall, a place where the trade unions used to meet. It was a meeting of the ANC, the African National Congress, to discuss the defiance of unjust laws. The hall was full of very exuberant members of the ANC. They were dancing and singing, there were speeches, and all of the great leaders were there on the stage. I had my first Leica and I must have photographed for two hours, two and a half hours furiously, and then suddenly I realized that this was a very long piece of film. I opened the back of the camera and the film hadn't engaged on the sprockets. I had my first rather bitter lesson in not being a photographer of events. Gradually I realized that I wasn't born to be a photographer of events. I didn't have the guts to be in situations of great physical danger. I didn't have the approach, I didn't have the technique, and ultimately I wasn't actually very interested in events. The events were the culmination of conditions. It was the conditions which held my interest. That understanding came gradually. It wasn't an overnight revelation, but it led me gradually into doing the kind of work that I have done.

By the 1960s, I had become a full-time photographer. I had no clients and I had very little experience. I set out on two projects that eventually became books. Each of them really demanded its own approach. One was to photograph people called Afrikaners, people who largely supported and brought into being the policy of apartheid. The other project was an essay on the dying gold mines near Johannesburg in South Africa.

I was born and brought up in a gold-mining town. My father's business as a men's outfitter was heavily dependent on the mines, and they more or less dominated our lives. I knew very little about them. So here I was an adult, with no clients, and I set out to look at these dying mines. I became interested in an operation called shaft sinking, the sinking of the shaft, the deep hole in the ground that becomes the shaft. The shaft provides access to the underground workings for men and machines and the conduit up which they haul the gold-bearing ore. It is a hugely audacious, dangerous feat of modern technology. It's very primitive but at the same time very modern. I set out to photograph that. I required the barest minimum of equipment because the conditions underground are extremely arduous. You're faced with a lot of flying water all the time to keep down the dust. You're in a position where you have to be very agile to keep out of the way of the men.

They work on bonuses so they couldn't care a bugger about anybody who gets in the way. You have to work fast and simply. I used a couple of Leica M-2 cameras. I learned to load them under my oilskins, a heavy waterproofed garment, without even looking at them. You can't use an underground camera because you can't reload under water. With a Leica at least you can reload. So I suited the equipment and the approach to the subject matter.

The work I did on the shaft sinking helped me with my later project that became a book called *The Transported of KwaNdebele*. Both of those projects involved working under conditions of extreme difficulty in regard to light. I don't use flash, and so once you've learned to cope with one situation of that kind, then the others are not that difficult. The shaft sinking was much more difficult because it was physically dangerous and the light was constantly changing.

The Transported of KwaNdebele was one of twenty essays by twenty photographers who were each asked to contribute an essay for the Carnegie Inquiry into Poverty that took place in 1983 in South Africa. There had been an inquiry by the Carnegie Corporation in 1929 and '30 which looked into poor white poverty. Now there was a new inquiry in 1983–84 that examined black poverty. I was asked to look at what was called homeland transport. The homelands were the tribal reserves set aside for the black tribes of South Africa, and those reserves under the apartheid government became states, satellite countries. The government hoped to turn them each into a separate country with its own constitution, its own parliament, its own voting system, the whole thing. It was fundamentally an attempt to push black people out of white South Africa, into enclaves of black South Africa where they could be kept and controlled. Their labor, however, was necessary in white South Africa, so a provision was made for the blacks to travel from those black homelands to white industrial complexes.

People from the homeland of KwaNdebele had to travel from about 80 to 200 kilometers (50 to 125 miles) to and from work every day. There was no railway line, there was no fast track. They had to travel by bus. This meant that some of them had to get up at about two o'clock in the morning in order to be in line for a bus at about a quarter to three in the morning. At about six o'clock, the bus would get into Pretoria, which was the industrial complex that they were going to. They would then have to travel another hour, some of them by bus, train, or taxi, to get to the work place to be at the gate at seven o'clock. They would repeat that journey in the evening. Some people were therefore traveling up to eight hours per day and putting in an eight-hour shift at work.

Joe Lelyveld of the *New York Times* was also interested in homeland transport, and so we made a bus journey together. The public relations officer of the utility company arranged permission for us to join a bus from KwaNdebele to Pretoria. We boarded at about 2:45 a.m. deep in KwaNdebele and traveled to Pretoria. It was one of the most moving experiences that I've ever had. People got onto the bus and I asked their permission to photograph. I asked if there was anybody who didn't want to be photographed and they all gave their permission. Frankly, they were all far more interested in trying to find themselves a comfortable way to sit so they could get back to sleep. After a while the bus became so crowded that I couldn't ask people and I was wedged in. People were actually lying on the floor and sleeping. I couldn't move. The driver, Joe, and I were probably the only people on the bus who were still awake. Others were sleeping a very uncomfortable kind of sleep.

I had prepared myself for this journey. I realized that standing in what would probably be almost total darkness and traveling on bad roads in a bus not built for comfort, I would certainly not be able to use a tripod. In order to work on a moving vehicle and keep the camera steady, I got myself a piece of nylon belt, long enough to go from under my shoe to my forehead. I fixed a tripod screw to the top of it that went into the base plate of my Leica. I was able to pull it taut, bringing the camera to my forehead. I then became a kind of moving tripod, because I could move and sway with the bus and shoot at anything from about a 1/15 to a half a second. I was using the fastest film I could get. At that time it was the film Kodak had developed for police use, Recording Film, which had a rating of about 1600 ASA. That's what I shot on the bus. On this particular bus, the first bus I traveled on, there were two interior lights: a little red one near the front and a green one near the back, that was all. Between those two lamps, and the light of other buses and motorcars on the road that came through the windows, I was able to expose for the work that I did.

I used a Pentax spotmeter which is pretty sensitive and estimated exposures. Frankly, in that kind of light an exposure meter doesn't get you very far. You've got to use your gut and trust luck. I work on the old-fashioned principle that if you are shooting on negative film, you expose for the shadows and I used to develop for the shadows as well, so I would end up with very dense film. I would much rather have a dense piece of film than one with nothing on it. You can't print what isn't there. But if you've exposed generously you can print. That's what I did. Most of that work was reasonably well exposed although it was made in almost no light. I think my fastest lens was a 35 mm f/1.4.

It was quite scary in that I didn't know what I'd get and I didn't know whether the damn stuff would come out. I don't remember how much I shot, but not a great deal. I'm not a machine gunner. I went in October 1983, and then in February '84 I went back and did the reverse journey and did some other photographs of the people standing in line at the bus stops. In all, I don't think there were more than four or five rolls of film, perhaps five or six but certainly not twenty or thirty rolls.

In 1976 I suggested to a magazine editor that he do an essay on white South Africans. I'd been in the States and Canada and people had said, "Who the fuck are these white South Africans? They're the cause of all this trouble there, you know." I came back and told the editor, "There is real interest in white South Africans and who they are." He eventually said, "Please do a piece on that, do an essay." I was going to get on my motorbike and travel around the country with a camera. I didn't have a really clear idea of what I would do with the white South Africans. I suddenly realized I had been doing a microcosm of white South Africa already. I had been photographing the white community of Boksburg, mainly public events. I would make it my business to be at these events, get permission if necessary to be there, tell people what I was doing, then just set myself up, and wait and wait and wait—and eventually get the photographs that I wanted.

Boksburg is about 14 miles from where I live so it was a nice easy motorbike ride. The shoot was one of the most difficult things I've ever done because these people were my people. It's the same type of community as the one that I grew up in. It was, therefore, very difficult to photograph it. There's a knife's edge between taking the mickey out of people and showing them living their lives as they are. Fundamentally, what I was looking at was the question, how is it possible to be law abiding and decent, which is what most of these people were, and yet at the same time be complicit in a system that is basically evil and mad. It was tough, I must say.

I once spent three days on a street corner photographing. There was a white man watching me all the time. I was absolutely sure he was from the security police. But I'm also equally sure he never understood what I was doing. He must have been driven mad. Somebody had told him to go and watch that stupid Jew, but he couldn't make out what the hell I was doing. I was just standing on a street corner taking photographs of ordinary life. There was nothing sinister. They never quite understood what I was about.

During the years of apartheid, to have a white skin gave you a lot of privileges. The security police, generally speaking, were fairly easy on whites, provided you didn't throw bombs or become a political activist, and weren't too much in the forefront of the news as a news photographer. So, unlike my colleague, Peter Magubane, who got himself beaten up many times and shot, I was never in the firing line. On a number of magazine assignments, I had confrontations with security police, but they were, for the most part, a fairly mild kind. They would take me in for questioning, speak to me for a couple of hours, and we would part. I knew that I was sometimes under observation. You had to be careful what you said and to whom you said it, and you watched your telephone. I was never really under threat because I was doing work that was somehow oblique. It wasn't a direct confrontation with the regime; they never quite knew what to make of me.

I maybe shot a hundred rolls of film for the essay that would become the book *In Boksburg*. I did a bit of 35mm, one or two shots on 4 × 5, but most of it was on 2¼ square. I would sit down with the contacts all the time. When I'm working on a project I tend to have either rough prints or the contacts right next to me at my computer and next to the phone at my desk. While I'm talking to people I'm looking at the work. If I go to the lavatory I take them with me. Gradually they sort of seep in and I seep into them. I find that there is quite a long process of editing. It is not easy and it's terribly important to me, because when I look at the first contacts as they come out of the hypo I'm thrilled. Amazing, they actually came out. Then there's a cooling off. The cooling off goes into a deep decline and there's a sort of depression. I'm reasonably sure that I'll come out of the depression and look at them again and get onto solid ground. That process is quite a painful one, but it's very necessary. It enables me to get down eventually to the bedrock of what I want. I don't think there is any easy way of describing that process except that I know very often I change my mind about pictures.

I see myself as an unlicensed, self-appointed social critic of the society in which I live. I use the camera as a means for making these observations. I'm moved to look at the underbelly of things, the conditions that give rise to the events of my country. When apartheid came to an end in the early '90s, a lot of us were suddenly faced with the situation that we no longer had an enemy. It was very easy, in a sense, during those years of apartheid to take photographs. We had a very clear-cut enemy. For some of my colleagues this was really quite a serious change in the whole climate of South Africa. For me it was not more than a blip on the graph, because I realized that I had all those years been looking at values and I was still interested in them. During the years of apartheid, I was looking at what did we value under the system, how did we value it, and how did we express those values? Those were basically the things I was concerned with. I photographed numerous situations, but fundamentally each of those pieces of work, although they're different in their technical approach, is concerned with the same thing. In post-apartheid South Africa I've been doing the same thing. I've been looking at values in this new democracy of ours and how we express them.

Maya Goded

Tierra Negra

M aya Goded was born in Mexico in 1970, the daughter of a Mexican political activist and an American anthropologist. She began to photograph when she was 15 years old. In the early 1990s she journeyed to the coasts of Guerrero and Oaxaca, photographing daily life of the indigenous communities. Her project began because she wanted to discover the land where her granduncle had died while flying his airplane and where her father had lived for a few years fighting for his political ideals.

While traveling, she soon discovered that although the general Mexican population are white descendants of the Spaniards and have a strong Indian presence, there are other cultural influences that have been neglected or forgotten. Black people, largely unseen in Mexico, live in numerous villages. She describes this community as the third root of the melting pot that is contemporary Mexico. She tried to capture these minority communities' present-day customs and way of life, as a culture that is threatened with extinction.

Goded says, "I came to understand that as long as we continue to ignore ethnic minorities, which are part of our Latin America, we can hardly understand our present cultural reality in Mexico's visible third root." She recalls, "Throughout my travels, which lasted three years, I tried to grasp the strength of this culture, women who in spite of the hostile environment find the needed space to build families with strong

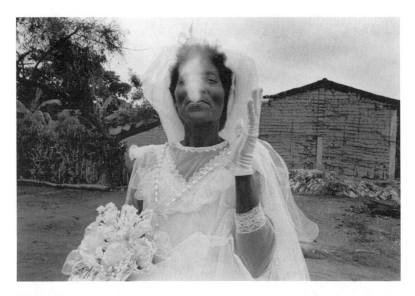

Tierra Negra, 1994
© Maya Goded

moral codes. The intimate co-existence between life and death brings us ever closer to the understanding of the human soul."

In 1993, a book of these photographs, *Tierra Negra*, was published in Mexico. Goded has been the recipient of an International Fund for Documentary Photography award and the W. Eugene Smith Fellowship Award for her work with prostitutes in La Merced, a downtown neighborhood of Mexico City and her hometown. A book of these photographs, *Good Girls*, was published by Umbrage Editions in 2006.

M y grandmother and my grandfather came to Mexico as emigrants from Spain during the Spanish Civil War. I grew up with stories about my grandfather's brother, because he was a very important part of my family. I didn't meet him for a long time because he was in jail in Spain, but eventually, my grandfather was able to bring him to Mexico to live. My great uncle was an adventurer and a pilot in the Costa Chica zone in Guererro and Oaxaca. He would visit my father and my niece and tell many stories about these villages. My father grew up with these stories. My grandfather's brother crashed his airplane in this part of Mexico, and my father had to go the village where he died to reclaim his body. These adventures were part of my family's lore

When my father married my mother, an anthropologist from the United States, she came with him to Mexico. They had this fantasy about these villages. In fact, they had the only book that existed about these villages. The book and these fantasies intrigued me when I was young, and I always wanted to go and see that part of Mexico.

Ever since I was little I have been very visual. I had problems with language; I was not a good writer. I was better visually, so I painted all the time. When I was older, I studied sociology, painting, and design. Once I took a photography class and decided photography was the best. I could, in a way, combine both language and art. Since I was not a good writer, but more capable visually, it was perfect.

As a young photographer in Mexico, I admired Graciela Iturbide. I actually called her on the phone one day and said "I want to meet you and show you my work." She told me "If you want to be a photographer, you have to be a photographer all the time." She suggested that I look for a job in the Instituto Nacional, and so I did. The Instituto Nacional gave me a scholarship and I made the decision to be a photographer—nothing else I could do. There was no other way to better express myself than through photography.

In my early years as a photographer, I was really very close to Graciela Iturbide; it was a very strong relationship. During that time, she was the only person I showed my work to. I thought later on that should I make myself more independent, because sometimes your teachers become very strong in their way of looking at things and you have to distance yourself so you can find your own way of seeing.

At the beginning of my career, I worked as a photographer for the Instituto Nacional Indigenista. They didn't pay well, but they did give me money to travel and for film. It was a perfect job for me. I was traveling all over Mexico and working in many villages. One day I worked very near Costa Chica and was surprised to see that the villagers had black skin. At the Institute, they were not helping these villages and they didn't give money to the people because they were not Indian. I went to my boss and asked what he thought about me doing a big story on the Mexican black population. He said he was not interested.

I wrote a project proposal anyway: to work for one year photographing the black population in Mexico. Success. Nobody had photographed these villages, which are located on the Pacific coast of Mexico, near Acapulco. The Instituto sent me to investigate and photograph. I began to work in these villages, the villages that my family had talked about, the villages that had filled me with their fantasies.

The place I liked the most was Guerrero, which has a black population, but it is also very mixed. Guerrero was difficult to photograph because there was a strong tension between the Indians, the blacks, and the whites, a very conflicted relationship between the three groups. I learned how to work in these communities. To walk on the streets of the village as a single woman was not done, because the townspeople would think I was a hooker. The only women who worked and walked by themselves in villages were prostitutes. I had to talk to the leader of the community and tell him I wanted to photograph these communities. In some villages they called everybody together at night, when they had finished their work. Mostly men came and I explained to them what I was going to do and how my assignment was important. I asked permission to photograph their traditions, their life. It worked, because one day somebody knocked on my door and said, "Oh, I'm going to do this. Do you want to try to photograph?" Little by little they were beginning to accept me as a photographer of the villages.

The first trips lasted for one month, and I concentrated on small villages. I knew that there was a priest who worked in the communities, so I talked with him about my project and told him that I wanted to meet people in the villages. He showed me some villages, and I spent a lot of time with him. So he wouldn't have problems with the villagers when they saw him with me, he told the villagers I was going to be a nun. But that story became a problem. When a woman died, the villagers called me to come, and I didn't know anything about what a nun would do. The situation was getting too convoluted—it was not the truth. As I stayed on, I had to explain who I really was.

When I began in the villages I stayed in a small, one-room clinic. But then I met women and they invited me into their houses. In each village, I chose two or three women to get to know well, so I could work more deeply and meet more people.

I shoot very slowly and don't use much film. I only have one camera, a 35mm with a 28mm and 35mm lens. Sometimes you have very good luck and you use a lot of film and sometimes you almost don't photograph anything. I was not in a rush. Sometimes there are no photographs at first and you meet people—I really prefer that way. Building relationships was more important, and then maybe on the next trip I would make more photographs.

I also began to write things that happened to me. But when I published *Tierra Negra,* I didn't put any of it in, because at that time, I thought it was not very important, even wrong. I had written about what happened, people's names, their stories, things that I thought were interesting. Because I always met so many people I wanted to keep track of who they were in the village and when I returned, I would know their names and remember things about them and the places. They told me about a lot of things, and shared songs. They liked to play with words and they often said very funny things. Sometimes the villagers wrote poems, because they like to write poems. They weren't very poetic, but those things can give you ideas of what is important in their culture, what you can photograph. All these everyday details make a richer work and in my next project I want to include all that information in the book.

Many of my ideas for the project had come from my uncle's stories. But the villages I saw were a completely different reality from those stories. Everybody said those things happened years ago and nobody did them any more. I decided to just take my photos and relax and try to see other things. It's funny because as I began to do this project, I had a friend, and she went on vacation where I was working. She wanted to see the villages I was photographing. When she came back home she told me "I had other ideas when I saw your photographs, and when I saw the same village, it seemed like it was another place." It's completely the way you see the things and what you concentrate on. If you are a woman or if you are a man can really make a difference. I was more into the families and the women in the villages and not in the fields working. I liked to spend time in the houses with the women. The women in these villages are very strong. They get married very young and the men are very macho.

The relationship between men and women in the villages is very complicated. In one village, if a man likes a woman, he will go with a lot of the men on horses, take the woman, go to a field, and have sex with her. If she is a virgin, they set off firecrackers in the town. All the town then knows that she is a virgin and the men are going to want to marry her. If there are no firecrackers, everybody knows that she's not, and that woman is not going to have a good husband in that village. Most have to go to another village and go to work in another place, because the men of her home village would rape her.

I didn't want to do a book on only the women, but because the situation was a little complex, I got closer to the women. I would do whatever they told me. If one advised me, "My husband is not a very good man. Don't go with him," I didn't. The women were always together and they accepted me in the community.

The image of the woman smoking was a woman dressing herself for a party. I took the picture because she was old and smoking in front of all the village and she didn't care. She did whatever she wanted. At the time, we were very happy and having fun, a good time. I liked this woman because she had children and she was getting married and she was old for marriage. So she was, in her way, like a feminist of this village.

It's hard for me to choose my favorite photograph. For me it's difficult to separate the photo from the thing that you lived. But one photo

I like was taken when a woman and I were talking and the woman was asking me about the world. That day we had gone to the beach to swim and were relaxing. We were looking at the sea, and she was asking me how the world is made. If she swims, is there an end? We had a coconut on the beach. Using the coconut, I was trying to explain how it was. I took a photo where the horizon line was very unusual. There was a place the horizon looked like it was going to end in the air. It was going to finish something.

All in all, I really enjoyed the women because they were not so important in the village hierarchy. They don't have a lot of power. The men rape them and then they have to go to another house. But as the women get older and older, they begin to have more and more power in the family. They really have a very big sexuality in relation to their body, and they begin to do whatever they want. I really enjoyed drinking with them and joining their parties. I like to hear the music of the places I photographed. Sometimes I was more into dancing instead of photographing. But sometimes that also helped me get photos.

I do everything while I photograph. That's why I like to do documentary. I observe, but I like to be in the world too, really get into it. I like to participate when I am photographing. I am not a photographer who doesn't want anybody to see me, who doesn't join in and wants people to think I am only looking.

I like to live with the people I am photographing. That's why maybe a lot of the photos are women, and the people are looking at me. I like the relationship between us. Most of the time we're playing because we're in a moment that I am enjoying and participating in.

I always gave the villagers photos when I was photographing their village. Every trip I took photos and they put them in their houses. I love to see the photos in their houses. It also let them have an idea of how I photographed them. One day two women told me that they had ideas about a photo they wanted me to make: they would ask all their grandchildren to be there, and one of the women would pour a big bucket on top of her head. We did it. The water was spilling all over her blouse, and it was very sexy, a great idea. But I didn't include the shot because it wasn't a great photograph. It was better as an experience. Sometimes they really did have good ideas, and it was also a way to play and let them propose things and bring those ideas to the photograph.

I used to develop and print everything. Nowadays I don't have time and that's sad. When I used to do this work, I would come back home and spend weeks in the darkroom. All day printing. You can think more in the darkroom, see what you did. You can concentrate. You can see what things you are interested in, what you want to do the next time you go. Nowadays I am rushing around so much that I don't have this time in the laboratory and that means no time for reflection. Now I do it on the computer. It's not the same because in the darkroom I could really concentrated on what I had done.

Recently I've been looking at a lot of books and text. It's like an obsession, looking at how the text and the photos go together, or not, and in which way. During this project I learned how to get into a community. I don't know how you teach that in school, but I think it's very, very important, the most important thing. I learned it with this work—how to get into the community and how to work with the people directly, how to get near people and gain confidence.

It's funny that in Mexico City they saw these photos and all the people thought the location was Cuba, not Mexico. Nobody thinks about this part of Mexico. It's always the Indians and the whites. All my trips were very impulsive and I photographed whatever I liked in the moment. But now maybe with time I see some aspects that I would like to finish. Recently I had to look for my contacts again and I came across some other photos that maybe I would like to use. It's a project that I think that I didn't really end. I would like to work a little bit more on it. When I look back at this project now, I think I shot less film than I should have. I would have liked to get a little bit more into the relations of the woman and the macho thing. You do in your life very few books and I think you have to try to do what you think works.

Afterword

Witness in Our Time

Social documentary photography offers the future a view of the past, and a voice to the dispossessed. It bears witness in an age when publications turn toward entertainment and celebrity photography and when individual expression is often drowned out by huge media companies. It amazes me that an individual with a camera still has a powerful and enduring voice.

Many of us have a moment when we see a photograph that captures an age or an event, and analyze it for clues about ourselves and our world. In the beginning I was attracted first as a viewer. My path toward documentary photography began as a slow curiosity. I was drawn to an image that is still vivid in my mind's eye, an image that was unlike anything I had ever seen. I realized then that the world could be captured and closely scrutinized in a single still moment.

I was distraught taking the bus home from seventh grade that November afternoon. It had been announced over the school loud speaker at my junior high school that President John F. Kennedy had been shot. I grew up under Eisenhower but have little childhood memory of him. JFK was something else. I remember the photographs of the young Senator from Massachusetts. I collected campaign literature, and I remember, like a dream, a campaign motorcade one block from where I lived—the sirens, the black cars, the photographers with their cameras all clamoring for a picture as the candidate's car rolled by.

River Baptism, Moon Lake, 1989
© Ken Light

School was dismissed early that afternoon of November 22 so that we could go home to our families. The tragedy disoriented us all. Time stood still. Our lives had been filled with images and reaction to the cold war, like the Cuban missile crisis. Might the air-raid drills for which we would cover our heads and duck under our desks to survive the fire and atomic radiation become a reality?

When I arrived home the black-and-white television's news coverage was fixated on Walter Cronkite and frantic images of the Dallas hospital, reporters, and spectators in total chaos. Regular broadcasting all but ceased to exist for days.

Then it happened. They were moving Lee Harvey Oswald, the assassin, through the garage of the Dallas police headquarters and, out of nowhere, right in front of my eyes, *bang,* he was shot dead. Hysteria. For me and my generation, it was the first time such a horrific act had been brought into our homes.

That next day the *New York Times* ran a photograph on the front page by *Dallas-Times Herald* photographer Bob Jackson. I still have that newspaper tucked away. It is yellowed, but it holds the memory of that November day when all America stopped. As photography will do, it crystallized the event. Weeks and even years later, I would look at that photograph, relive the assassination of JFK and the murder of Oswald, and ponder their meaning.

The '60s was a time of overwhelming political upheaval. The Cuban missile crisis; the Civil Rights movement; the assassinations of Malcolm X, Dr. Martin Luther King Jr., and Robert Kennedy; the riots in Watts, Detroit, and Newark; and the Vietnam War. All these events entered my life through photographs in the daily newspaper and *Life* and *Look* magazines.

I had a camera that my father, an amateur photographer, gave me, but I had no sense of what I could do with it other than photograph family, friends, and the occasional tree. Despite being drawn to the powerful images of my time, it never occurred to me that I could make them. In high school not much caught my interest. I worked in a darkroom with my best friend, Carl, but we had no formal training and little understanding of the technical side of photography. Once we developed film at 120 degrees and wondered why it was completely overexposed.

The Vietnam War was raging when I graduated from high school and I left for college in Ohio in 1969. The Oswald photograph was nothing compared to the photographs and TV broadcasts of the Vietnam War. Every night I saw the war up close on television and the next day I could look more deeply at the images in the morning newspaper —like Eddie Adams's photograph of a Viet Cong terrorist being shot point blank or Nick Ut's photo of young Vietnamese children napalmed by friendly fire.

Opposed to the war, I threw myself into the fray like so many others of my generation. I helped organize the Vietnam Moratorium; we sent dozens of buses from my college to Washington, D.C., to protest. I brought my camera with me, more by accident than design. I made some images of a candlelight march in front of the White House and the thousands of students protesting.

Slowly, I began to understand how the camera could help tell the story of my world. I found excitement and a creative connection. But I started to notice there was a difference between what I was trying to do and what I was seeing in newspapers and magazines. The newspaper and magazine photographers I would meet at demonstrations were interested in making a quick photo. They felt no sense of being a historical witness. They were good at what they did, but most seemed uninvolved and disconnected from the people and the events unfolding in their viewfinders. Many of their editors saw us as dirty unpatriotic hippies and the stories and images that they published often echoed these sentiments.

In late April 1970, President Nixon secretly invaded Cambodia. America's colleges exploded in massive demonstrations and riots. I learned that a major protest was being organized, and I traveled to Ohio State University in Columbus to photograph the students. Rioting broke out. National Guardsmen with fixed bayonets lobbed tear gas and made hundreds of arrests.

Armed with a single 35mm camera with a 50mm lens, a press pass pinned on my green army surplus fatigue jacket, a few rolls of Tri-X, and a gas mask, I began to photograph the melee: close ups of students lobbing tear gas canisters back at the National Guard and police; Ohio highway patrol officers clubbing students; and troops with loaded and bayoneted rifles advancing toward the thousands of rioting young people.

Late in the afternoon I focused my lens on a student pulled in two different directions by police officers. Suddenly I felt four hands on my shoulders. I quickly turned around to find two helmeted highway patrol officers, their eyes peering at me through the dense plastic of the gas masks jutting from under their helmets, telling me in garbled voices to come with them. I pointed to my press pass, but one of the officers ripped it off my jacket, tore it up in little pieces, and threw it up in the air like party confetti. They handcuffed me, marched me to the paddy wagon and sent me to jail with some three hundred others. I was charged with a felony—inciting to riot. For the first time I realized that making photographs carried some risk, and that powerful forces might actually want to stop such endeavors.

My camera and exposed film were placed in a brown paper bag with my name on it. To this day, I marvel that my film was still there when I was released from jail that evening.

While these events were overshadowed by the killing of four students at Kent State University a week later, my photographs of the Ohio State riots appeared in the alternative press that was flourishing. Some of the photos were published on posters and in a few books. A photographer had been born.

Over the next year I discovered others who had witnessed their time —Robert Capa with his Spanish Civil War reportage, Lewis Hine's pioneering study of child labor, and the Farm Security Administration images of America's Depression. I read how the publication of Jacob Riis' photographs in the 1870s of the squalid Mulberry Bend Slum in *How the Other Half Lives* had led to massive urban renewal of the slum by Theodore Roosevelt, then the governor of New York.

I began to see how long-term projects such as these could show a more in-depth presentation of issues. Ironically, many of the magazines that had a small commitment to the longer narrative essay began to falter in the '70s. *Look* and *Collier's* magazines were already gone. *Life* magazine soon closed.

About this time, Robert Capa's brother, Cornell, founded the Fund for Concerned Photography. He had organized shows of social photography, and published two volumes of *The Concerned Photographer* (Grossman, 1968) book series, which became my well-thumbed bible. The introduction he wrote profoundly moved me.

> Today so many pictures are being taken that no one is really interested in what has gone on before. Man's witness of his own times dies with

him. Added to that, the technological advances in camera design have made photography seem easy. It has become so popular—so used and abused—that because of its popularity, it is in danger of losing its own self-respect as well as the trust and confidence of viewers in its veracity and artistry. The role of the photographer is to witness and to be involved with his subject. There are many concerned photographers all over the world whose work will provide the visual history of our century—the first century of which such a documentation will exist. The concerned photographer finds much in the present unacceptable that he tries to alter. Our goal is simply to let the world also know why it is unacceptable.

Cornell's manifesto and publication gave me direction and focus, showing me that it was possible to make important visual statements and survive as a photographer. I was elated when Cornell, in 1973, bought ten of my prints for ten dollars each for the Concerned Photography collection. I felt I had become part of a community.

Other photographers' work had also came to my attention. Danny Lyon's projects, *The Movement* and *Conversation with the Dead,* breathed new life into documentary photography in the late 1960s. Bruce Davidson's *East 100th Street* liberated photographers to create images far from the typical photojournalism of the day by using a large-format view camera and strobe lighting. Larry Clark's *Tulsa* showed the photographer as biographer. W. Eugene Smith created *Minamata* showing photographers that the lone voice of the photographer was still viable.

I soon realized that a handful of contemporary photographers had moved outside the generally proscribed role of photojournalism. Like earlier twentieth-century photographers they were witnessing their time. Photographer Lewis Hine had said, "There were two things I wanted to do. I wanted to show the things that needed to be corrected. I wanted to show the things that had to be appreciated." Like Hine, this new generation of photographers was actively partisan in a time when editors and academia were telling us to separate our personal feelings from our images. Editors also began the slow move to limit photography merely to illustrating stories, a format that is prevalent today. Photographer Walker Evans once said, "We need more than illustrations in the morning paper of our period." How true it now seems.

As the Vietnam War ended, I turned to other subjects. I now look back in wonder at my naiveté. I had been filled with passion and rage of what I saw happening in my country in the '60s, but I had little understanding of how to support myself as a photographer or even to conceive what a life in photography might mean. The movement photography that I had done the last many years now seemed so narrowly focused. I had believed that my voice was important and that photography might change the things I had seen, but now I was consumed by what I saw as a bigger picture for my photography. I wanted to look more deeply at America with my camera and sustain long-term projects.

I worked in a warehouse and did design and paste-up at night for a weekly free circular, so that my daylight hours would be available for photography. I took a few freelance assignments, but I wanted to remain independent without an editor or employer to dictate how I should tell my stories.

I photographed DeWitt Clinton High School in the Bronx, where I learned to navigate the bureaucratic morass and to connect with my subjects. A year later I began to photograph industrial workers who were exposed to dangerous working conditions in decaying foundries and factories, a project which lasted six years and led to a staff position creating labor images, posters, multimedia slides shows, and a series of 16mm documentary films about occupational health at the Labor Occupational Health Program (LOHP) at the University of California, Berkeley. I had my first exhibitions. I had begun to forge a life as a social documentary photographer.

However, when I tried to find a publisher for a book of the industrial workers photographs, one book editor told me, "Workers don't buy books."

In 1978, I started photographing migrant and child farm labor. A friend and fellow photographer Bill Owens tried to discourage me, saying that Dorothea Lange had done this already and had done it well. Documentary photographers are often met by such comments, but I believe that each generation needs to reexamine important issues despite what has been done before. I was amazed to find that so little had changed since the days of Lange's work. This strengthened my conviction to see, reveal, and support those trying to make change. Organizations like the National Migrant Ministry and the United Farm Workers Union used my work to illustrate their cause. I was awarded three National Endowment for the Arts (NEA) grants and my first NEA photographer's fellowship to help complete the farm-worker photographs. They were published in two books, *With These Hands*, with a foreword by Cesar Chavez, and *In the Fields*, with text by Paul Taylor, Dorothea Lange's husband and partner.

In 1982, the farm-worker project led me to the U.S.–Mexican border, where I documented the thousands of "illegal aliens" crossing into the United States. Like a visual puzzle, I looked for pieces of this amazing journey that could be edited and sequenced in an in-depth presentation. I received a second NEA photographer's fellowship to photograph conditions in rural Mexico. This body of work traced the journey from rural Mexico across the border and to a new life in Southern California. It was published by Aperture as *To the Promised Land*.

In 1989, after some friends commented about the deplorable conditions in Mississippi, I turned my camera to the Mississippi Delta. I had seen or read little about this part of the country and found the region to be so important to the fabric of contemporary American life, as well as a startling and amazing place. Over the next four years I photographed the effects of poverty and a century of neglect in the region. The end result was *Delta Time*, published by the Smithsonian Institution Press.

In 1994 I collaborated with writer Suzanne Donovan. She had orchestrated and gained access for us to Texas Death Row in Huntsville, where I spent a year photographing. It was a great challenge to show this world, and remain connected to the real world outside, where the men I had photographed committed unspeakable crimes. Many of the inmates I photographed have since been executed. This work was published in the book *Texas Death Row*. By that time I was a member of the photo agency JB Pictures, and with agency support, the work reached a global audience that I could have never imagined at the beginning of my career. My images were published in a six-page portfolio in *Newsweek* and in a similar manner in England, Germany, Korea, Japan, Switzerland, Italy, Spain, Venezuela, Finland, and other countries. As a result, I was invited to speak about my experience to many groups and organizations all over the world.

Four decades after my first published images, I am still photographing though now I also teach and curate photography exhibitions. I have tried to get my work into as many venues as possible—in publications, slide shows, posters, exhibitions, magazines and books, and on the web at www.kenlight.com. But making photographs and trying to attain publication continues to be one of my most difficult challenges.

I think back to a comment that Jacob Riis made almost a century ago: "For more than a year I had knocked at the doors of various magazine editors with my pictures, proposing to tell them how the other half lived, but no one wanted to know." Photographers today continue to face the same problem; images must fit onto a convenient news peg for editors to even be interested in them. It's not enough now to have a good project or visual story. Museums continue to largely steer away from contemporary photographs that have a human or social connection.

Many of the questions I reflected on in my early years continue to be debated—they have been part of the fabric of documentary photography since its inception. One day, while looking at old issues of the Photo League's Depression-era newsletter, *Photo Notes,* I noticed discussions on how work is created; how photographers create a photographic life; and how to continue to spread the idea of social photography. I recognized from this that each generation struggles with similar concerns, and that my generation should weigh in with their ideas and knowledge to create a record for the coming generation.

As the idea for *Witness in Our Time* began to form, I realized that my many years of photographing had given me an opportunity to look more closely at these same questions, ones my students had been also raising. A contemporary record of those issues would be a valuable resource to fuel the dialogue and discuss the visual language of documentary photography. A book would give me the opportunity to talk with and question my peers. A book might also bridge generations of documentary photographers and inspire the next. My interest in interviewing social photographers was as a kindred spirit and fellow photographer, not as an art historian or critic. Most of those interviewed were friends and colleagues. Sometimes this made it easier, sometimes more difficult.

Two of the most difficult questions I faced were who to include in this book and how to explain the many who are missing. I interviewed many more than the twenty-nine photographers, editors, and curators included in this book. My goal was to interview those who had not only made humanist and socially engaged photos, but who had also been socially active. I tried to avoid those who had simply been given interesting assignments related to social causes. I wanted those who had used their camera to bear personal witness to injustice. Those included are but a small part of the documentary family. The choice was often predicated on accessibility to the photographers and my personal knowledge of their work. I wanted to include both the well-known and those less recognized. I tried to find a few who had moved away from photography, but had once created work that inspired, and those who were just emerging.

Danny Lyon wrote me "My mind is far away on other things—I just couldn't do it, sorry." Interviews with Gilles Peress, Markéta Luskaová, and Cornell Capa, whose work with the Fund for Concerned Photography had inspired me, were not satisfying to either party. Arthur Leipzig, James Nachtwey, and Roland Freeman proved difficult to pin down. For various reasons, it wasn't possible to include interviews with photographers Ben Fernandez, Jason Eskenazi, Nubar Alexanian, filmmaker-photographer Leo Seltzer, and Jocelyne Benzakin, founder of JB Pictures. Sometimes I missed an opportunity. When Josef Koudelka came to my house, we talked for many hours, but a friend had warned me ahead of time that he would never let me tape a conversation so I never asked. I also accepted the same warning about Roy DeCarava, which to this day I regret.

Many photographers in the photojournalists' agency Magnum have worked deeply within the social documentary tradition and they created a special problem: so many have done work that I admire that this project easily could have become a Magnum book. Michael Hoffman the genius behind Aperture spoke at length about the many risks of publishing important socially oriented books. Rather than include his words, I chose to include Aperture's important books in the bibliography. I tried to choose photographers from a variety of countries and cultures, but travel costs, and in some cases, communication were prohibitively expensive and difficult. The majority of the image makers in this book are from the United States, where the tradition of social photography is strong.

One early morning, as I sat in my shabby little motel room in West Virginia working on my book *Coal Hollow* and waiting for a Klu Klux Klan rally to start, I realized that I was four hours away from where my photographic journey had begun in 1969. I thought back to those early moments with the camera and how far photography had come. Few cameras back then had built-in light meters; strobes were cumbersome and unsophisticated; and we still developed with chemicals. Digital cameras, computers, cell phones, electronic mail, and the web were not yet invented. Few, if any, photography galleries even existed, and the idea of buying original photographic prints was just on the horizon.

Much has changed in our world since those days and even more since this book was first published in 2000. It has been a time of new and remarkable possibilities opening up, but also many doors closing. Could we have ever imagined a world without film or the wet darkroom? Who would have thought that traditional photo venues that we had become so comfortable with and dependent on for our livelihood would disappear? *Look* and *Life* magazines have closed. A number of photo agencies have been bought out. Some people have even called the very nature of photography into question. Is the amateur citizen journalist the new model or will Dirck Halstead's Platypus model, "this strange new breed—newspaper and magazine photographers with the skill to shoot with a video camera and still camera" be the future? The traditional business model for sustaining our photography is to license our own images, but flagrant image sharing by Internet users has severely compromised that model. The delivery vehicle for visual stories is also rapidly evolving. You might be reading this as an e-book on a tablet or flexible computer screen.

But what of documentary? What will happen to those of us who have embraced the tradition, this deeply shared humanity of witnessing a moment in human history? Fred Ritchin asks, "Why don't we see this as a Golden Era set of possibilities as opposed to walking around in the doom and gloom? An expanded documentary photography could still bring us to greater understandings and to a greater sense of who we are. It is not just the history of photojournalism/documentary, but it's the challenge of photojournalism/documentary. That is where you need creativity, innovation, intuition, and ideas. We're too mired in our past and our past glories. If we could create something instead of all of us trying to be like the photographic heroes of the twentieth century, we could really move forward."

Fred raises important ideas that we too often ignore or even fear. As an educator, writer, and photo editor, his outsider perspective is important to consider. Might this be a new "Golden Era" for documentary photographers or will we lose control of our own destiny?

It is sometimes hard to fully embrace the digital world when it feels like Pandora's box is open. Our livelihood is threatened by media mergers, disintegration of the agency model, and widespread violation of our photography as intellectual property on the web. The oft-suggested path of financing projects with grants and nonprofit partnerships is just not that easy.

In particular, the newfound disregard for authorship has created profound issues. Recent books and essays by digital pioneers such as Jaron Lanier (*You Are Not a Gadget,* Knopf, 2010) have opened the debate about "Digital Maoism" and the disaster related to free culture that have altered the models. Lanier and other Internet visionaries are beginning to see this as an evil to our culture and our democratic society.

Ironically, despite the current state of documentary/photojournalism, more and more young photographers are embracing the documentary tradition. This gives me hope that it will continue with new ways of telling stories and reaching our audiences, and yes, we will find ways to support our work. We do not have to become victims of technological change. Documentary photography remains a kind of cultural glue that continues to hold us together. Melanie Light, writer and Executive Director of Fotovision, has written "in this day of secularism, the visual media of journalism and documentary photography can also serve as one vehicle through which we can each find our humanity, our spiritual and human connections to each other. We are reminded that despite the tsunami of imagery around us, we are challenged by each visual encounter to check in with ourselves, touch base with our intention and perhaps strive to adjust it toward a more intelligent, more humanist goal."

Just recently I have finished photographing in California's Central Valley using film and printing in a wet darkroom. I also scanned and photoshopped the negatives to make digital files. Though the images will be published in an offset duotone book, the new digital possibilities are staggering. Working with newsweek.com, the work was published online as "The Valley of Shadows." It generated 3.3 million page views and was linked to and from numerous websites reaching an immense audience that I could have never imagined a few years ago.

It has been four decades since I created my first images. My colleagues and I continue to struggle to photograph issues and get our work seen. Over the years critics have questioned the need for social documentary work and the need to witness: "It's been done before" or "After all, doesn't TV do it better?" Others see the need to construct a more contemporary avant-garde vision for photography. But the humanist vision in photography maintains its relevance because it is a way for people to connect with their own experiences.

W. Eugene Smith said "Never have I found the limits of the photographic potential. Every horizon, upon being reached, reveals another beckoning in the distance. Always, I am on the threshold. Photography is a small voice, at best, but sometimes one photograph, or a group of them, can lure our sense of awareness."

As the photographers and editors in this book show, the need to inquire, to express and to witness one's world, will always, even under the most dangerous, economically difficult, and technologically challenged times, endure.

Bibliography

Dotter, Earl. *In Our Blood: Four Coal Mining Families.* Washington, D.C.: Highlander Research and Education Center, 1979.

———. *The Quiet Sickness: A Photographic Chronicle of Hazardous Work in America.* Washington, D.C.: American Industrial Hygiene Association, 1998.

Ferrato, Donna. *Living with the Enemy.* New York: Aperture, 1991.

———. *Love & Lust.* New York: Aperture, 2005.

Fink, Larry. *Boxing.* New York: powerHouse, 1997.

———. *Forbidden Pictures.* New York: powerHouse, 2004.

———. *Runway.* New York: powerHouse, 1999.

———. *Social Graces.* New York: Aperture, 1984; powerHouse Books, 2001.

———. *Somewhere There's Music.* New York: Damiani, 2006.

Freedman, Jill. *Circus Days.* New York: Harmony Books, 1975.

———. *Firehouse.* Garden City, N.Y.: Doubleday, 1977.

———. *Ireland Ever.* New York: Harry N. Abrams, 2004.

———. *Old News: Resurrection City.* New York: Grossman Publishers, 1970.

———. *Street Cops.* New York: Harper & Row, 1981.

———. *A Time That Was: Irish Moments,* New York: Random House, 1987.

Goldblatt, David. *In Boksburg: The South African Photographic Gallery.* CITY: Gallery, 1982.

———. *David Goldblatt Photographs.* Rome: Contrasto, 2006.

———. *Intersections.* New York: Prestel, 2005.

———. *Lifetimes under Apartheid.* Alfred A. Knopf, 1986.

———. *South Africa: The Structure of Things.* New York: Monacelli Press, 1998.

———. *The Transported of KwaNdebele: A South African Odyssey.* New York: Aperture, 1989.

Goded, Maya. *Good Girls.* Brooklyn: Umbrage Editions, 2006.

———. *Plaza de Soledad.* Barcelona: Lunwerk, 2006.

———. *Tierra Negra*. Mexico: Consejo Nacional para La Cultura, 1994.

Iturbide, Graciela. *Asor*. New York: Little Steidl, 2008.

———. *Eyes to Fly With*. Austin: University of Texas Press, 2006.

———. *Fiesta und Ritual: Graciela Intrubide Mexiko*. Bern: Benteli, 1994.

———. *Graciela Iturbide*. London : Phaidon, 2006.

———. *Images of Spirit*. New York: Aperture, 1997.

———. *Juchitán de las Mujeres*. Mexico, D.F.: Ediciones Toledo, 1989.

———. *Los Que Viven en la Arena*. Mexico, D.F.: Institutio Nacional Indigenista: FONAPAS, 1981.

———. *En el Nombre del Padre*. Mexico, D.F.: Ediciones Toledo, 1993.

———. *Torrijos: The Man and the Myth*. Brooklyn: Umbrage Editions, 2007.

Jacobson, Colin, ed. *Underexposed: Censored Pictures and Hidden History*. London: Vision On Publishing, 2002.

Kratochvil, Antonin. *Antonin Kratochvil*. CITY: Torst 2003.

———. *Broken Dream*. New York: Monacelli Press, 1997.

———. *Incognito*. Santa Fe: Arena Editions, 2001.

———. *Persona. Portraits*. Bratislava, Slovakia: Slovart, 2006.

———. *Supravvivere*. Italy: Motta Editore, 2001.

———. *Vanishing*. CITY: de.MO, 2005.

Light, Ken. *Coal Hollow*. Berkeley: University of California Press, 2006.

———. *Delta Time*. Washington, D.C.: Smithsonian Institute Press, 1994.

———. *In the Fields*. Oakland, Calif.: Harvest Press, 1982.

———. *Texas Death Row*. Jackson, Miss.: University Press of Mississippi, 1997.

———. *To the Promised Land*. New York: Aperture, 1988.

———. *With These Hands*. New York: Pilgrim Press, 1986.

———. *Witness in Our Time: Working Lives of Documentary Photographers*. Washington, D.C.: Smithsonian Institution Press, 2000, 2010.

Magubane, Peter. *Black Child*. New York: Alfred A. Knopf, 1982.

———. *Dress and Adornment*. African Heritage Series. Cape Town: Struik Publishers, 2003.

———. *Magubane's South Africa*. New York: Alfred A. Knopf, 1978.

———. *Soweto: The Fruit of Fear*. Trenton, N.J.: Africa World Press, 1986.

———. *Vanishing Cultures of South Africa: Changing Customs in a Changing World*. New York: Rizzoli Books, 1998.

———. *Women of South Africa: Their Fight for Freedom*. CITY: Little, Brown & Co, 1993.

Mark, Mary Ellen. *A Cry for Help: Stories of Homelessness and Hope*. New York: Simon & Schuster, 1996.

———. *Exposure*. London: Phaidon, 2005.

———. *Extraordinary Child*. Reykjavik: National Museum of Iceland, 2007.

———. *Falkland Road*. New York: Alfred A. Knopf, 1981.

———. *Indian Circus*. San Francisco: Chronicle Books, 1993.

———. *Passport*. New York: Lustrum Press, 1969.

———. *The Photo Essay*. Washington, D.C.: Smithsonian Institution Press, 1990.

———. *Photographs of Mother Teresa's Missions of Charity in Calcutta, India.* Carmel, Calif.: Friends of Photography, 1985.

———. *Portraits.* Washington, D.C.: Smithsonian Institution Press, 1997.

———. *Seen behind the Scene,* London: Phaidon, 2008.

———. *Streetwise.* Philadelphia: University of Pennsylvania Press, 1988.

———. *Ward 81.* New York: Simon & Schuster, 1979; Damiani, 2008.

McCullin, Don. *The Destruction Business.* CITY: Open Gate Books, 1971.

———. *Don McCullin.* CITY: Trafalgar Square, 2003.

———. *In England.* New York: Thames & Hudson, 2008.

———. *India.* London: Jonathan Cape, 1999.

———. *Is Anyone Taking Notice.* Cambridge, Mass.: MIT Press, 1973.

———. *McCullin in Africa.* London: Jonathan Cape, 2005.

———. *Open Skies.* New York: Harmony Books, 1989.

———. *Sleeping with Ghosts.* New York: Aperture, 1996.

———. *Unreasonable Behavior.* New York: Alfred A. Knopf, 1992.

Meiselas, Susan. *Carnival Strippers.* New York: McGraw-Hill Ryerson Ltd., 1976.

———. *Encounters with the Dani.* New York: ICP Steidl, 2003.

———. *Kurdistan: In the Shadow of History.* New York: Random House, 1997.

———. *Nicaragua.* New York: Pantheon Books, 1981.

———. *Pandora's Box.* CITY:Trebruk Publishing, 2002.

———. *Susan Meiselas: In History.* New York: ICP Steidl, 2008.

Mieth, Hansel. *The Heart Mountain Story: Photographs by Hansel Mieth and Otto Hagel.* Los Gatos, Calif.: M. Inouye, 1997.

———. *Simple Life: Photographs from America, 1929–1979.* Stuttgart: Schmetterling Verlag, 1991.

Miller, Wayne F. *Chicago's Southside.* Berkeley: University of California Press, 2000.

———. *Wayne F. Miller: Photographs 1942–1958.* New York: powerHouse, 2008.

———. *The World Is Young.* Japan: Fukuinkan Shoten, 1999.

Owens, Bill. *Bill Owens.* New York: Damiani, 2008.

———. *Leisure.* New York: Fotofolio, 2004.

———. *Our Kind of People.* New York: Simon & Schuster, 1975.

———. *Suburbia.* San Francisco: Straight Arrow Press, 1972.

———. *Working.* New York: Fotofolio, 2009.

Partridge, Rondal. *Quizzical Eye.* Berkeley: Heyday Books, 2003.

Richards, Eugene. *50 Hours.* Wollaston, Mass.: Many Voices Press, 1983.

———. *Americans We.* New York: Aperture, 1994.

———. *Below the Line: Living Poor in America.* Mount Vernon, N.Y.: Consumers Union, 1987.

———. *The Blue Room.* London: Phaidon, 2008.

———. *Cocaine True, Cocaine Blue.* New York: Aperture, 1994.

———. *Dorchester Days.* Wollaston, Mass.: Many Voices Press, 1978.

———. *Exploding into Life*. New York: Aperture, 1986.

———. *The Fat Baby*. London: Phaidon, 2004.

———. *Few Comforts or Surprises: The Arkansas Delta*. Cambridge, Mass.: MIT Press, 1973.

———. *The Knife and Gun Club: Scenes from an Emergency Room*. New York: Atlantic Monthly Press, 1989.

———. *A Procession of Them*. Austin: University of Texas Press, 2008.

———. *Stepping through the Ashes*. New York: Aperture, 2002.

Ritchin, Fred. *After Photography*. New York: W. W. Norton, 2008.

———. *Mexico through Foreign Eyes, 1850–1990*. New York: W. W. Norton, 1993.

———. *In Our Own Image: The Coming Revolution in Photography*. New York: Aperture, 1990, 1999.

———. *In Our Time: The World as Seen by Magnum Photographers*. New York: W. W. Norton, 1989.

———. *An Uncertain Grace: The Photographs of Sebastião Salgado*. New York: Aperture, 1990.

Rodriguez, Joseph. *East Side Stories: Gang Life in East LA*. New York: power-House, 1998.

———. *Flesh Life: Sex in Mexico*. New York: powerHouse, 2006.

———. *Juvenile*. New York: powerHouse, 2003.

———. *Still Here: Stories after Katrina*. New York: powerHouse, 2008.

Rosenblum, Walter. *Lewis Hine, Ellis Island: Memories & Meditations of Walter Rosenblum on the Life & Work of an American Artist*. Toronto: Lumiere Press, 1995.

———. *Walter Rosenblum*. Dresden: Verlag der Kunst, 1990.

Salgado, Sebastião. *Africa*. CITY: Taschen, 2007.

———. *The Children: Refugees and Migrants*. New York: Aperture, 2000.

———. *The End of Polio: A Global Effort to End a Disease*. New York: Bulfinch, 2003.

———. *Migrations: Humanity in Transition*. New York: Aperture, 2000.

———. *Other Americas*. New York: Pantheon, 1986.

———. *Sahel: The End of the Road*. Berkeley: University of California Press, 2004.

———. *Sahel: L`Homme en Détresse*. Paris: Prima Presse, 1986.

———. *Terra: Struggle of the Landless*. London: Phaidon, 1997.

———. *An Uncertain Grace*. New York: Aperture, 1990.

———. *Workers: An Archaeology of the Industrial Age*. New York: Aperture, 1993.

Sheikh, Fazal. *A Camel for the Son*. Vol. 1. International Human Rights Series. Rotterdam: Netherlands Photo Institute, 2001.

———. *The Circle*. Göttingen, Germany: Steidl, 2008.

———. *Tf. Editores*. Madrid: PUBLISHER, 2005.

———. *Ladli*. Göttingen, Germany: Steidl, 2007.

———. *Moksha*. Göttingen, Germany: Steidl, 2005.
———. *Portraits*. Göttingen, Germany: Steidl, 2009.
———. *Ramadan Moon*. Vol. 2. International Human Rights Series. Rotterdam: Netherlands Photo Institute, 2001.
———. *A Sense of Common Ground*. Zurich: Scalo Verlag, 1996.
———. *The Victor Weeps: Afghanistan*. Zurich: Scalo Verlag, 1998.
Singh, Dayanita. *Blue Book*. Göttingen, Germany: Steidl, 2009.
———. *Go Away Closer*. Göttingen, Germany: Steidl, 2007.
———. *The Home and the World*. Göttingen, Germany: Steidl, 2008.
———. *Myself Mona Ahmed*. Zurich: Scalo Verlag, 2001.
———. *Privacy*. Göttingen, Germany: Steidl, 2003.
———. *Zakir Hussain: A Photo Essay*. New Delhi: Himalayan Books, 1987.
Tucker, Anne Wilkes. *Brassaï: The Eye of Paris*. New York: Harry N. Abrams, 1999.
———. *Chaotic Harmony: Contemporary Korean Photography*. CITY: PUBLISHER, 2009.
———. *Louis Faurer*. London: Merrell Publishers, 2003.
———. *Robert Frank: New York to Nova Scotia*. New York: New York Graphic Society, 1986.
———. *This Was the Photo League: Compassion and the Camera from the Depression to the Cold War*. Chicago: Stephen Daiter Gallery, 2001.
———. *The Woman's Eye*. New York: Alfred A. Knopf, 1973.
Vignes, Michelle. *Bay Area Blues*. San Francisco: Pomegrante, 1993.
———. *The Blues*. San Francisco: North Beach Press, 1986.
———. *Oakland Blues*. Paris: Marval, 1990.

Index